WHAT WASHINGTON SAID

HARPER TORCHBOOKS
HARPER & ROW, PUBLISHERS
NEW YORK, EVANSTON, SAN FRANCISCO, LONDON

WHAT WASHINGTON SAID

Administration Rhetoric
and the Vietnam War:
1949-1969

F. M. KAIL

For Wendy

WHAT WASHINGTON SAID
Copyright © 1973 by F. M. Kail
All rights reserved. Printed in the United States of America. No part of this book may be used or reproduced in any manner without written permission except in the case of brief quotations embodied in critical articles and reviews. For information address Harper & Row, Publishers, Inc., 10 East 53d Street, New York, N. Y. 10022. Published simultaneously in Canada by Fitzhenry & Whiteside Limited, Toronto.

First HARPER TORCHBOOK edition published 1973

LIBRARY OF CONGRESS CATALOG CARD NUMBER: 73–2057

STANDARD BOOK NUMBER: 06-131760-8

DESIGNED BY ANN SCRIMGEOUR

CONTENTS

The time has come for some new initiatives. Repeating the old formulas and the tired rhetoric of the past is not enough.

PRESIDENT RICHARD M. NIXON
MAY 14, 1969

FOREWORD

HAROLD D. LASSWELL

The author of this book believes that public officials and private citizens are able to learn from American experience in Southeast Asia, and especially from the waging of an undeclared war in Vietnam, Cambodia, Laos, and elsewhere.

Kail makes part of this learning relatively easy. He spreads the public record before us from 1949 on. The record is complete and is readily verifiable. That the public media imputed a statement to the president or to his principal advisors can be definitely established. Obviously it is the public, not the private and still controversial record, that has affected public perspectives.

We are reminded that presidential statements are political acts. Professional players of the great game of politics take this for granted. The occasional player, however, may lose sight of this. An act is political when it is intended to win support for the actor or to weaken the position of his opponents. It is not implied that the act is aimed exclusively at obtaining a political result, or that the only significant consequences of the act are political. When the president delivers a memorial eulogy in Arlington National Cemetery, he performs a ceremonial act of respect and gratitude, yet the political overtones are unmistakable. Clearly the nation's power in the world arena is contingent on the support of those who put their lives on the line. No party politician spurns an opportunity to improve his image by appearing in a ceremony in which the common identity is reaffirmed.

Our attention is focused on the language of politics in a matter of enormous importance in foreign policy. Some lessons relating to the language of politics are very old. Between crises they grow dim, and must be relearned. For example, a remarkable fact about public life in the United States is our ambivalent attitude toward political power. This ambivalence is reflected in the use of language. Power is usually treated in terms of "either-or," rather than "more or less." For instance many Americans are startled by the idea expressed above that a Memorial Day ceremony is not exclusively honorific, that it has foreign and domestic power implications.

In the same "either-or" vein are assertions that world affairs are only to be understood as "naked," not "lawful," power. Analytically, it is possible and useful to distinguish effective control when it is "authoritative" ("lawful") from control when it is not. That these distinctions are tacitly accepted is suggested by the concern of public leaders to defend the legality, morality, and expediency of their position. True, specific arguments may be freely invented or dropped as they were in controversies over Vietnam. It is the strategy of justification that stays constant. In their turn opponents adopt a tone of righteous indignation when they accuse the chief executive of violating the constitutional separation of powers, or riding roughshod over international norms that censure genocide and aggression.

There is, in fact, reluctance to refer flatly to power, and particularly to "our" power. Nevertheless, it is permissible to discuss the subject if it is treated in ideological terms. The political language of 1950 acknowledged not the fundamental division and militancy of the world power arena, but the supposedly overwhelming role of ideology in creating divisiveness. Communism was treated as an unchangeable threat. Such an interpretation made ideology the sole unchanging variable or variable-cluster in the entire social process. When we recall past fluctuations in religious and secular ideologies, this assumption is far from persuasive.

Kail's case study may be veiwed as an account of the flexibility of many components of American ideology. He shows how ideology was redefined and adapted by public officials to fit their changing perspectives of the political requirements of situations. The author wisely refrains from attempting to pass judgment on the "sincerity" of public leaders, but presents our political process as an endless exercise in persuasive advocacy, whether the target of persuasion is a diplomat, a judge, or a member of the anonymous public.

The book provides data that verifies another basic proposition about persuasive communication. Formulated as a principle the proposition is "Never arouse specific expectations that you cannot fulfill." Restated as a scientific assertion the proposition becomes "When specific expectations are perceived as unfulfilled, the attributed source of expectation loses credibility." For instance, so much false prophecy was current in the Vietnam war that it began eventually to smell of fraud.

Another lesson can be relearned from the record. In bodies politic where dissent traditionally receives a substantial measure of legal and moral protection, strategies of suppression are signs that national policy is vulnerable to challenge on grounds of principle, fact, or both. In a relatively democratic public order officials are required by principle and expediency to maintain a supporting coalition by relying for the most part on openness and persuasion.

Old hat? True—so long as hats are worn. What if hats themselves are obsolete? Is it probable that circumstances are changing so fast that executive power can act, and act irreparably, before the inner and outer voices of doubt or dissent are able to make themselves effective?

Perhaps the odds can be shortened if a continuing appraisal of public policy is made more prompt, systematic, and selective. This implies that Congress must be more adequately equipped with agencies of planning and appraisal of American policy in the contexts of national and world development. Implied also is improvement of the voluntary, civic order to include more competent and immediate coverage of the same context. If knowledge is power, we are traditionally opposed to allowing it to become a monoploy of the presidency or the Congress, or of giant corporate interests outside government. Implied is the willingness of American intellectuals—in their role of knowledge specialists—to go beyond the role of clients serving various interests, and to act as responsible citizens. Presumably they are able to use their professional associations, for instance, to examine and report on the social consequences and policy implications of knowledge.

Kail's analysis shows that some components of the American

ideological system continue to distort policy judgments. We do not like to acknowledge the degree of truth suggested by terms like "self-righteousness" or "arrogance." Despite a complementary tradition of self-doubt and self-examination, the inflation of the self continues to deflect attention from important realities. After all, our national "self" is not removed by many years from chronic subordination to Europe, and from the use of simple bombast to overcome a gnawing sense of inferiority. Asia was one continent where we turned to confirm our uncertain sense of greatness and mission. Our missionary, medical, educational, and "open door" activities were perceived as civilizing tasks. No doubt we have been plagued in recent years by compulsions to overcome our frustrations in East Asia and to complete our manifest destiny. There is little question that recent events call for a monumental reappraisal of our national identity, value goals, and factual expectations.

The present volume contributes to this national mood of reevaluation. It is a masterpiece of self-effacement on the part of the author. He allows our officials to efface themselves.

INTRODUCTION

It is possible that if the press were sufficiently controlled and the citizenry sufficiently insulated a government could wage a distant war and no one would know.

This has not, however, happened in Vietnam. Although there have been efforts to shroud United States operations in Southeast Asia in secrecy and attempts to stifle information, the crusade for Indochina, in part because of the resourcefulness of the media, in part because of basic democratic guarantees, has not been a closed but an unusually open affair. The American consciousness is ridden with images of pillage, atrocity, and disastrous error memorialized by the camera; it is numbed by the millions of words which have been spent in glorification, analysis, and description of the daily adventures. The pictures and commentary have shaped the national perspective and defined the collective experience. For this, the most unpopular war in U.S. history, has also been the most visible and widely discussed.

The pages which follow examine Washington's role in that discussion, comprising a study of the public rhetoric to complement the Pentagon Papers' treatment of communications passed in private. The source for the material is the *New York Times*.* The spokesmen are the principal civilian officials responsible for articulating American foreign policy: the president, the vice president, the secretaries of state and defense, the ambassador to South Vietnam, the representative to the United Nations, and their respective deputies and staffs. The

* The reader who wishes to trace a particular quotation back to the *New York Times* edition from which it was taken need only add one day to the date referred to in the text.

period is the two decades from the spring of 1949 through the spring of 1969, that is, from the Truman Administration's initial expression of support for the French-sponsored regime of Bao Dai to the Nixon Administration's first and only comprehensive defense of American intervention.

The book is composed of a series of essays that need not be read in any particular order. The first chapter opens with an exploration of the historical background leading to U.S. recognition of Saigon; the last closes with a collection of articles on the origin and substance of, and reactions to, domestic dissent. The intervening sections deal with the themes which over time came to dominate the rhetoric, themes arranged according to one of four questions to which they were responsive:

>Who is the enemy?
>What is the nature of the war?
>Why must we struggle?
>How did America become involved?

Throughout are scattered a myriad of quotations illustrating the particular language by which the people of the United States were made acquainted with the struggle for Indochina.

This is not the only work which could have been written on the rhetoric of the Vietnam War, and there are limits to both its design and its scope. It does not treat the whole area of military jargon. It leaves open any consideration of the real thoughts or beliefs of individual spokesmen. It can be regarded neither as a theoretical nor a polemical tract. It is, however, the only detailed chronicle of what Washington, over a generation, has had to say about America's involvement in Southeast Asia.

But it is more than just a chronicle; it offers insight as well into the dynamics of government oratory. It points up the correlation between the emergence and development of an official argument and the progressive increases in the U.S. military role. It adduces evidence which supports the inference that strategy sessions were held to determine the emphasis and thrust of efforts to educate the home front on the issues. It suggests that speechwriters' decisions as to what facts to select, what phrases to choose, what analogies to draw were based not upon standards of clarity and precision but upon the anticipated persuasive impact that their statements would have. It reveals political rhetoric to be what it has always been in wartime—propaganda, a systematic attempt by the government to promote its favored perspective. It should prove, therefore, not only to be of use to academics and public figures, but to be of interest to all who have been the targets of this campaign, to all who have lived through—and are still enduring— the tragedy of Indochina.

F.M.K.

CHAPTER ONE

AT THE BEGINNING

THE HISTORICAL BACKGROUND

France assumed control of Indochina in 1887 and over the years that followed, with a singlemindedness and lack of vision that was startling, reduced it to its imperial will. Through ruinous trade restrictions, erratic industrialization, forced production and consumption, and high taxation, the economy was thoroughly exploited; colonies were regarded as existing solely at the pleasure and for the financial benefit of the mother country. Though Paris had revolutionized Western thought by exposing Europe to the philosophy of reason, it subjected the people of Southeast Asia to governments committed wholly to reaction and arbitrary rule. Political parties and trade unions were outlawed; civil liberties in general and freedom of the press and assembly in particular were circumscribed; the administrative hierarchy was entirely closed to the local population. Having piously and unasked undertaken to uplift the backward peasants, the French introduced legal, social, and educational reforms. Rather than civilizing the natives, however, these changes succeeded only in destroying indigenous institutions and generally undermining the Vietnamese culture that was already there. Decades of such foreign domination nurtured within the Indochinese an understandable frustration and a contempt for outsiders. At the end of the Second World War these long and deeply felt emotions found an outlet for expression.

Though by mid-1945 there were a number of groups which sought to lead the movement for Vietnamese independence, only one effectively could: the Vietminh. A popular front coalition, it had been formed in 1941 at the instigation of the Communist party of Indochina and operated, from the beginning, under the direction of Ho Chi Minh, the party founder and a veteran Marxist. Because it was better organized and better staffed than the other groups, it alone was able to capitalize on the fortuitous circumstances of the late summer when, with the French displaced by the Japanese, and the Japanese defeated by the Americans, there was no one in a position to govern the country.

The Vietminh seized the initiative in August 1945. On the seventh its guerilla forces were declared a "liberation army"; the next week the call was issued for a general insurrection; by the fourteenth rebel soldiers had captured military stores and public buildings in Hanoi and taken over the city. In an effort to increase and deepen popular support a representative assembly was convened on August 16 which appointed a "People's National Liberation Committee" headed by Ho Chi Minh to oversee the revolution. Several days after that the hereditary Emperor Bao Dai abdicated, transferring his divine authority to the new provisional government. On September 2, as Japan surrendered to the United States aboard the U.S.S. *Missouri*, the Democratic Republic of Vietnam was proclaimed in Tonkin.

France did not simply acquiesce to these events but began operations to reclaim Indochina before the start of fall. Her progress, while sustantial, was uneven. In the South, where the Big Three had assigned the British to oversee pacification, success was immediate. The British military commander, in flagrant disregard of instructions not to get "involved in keeping order," supplied the French garrisons with weapons and, with the unlikely aid of the Japanese, launched a campaign to undo the Vietminh revolution. In the autumn Paris regained control of Saigon, having expanded it by winter to include most of the territory below the sixteenth parallel. In the North, by contrast, France was stymied. There, in accord with the same allied agreements, China was in charge, and the Chinese, having suffered under European colonialism for a hundred years, were not disposed to midwife the rebirth of an empire; nor, with an occupation army of 180,000, was their disposition likely to be changed. For six months, therefore, while Paris sought to come to terms, Chunking observed a benevolent neutrality: the Vietnamese continued to direct the civil administration of the region, while the French, interned during the war, remained confined to quarters. When at the end of February, France had conceded enough to get China to withdraw, the Democratic Republic had established a northern base of power.

In early 1946 with the Vietnamese entrenched in one half of the country and the French in the other, and with neither side having the resources or inclination to force a showdown, Paris and Hanoi resorted to diplomacy. On March 6 an understanding was reached: France would recognize Vietnam as a "free State" within a "French Union" and would conduct a referendum to determine if the three Vietnamese provinces—Tonkin, Annam, and Cochin-China—would be united; Vietnam, in return, would permit French troops to reenter the North peaceably. The agreement, though it averted war, settled nothing. Each side had gained a point: France had reasserted its presence in Southeast Asia; the Democratic Republic had won recognition. But the fundamental problem was still unsolved: how to satisfy Vietnamese demands for independence without denying France hegemony over Indochina. The March accords were not a reconciliation, but only the hope that in time a reconciliation would come.

That hope proved to be short-lived. Though Vietnamese officials were prepared to honor the compromise, the colonial administration was determined to subvert it. In the spring the

French high commissioner supervised the formation of an autonomous state in Cochin-China, despite the Paris promise that national unification was a question to be decided by the people through election. During the summer he sabotaged critical discussions between France and Vietnam at Fontainebleau by staging a rival conference of competing Indochinese minorities in Dalat. That autumn, choosing a minor harbor incident as his pretext, he ordered the aerial bombardment of Haiphong in which 6,000 civilians were killed. By late November 1946, war in Indochina had become inevitable. The Vietnamese in the end precipitated it: on December 19, in response to a directive to disband, the Vietminh militia attacked the French stationed in Hanoi. The ultimate responsibility, however, lay with France; the imperial bureaucracy, with its open and unremitting policy of antagonism, had made violence seem the only answer.

In 1947 Hanoi nevertheless made several offers to reopen talks, but they aroused little interest. Paris by then wanted an alternative to dealing with Ho Chi Minh rather than a resumption of contacts. It sought a replacement, someone capable of rallying the Vietnamese with a program more to the liking of France, a person equally popular, but not so intractably nationalistic. Its search eventually led to Hong Kong and the residence-in-exile of the former Emperor of Annam, Bao Dai. A member of a respected royal family, the ex-mandarin had inherited a devoted following; his flexible approach to politics, his service successively in colonial, fascist, and revolutionary regimes, suggested a strong tendency to accommodate principle to expediency. Given French purposes he was an ideal figure—a man of stature and few convictions.

Negotiations opened in the spring of 1947 and, while they took longer than anticipated, dragging on for more than twenty months, their results wholly fulfilled Paris's expectations. On March 8, 1949, in an exchange of letters with the president of the Fourth Republic, Bao Dai agreed to lead a Vietnam "united," "independent," and deferential to the economic and political interests of France; that is, he accepted the terms which two and a half years before had been offered to and rejected by Ho Chi Minh.

Despite the preoccupations of the Second World War, America was not indifferent to the situation in Southeast Asia, and long before it was over President Roosevelt began to consider the question of Indochina's future. His conclusions, though never publicized, were well-known to his associates and the Allies. Regarding French administration of the region as having been disastrous, he was opposed to the resurrection of a Gallic Empire. As early as January 1943, he declared that the United States would not be "wheedled into the position of accepting any [post war] plan that will further France's imperialistic ambitions."[1] A year later, in a memorandum to Secretary of State Cordell Hull, he was even more direct and emphatic:

> Indochina should not go back to France. . . . France has had the country . . . for nearly one hundred years and the people are worse off than they were at the beginning. . . . France has milked it. . . . The people of Indochina are entitled to something better than that.[2]

The "something better" was independence and the end of French rule. To achieve it, he favored the creation of an international trusteeship, recommending a commission made up of "a Frenchman, one or two Indochinese, and a Chinese and a Russian, because they are on the coast, and maybe a Filipino and an American."[3]

The military's maneuverings in the Pacific were in harmony with the president's anticolonial inclinations. When the Japanese staged a coup against the French in Indochina on March 9, 1945, United States Theater Headquarters ordered that no supplies or air cover be given the retreating forces. By May the Office of Strategic Services, which had established initial contact with the Vietminh some months before, had started providing the guerillas with small amounts of weaponry, money, and communications equipment in return for intelligence about the enemy. Throughout August and September, the critical period during which the Democratic Republic of Vietnam (D.R.V.) was being formed, American personnel stationed in the area gave advice, technical assistance, and open encouragement to the rebels, and thereby lent apparent official approval to their cause.

Though the men in the field cooperated with the nationalists into October—at the beginning of the month an American major and general appeared with the revolutionary leaders at a mass rally in Hanoi—their activities had been undercut and superseded by the professional politicians; Washington had abandoned any idea of "liberating" Vietnam the previous spring. Whatever Franklin Roosevelt's aspirations may have been, they were finally only aspirations, not government policy, and on May 8, 1945, within weeks of his death, the Truman Administration assured Paris that the United States had never, "even by implication," questioned "French sovereignty over Indochina"[4] and implied that it would not do so in the future.

The decision not to get involved in southern Asia held for almost four years, sustained by a nagging and paralyzing uncertainty about whom to support. The Democratic Republic had earned respect for having galvanized a popular and progressive resistance movement, but to embrace it was to approve the known Communist connections of its leadership. There was little applause for France's imperialistic pretensions, yet to antagonize her was to jeopardize the success of plans for European recovery. Bedeviled by ambivalence, Washington remained neutral, evenhandedly refusing French requests for matériel and Vietnamese appeals for diplomatic intervention, observing in public a discreet silence. Secretary of Defense Marshall epitomized the nation's noncommittal attitude at a news conference on February 7, 1947; he confined his discussion of the Indochina crisis to an expression of hope that "a pacific adjustment of the difficulties could be found."

Much of the ambiguity had been resolved by 1949. Soviet initiatives in Central and Eastern Europe convinced the government that communism, rather an ideological eccentricity, was a mortal danger to the free world. France, as a result, assumed even more importance as a link in Western security, while the D.R.V., with its Marxist affiliations, became even more suspect. Against the background of these Cold War reconsiderations, the United States verged on a commitment at mid-year. On June 8 the State Department welcomed "the formation of the new unified state of Vietnam," taking note of Bao Dai's "sincere efforts to unite all truly nationalist elements within Vietnam" and hailing the "statesmanship" displayed by both Paris and Saigon. Having proceeded that far, however, Washington went no further. There were still reservations. It remained unclear how closely tied Ho Chi Minh was to Russia and how really free Bao Dai would ever be of France.

Then in late 1949 the red armies of Mao Tse-tung spectacularly achieved control directly across the Vietnamese border. Containing communism in Asia suddenly became a fixation, and anticolonialism was displaced to the periphery. At the end of December Mr. Truman decided to oppose the Vietminh and aid the French. A month later that policy was publicly realized.

On January 29 the government, in an unusual move, announced its intention of "establishing closer relationship" with the Saigon regime. When the Soviet Union recognized the Democratic Republic the next day,Washington advertised that act as proof that Ho Chi Minh was not a patriot, but a servant of the Kremlin. "[T]he fact of recognition by Moscow," the State Department contended on the thirty-first, "should effectively destroy any illusions of Ho Chi Minh as a purely Nationalistic leader and place him in his true position as an agent of world communism." Dean Acheson carefully repeated that assessment on February 1:

> Soviet acknowledgment of his movement should remove any illusions as to the "Nationalist" nature of Ho Chi Minh's aims and reveals Ho in his true colors as the mortal enemy of native independence in Indo-china.

Speaking in Jakarta on the third, the U.S. Ambassador at Large, Dr. Phillip Jessup, reiterated it:

> Soviet recognition is clear confirmation of the fact, which we have been aware of for some time, that Ho Chi Minh is a Communist agent trained in Moscow . . . not a representative of the nationalist aspirations of Viet Nam.

Meanwhile in Paris, the French Assembly after eleven months of delay ratified the Elysee Accords on February 2 and legally confirmed the promise of independence extended in March. Though this event did not elicit a comparable official barrage, being too long overdue to indicate anything other than France's reluctance to part with her empire, it too had significance; for if Russian recognition of the D.R.V. made it appear justifiable for America to assist Bao Dai, French ratification of the accords made it diplomatically possible. On February 7, therefore, in a not surprising climax to the week's activity, Washington established relations with Saigon: it declared that France's efforts to "promote political stability and the growth of effective democratic institutions" in Indochina would not "be hindered by internal dissension fostered from abroad" and thereby served notice that the future of Southeast Asia had become a cause of importance to the United States and the entire free world.

THREE WORDS

Three words emerge as central to understanding Washington's case for American involvement in Southeast Asia: communism, aggression, and freedom. Each had become familiar in other contexts, and by 1950 needed no introduction. The march of the Soviet Army across Eastern Europe in 1945, the uprisings in Greece and Turkey in 1947, the victory of Mao Tse-tung and the blockade of Berlin of 1949 stood clearly for communism. The attack on the Low Countries in 1939, the invasion of France in 1940, the destruction of the Pacific fleet at Pearl Harbor in 1941 represented aggression. The principles set forth in the Declaration of Independence, the Fourteen Points, and the Atlantic Charter symbolized freedom. The use of these words in the description of the struggle in Indochina, therefore, called up associations and stimulated reactions which had been learned before, associations and reactions related to what, in retrospect, were the less confused and more classic confrontations of the past.

Communism

At a luncheon meeting on April 19, 1965, Leonard Unger, the deputy assistant secretary of state for far eastern affairs, talked to the members of the Economic Club of Detroit about the rationale behind the stand being made by the United States in Vietnam. He observed that the Western powers had "checked Soviet expansionist moves in the past twenty years and now the Russians have too much to lose to think readily of precipitating a major war." He went on:

> If we can check the Communists in Asia until the time when they have too much to lose materially—until moderating forces have a chance to assert their influence—then the threat of war in Asia may also slowly fade away.

The unacknowledged source of this argument was Professor George Kennan. Eighteen years before, in an article that appeared anonymously in the summer edition of *Foreign Affairs,* he had prescribed

> that the main element of any United States policy toward the Soviet Union must be that of a long-term, patient but firm and vigilant containment of Russian expansive tendencies.

For two decades, officials explained America's mission in Indochina as part of this general effort to halt the advance of communism. Secretary of State Dulles told reporters on April 19, 1954, that it was essential "to assure that that area [of Southeast Asia] cannot be conquered by the Communists." At a news conference almost ten years later, on September 12, 1963, President Kennedy remarked, "But we've got a very simple policy in that area, I think the Vietnamese people and ourselves agree we want. . .the Communists to be contained." His successor, Lyndon Johnson, expressed the same hope on April 23, 1964, "that we could all unite in an attempt to stop the spread of and the envelopment—the spread of communism in that area of the world." Defense Secretary McNamara on March 12, 1965, called the Vietnam War "our struggle to halt Communist expansion in Asia." On February 19, 1966, Secretary of State Dean Rusk testified to the Senate Foreign Relations Committee: "What we face in Vietnam is what we have faced on many occasions before—the need to check the extension of Communist power." And on October 23, 1967, Vice President Humphrey declared:

> If our policy of mutual security and containment of Communist
> power in Europe has been right, the same logic and compelling
> reasons require the application of such a policy in Asia.

Though Washington's pronouncements on Vietnam reflected an undeviating opposition to communism, they also took
account of the distinctions between the Communists faced by
Presidents Truman and Eisenhower and those whom Presidents Kennedy and Johnson met. In the period from 1950 to
1954, the label "Communist" was much of the time an explicit
enough means of identifying the enemy for the public. The
unified, monolithic structure which it implied was reinforced in
phrases like the "the world Communist conspiracy,"[5] "the
Communist bloc,"[6] and "international communism."[7] The
locus of this Communist power was Russia: "a central will re-
sides in Moscow," John Foster Dulles explained on October 20,
1953, "and thus Moscow becomes the capital of all the captive
world." Asia-watchers saw in the defeat of Chiang Kai-shek the
movement of "China into the Soviet orbit,"[8] the creation of a
new, faithful "Chinese Communist ally."[9] The implacable purpose of all Marxists was said to be "to promote world revolution,
destroy freedom, and communize the world."[10]

In the early 1960s officials began to acknowledge a rift between the Russians and the Chinese. Secretary Rusk remarked
to the press on March 1, 1962, "We know of discussions, differences and problems that have occurred within the Communist
bloc." By March 26, 1964, the split had become more open and
acute, and Robert McNamara could tell the National Security
Industrial Association, "Communist China's interests are clear:
it has publicly castigated Moscow for betraying the revolutionary cause whenever the Soviets have sounded a cautionary
note." On October 25, 1965, presidential adviser McGeorge
Bundy observed that Moscow "ranks second only to the U.S. in
the frenetic propaganda of Peking." In the years that followed,
Peking's particular and militant vision of Marxism caused
speechwriters to allude to its doctrine specifically as "Asian
communism."[11]

The ideological differences that developed between China
and the Soviet Union signaled the end of the uniform party line

which the United States had come to expect in its dealings with Communists. It became clear that in Vietnam Russia's interests were different from China's, and Hanoi's were different from those of the other two. Russia wanted to avoid a major confrontation with the West and to rebut China's contention that it was guilty of bourgeois revisionism. China sought a victory by Hanoi to vindicate her position in the ideological struggle and to expand her influence with the nations of Asia. Hanoi aimed for the destruction of the regime in the South and the reunification of both Vietnams under a single northern government. As these differences were accommodated in the rhetoric, the incidence of references to communism declined, for it implied an identity of purpose which no longer existed within the socialist community; at the same time, and in parallel fashion, the use of more general labels, like "enemy," "foe," and "other side" increased.

To Washington the passing of the era of absolute Soviet hegemony and the emergence of polycentrism did not suggest that communism had ceased to be a menace; the menace persisted, but in altered form. Dean Rusk outlined a revised theory of the Communist threat in a speech given in May 1966.[12] He explained to an audience of foreign relations experts:

> Significant changes have occurred within the Communist world. It has long ceased to be monolithic, and evolutionary influences are visible in most of the Communist states. But the leaders of both principal Communist nations are committed to promotion of the Communist world revolution—even while they disagree bitterly on tactics.

On September 10, 1968, shortly after the Soviet invasion of Prague, President Johnson expressed a similar view. He told a gathering of the American Legion that some people

> concluded that changes of such magnitude were taking place in the Communist world that we could relax our vigilance, trusting that the Communists wanted the same kind of world that we Americans wanted.

He went on:

> The message out of Czechoslovakia is plain. The independence of nations, the liberty of men are today still under challenge. The

free parts of the world will survive only, only if they are capable
of maintaining their strength and capable of maintaining and
building their unity.

Although the international hierarchy had disintegrated, ultimate Communist objectives remained the same.

It was only seldom that communism was more than mentioned by American officials; a rich popular imagery already
existed, making technical and academic explication superfluous. On the few occasions on which they did discuss it, however,
the focus was always on a single aspect of Communist doctrine:
the endorsement of violence as an acceptable means of political
change. President Johnson put it simply during a news conference on November 2, 1967:

> The problem is with the Communist enemy who insists on con-
> tinuing the course that places us in Vietnam and that will keep
> us there until they decide that might does not make right, and
> they cannot gobble up weaker people because they are stronger.

The United States had reluctantly accepted the Communist
domination of Eastern Europe and China and would not interfere in those areas no matter how repressive the methods of
internal control became. But outside that sphere intervention
was appropriate. The refusal to tolerate the expansion of Communist power was couched not in terms of opposition to Communist social, economic, or political theory, but in terms of
opposition to Communist methods. The enemy in Asia was in
this respect the same enemy the United States had found in
Europe twenty-five years earlier. It was called communism
now, and had been called fascism then, but the differences were
largely semantic. In both instances America saw itself as defending civilization against those who would resort to force to
realize their ambitions. On September 17, 1953, John Foster
Dulles had described the war in Indochina as a war against
"Communist forces" who were "seeking to gain political power
by military violence." Fifteen years later,[13] Robert McNamara
said much the same about Vietnam: "we find ourselves engaged
[in Southeast Asia] in a conflict to preserve the principle that
political change must not be brought about by externally directed violence."

Aggression

For nearly half a century the international community has sought in vain to define aggression. The scores of meetings and conferences held on the question have produced nothing more spectacular than the tacit agreement that whatever definition finally emerges must comprehend the case of the unprovoked armed attack. The uncertainty which persists in the law has had an anomalous effect. On the one hand, there are very few instances in which it can be indisputably said that aggression has occurred; on the other, there is a virtually unbounded area in which that contention may be advanced and argued.

To both the Democrats and Republicans who were in office in the period from 1950 to 1954, the French Indochina war was a war of aggression. President Truman spoke of Indochina on March 6, 1952, as the place where "the free nations are holding the line against aggression." Secretary of Defense Charles E. Wilson spoke on May 5, 1953, of "stemming the tide of aggression" in the south of Asia. On May 7, 1954, General Eisenhower wrote that the battle showed that the West was determined "to resist dictatorial aggression."

During the Kennedy Administration, when fighting erupted again, the descriptions emphasized the guerilla aspects of the warfare. In an address before the United Nations General Assembly on September 25, 1961, the president reported that "South Vietnam is already under attack, sometimes by a single assassin, sometimes by a band of guerillas, recently by full battalion." The president told newsmen on February 7, 1962, "It's a . . . subterranean war, [a] guerilla war of increasing ferocity." On October 2, 1963, the White House reviewed the threat of "the externally supported and stimulated insurgency" in Southeast Asia.

The pattern shifted in 1964. With growing regularity the enemy's terrorism was identified as aggression. President Johnson, in a New Year's message to the Republic of Vietnam, reiterated America's continuing concern about the "terrorist aggression" in the South. On February 21, he pointed to the intensifying campaign of "terror and violence, directed and supplied by outside enemies," and warned that "this type of aggression is a deeply dangerous game." The White House promised on March 17 to do what was necessary to bring "aggression and terrorism under control." In an address before the American Law Institute on May 22, Secretary of State Rusk asserted that "in South Vietnam a major aggression is under way. I say 'aggression' deliberately." By the end of the speech he had repeated the charge twelve times.

Equilibrium was reestablished in 1965. Aggression became the principal symbol for hostile activity in Vietnam. It remained so for the next three years.

In April 1954, there was a possibility of a Big Power intervention in Indochina. In February 1965, the United States initiated its campaign of air raids over the North. In February 1966, a thirty-eight day bombing pause was suspended and the Senate scrutinized the administration's Far Eastern policies. In October 1966, Mr. Johnson met with the Asian allies and visited American troops at Camranh Bay. At each of these times, when the government was under special pressure to justify its position in Southeast Asia, it placed an unusual stress on the aggression being carried out by the other side.

The aggression to which it referred was not that with which the world had long been familiar. On April 5, 1954, Secretary Dulles acknowledged that the sort of "open" aggression which had occurred in Korea was not taking place in Indochina; the State Department, in its White Paper of February 1965, wrote of the warfare in Vietnam as a "totally new brand of aggression." The public had seen the dramatic aggression by invasion, the massive border crossings by national armies. It was now witnessing a more insidious aggression by proxy, an externally manipulated, internal revolution. Officials dismissed the differences, however, as differences in form, not in substance, differences designed to promote ambiguity; Secretary Dulles as well as Secretary Rusk called them differences contrived "to confuse the issue"[14] in the eyes of the world. For the essence of both the old and the new aggression was the same: an attempt by one state to destroy another militarily.

Both lawyers and politicians appreciate the subtlety of language. The lawyer's particular interest is in the meaning of words; the politician's, in their connotation. There were more technically precise ways in which Washington could have described the interrelationship between foreign and domestic elements in Southeast Asia than by characterizing the war as an aggression, but the gains in precision would have been offset by the losses in simplicity and emotional impact. "Aggression" said little about the detail of the daily face of battle, but it signified forcefully and economically that battle's dangers and importance. It was a compact formula for a complex truth. The truth, as Mr. Johnson recited it on July 28, 1965, was that

> this is a different kind of war. There are no marching armies or solemn declarations. Some citizens of South Vietnam, at times with understandable grievances, have joined the attack on their own government. But we must not let this mask the central fact that this is really war.

Freedom

From the beginning, freedom was an important element in Washington's rhetoric. On November 27, 1950, Dean Rusk, assistant secretary of state, voiced the hope that other countries would "make every contribution within their power to enable the Associated States and their partners in the French Union to accomplish their mission of freedom." A communiqué released by the Big Three Western foreign ministers on July 14, 1953, proclaimed that the defense of Indochina was "essential to the free world."[15] Undersecretary of State Walter Bedell Smith stated on February 23, 1954, that "the French Union Forces are the forces of freedom."

The freedom directly in the balance was that of the Vietnamese, and it was to their specific cause that officials most often addressed themselves. John Foster Dulles, on April 14, 1954, said the West sought for Indochina a peace which would "safeguard the freedom of its people." On February 7, 1962, President Kennedy told newsmen of the plight of the people of South Vietnam, "who, with the greatest courage . . . are attempting to maintain their freedom." In a message dated May 28, 1966, Secretary of State Rusk recounted to the Saigon Government the efforts being made "to help South Vietnam preserve its freedom."

On occasion, however, the war assumed far grander scale and proportion: the stakes were no less than the freedom of mankind. On April 23, 1954, President Eisenhower declared that Indochina had "become again a testing ground between dictatorship and freedom." President Johnson told the press on June 2, 1964, "this is not just a jungle war, but a struggle for freedom on every front of human activity." On June 11, a year later, Vice President Humphrey, pursuing the theme further, said that Vietnam was "part of the continuing struggle which we must be prepared to wage if we are to preserve free civilization as we know it."

There was never an attempt to move from this ringing oratory with its solemn proclamations to define precisely the meaning of its terms. It was never certain, for example, if "freedom" stood for the political independence of a state or the civil liberties of a population, or both, nor to what degree either of these conditions had been yet realized in the Republic of Vietnam. Neither was it made clear how the "preservation of freedom in Southeast Asia" differed, except verbally, from the "resistance to communism in Southeast Asia" or "stemming the tide of aggression in Southeast Asia" as statements of national objectives.

Washington only intended that the public, by association, regard the war in Vietnam as a fight for freedom. It did so not because in the abstract sense this was an appropriate characterization, but rather because it was a useful one. The phrase was designed to invest the war with a relevance, an importance, a worthiness, which it otherwise may have lacked. The nation was meant to relate the seemingly unique situation in Asia to this ideal central to America's cultural tradition. People were supposed to understand Vietnam as a young soldier had written Dean Rusk that he understood it:

> We are fighting for the freedom of these people, as we once fought for our own. Of these thousands of young Americans over here, we all take pride in fighting for the principles that made our country the greatest on earth.

On October 25, 1967, President Johnson cited this as a "clear and eloquent" expression of the U.S. purpose.

NOTES TO CHAPTER 1

1. Elliott Roosevelt, *As He Saw It* (New York: Duell, Sloan and Pearce, 1945), p. 116.
2. Cordell Hull, *Memoirs* (New York: The Macmillan Company, 1948), 2:-1597.
3. Samuel I. Rosenman, ed., *The Public Papers and Addresses of Franklin D. Roosevelt: Victory and the Threshold of Peace* (New York: Harper & Row, Publishers, 1950), p. 557.
4. *Diplomatic Papers,* 1945 (GPO, 1969) 6:307.
5. Eisenhower, January 7, 1954.
6. Dulles, April 11, 1954.
7. State Department, September 30, 1953.
8. Dulles, March 29, 1954.
9. Dulles, April 5, 1954.
10. Eisenhower, April 4, 1959.
11. Johnson, October 27, 1966.
12. Rusk, May 24, 1966.
13. McNamara, February 1, 1968.
14. Dulles, March 29, 1954. Rusk, February 18, 1966.
15. The phrase "free world" remained a speechwriters' reflex long after it had ceased to be appropriate or even fashionable to view the world in such moralistic and dogmatic terms. Though it never again was used as extensively as in the early 1950s—in 1954 it was invoked 30 times—the image of the "free world" was struck on thirteen occasions in 1966 and on four in as late as 1968.

CHAPTER TWO

WHO IS
THE ENEMY?

RUSSIA

The Truman Administration, during the first week in February 1950, left no doubt about its assessment of the realities in Vietnam: the Soviet Union was exploiting Vietnamese aspirations for independence as a means of expanding its empire in Asia. Phillip Jessup, the president's special envoy, had rehearsed the position in Jakarta, Indonesia, on February 6. "Stalin's program," he began, "is quite clear." He continued, "Russia is encouraging nationalism in Asia only as a step toward the subjugation of the people to the alien rule of Russian dictators."

The Republicans moved into the White House in January 1953. In the spring of 1954, as the fighting in Indochina reached a critical stage, the theory of a Moscow-based conspiracy was revived and given added substance and detail. It was presented first on March 29 by Secretary of State Dulles:

The Communists have, in these matters, a regular line which was laid down by Stalin in 1924.

And their scheme is to whip up the spirit of nationalism until it becomes violent. That is done by professionally trained agitators. Then the violence is enlarged by Communist military and technical leadership and by the provision of military supplies. And in these ways international communism gets a stranglehold on the people and it uses that power eventually to "amalgamate" them into the Soviet orbit.

The word "amalgamation" is the word which was used by Lenin and Stalin to describe their process. And it is this "amalgamation" which is being attempted now in Indochina.

He restated it in a televised address to the nation on May 7:

In the name of nationalism, the Communists are aiming to deprive the people of Vietnam of their independence by subjecting them to the new imperialism of the Soviet Communist bloc.

What's going on there in Indo-China is a perfect example of Soviet Communist strategy as applied to colonial and dependent areas. It is a strategy laid down many years ago by Lenin and Stalin and it is a strategy the Communists have practiced to take over much of Asia.

And on June 10, before an audience of Rotarians, he recited the theory again:

Stalin, in one of his classic lectures, which is now part of the Communist bible, outlines the strategy of "amalgamation" by means of "alliance with the liberation movement of the colonies and dependent countries." He outlines a two-phased program— a program of duplicity. In the first phase the communistic agitators are to whip up the nationalistic aspirations of the people so that they will rebel violently against the existing order. Then, before independence can become vigorous and consolidated in its own right, the Communists are to take over the new government and use the power to "amalgamate" the peoples into the Soviet orbit. . . .

What is going on in Indo-China is a classic example of the application of this Communist strategy.

These passages represent what proved to be the extreme view of Russian influence in Vietnam. The notion that the Soviet Union was the ultimate enemy, encouraging discord and fomenting rebellion, ended with the conclusion of the Geneva Accords on July 21, 1954.

The renewal of violence six years later was not ignored in Moscow, nor were Moscow's activities in abetting it ignored in Washington. During the years from 1960 to 1964 officials pointed to the political and moral support that the Russians lent to the insurgents' cause. They cited Soviet doctrine which, while no longer exhorting the export of revolution, remained openly sympathetic to revolutionary movements that were locally inspired. On February 17, 1962, in a speech billed by the Pentagon as a rationale for U.S. involvement in Southeast Asia, Defense Secretary McNamara focused on an address given by Premier Khrushchev at a party congress in January 1961; he noted that the Russian leader had endorsed "wars of liberation and popular uprising" as the most acceptable strategy for advancing communism in the atomic age, particularly embracing the struggle in Vietnam. He returned to that address during the spring of 1964.[1] Describing it as "one of the most important speeches on Communist strategy of recent decades," he reminded his audience of the key passages:

> Khrushchev stated: "In modern conditions the following categories of wars should be distinguished: world wars, local wars, liberation wars, and popular uprisings."
> He ruled out what he called "world wars" and "local wars" as being too dangerous for profitable indulgence in a world of nuclear weapons. But with regard to what he called "liberation wars" he referred specifically to Vietnam. He said: "It's a sacred war. We recognize such wars."

That September[2] Ambassador Maxwell Taylor testified to a House panel that an American withdrawal from South Vietnam would prove that "Khrushchev [was] . . . right in believing that [he has] . . . a new tactic, the war of liberation, which cannot be defeated by the strongest nation in the world."

In the latter half of the decade government reports indicated a growing Soviet military commitment. On June 3, 1965, the Defense Department announced, "A small number of Ilyushin-28 type aircraft have been observed on the ground in the Hanoi area." On July 6, 1965, the State Department disclosed that two Russian antiaircraft missile sites had been installed in the North. In a message to the Foreign Ministry in Moscow, dated July 23, 1966, the United States emphasized "that the Soviet Union has been supplying petroleum products used by North Vietnam." That October[3] the presence of Russian technical advisers was confirmed. Mr. McNamara wrote in his annual review for Congress submitted in February[4] 1968, that in the preceding year military and economic aid in Hanoi had come from "chiefly the Soviet Union" and had since 1965 "been steadily increasing." President Nixon commented in a news conference on March 4, 1969, that the Russians "furnish 80 per cent, 85 per cent of the sophisticated military equipment for the North Vietnamese forces." "Without that assistance," he added, "North Vietnam would not have the capability to wage the major war they are against the United States."

Yet, though from 1965 the scale of Russian assistance escalated greatly, during that same period references critical of the Soviet Union occurred at a steady and low level of intensity. The accounts of the discovery of Soviet matériel were notable for their objective content and the absence of even the most perfunctory denunciations. They were often presented in routine briefings by minor departmental officials, or in obscure and little publicized state documents. There was, in the face of considerable and damning evidence, a deliberate effort to minimize the significance of Moscow's assistance in Indochina.

That effort was not, however, confined to subtle shadings and understatement. On August 4, 1965, Ambassador at Large W. Averell Harriman declared, in what was to be only the first in a long series of such declarations, that the Russians "sincerely wanted peace" in Vietnam. McGeorge Bundy, the president's special assistant for national security affairs, said on January 16, 1966, "it has been made clear to us over a long period of time that the Soviet Government hopes there can be a peaceful settlement." On September 21, 1966, Mr. Johnson told newsmen that he had "felt all along that . . . [Moscow] would like to see a negotiated—negotiations and discussions rather than what's happening." On March 9, 1967, he repeated his feeling: "Yes, I believe that the Russians generally want peace." Two years later, on March 4, 1969, President Nixon agreed:

And I think I could say that, based on the conversations that the Secretary of State and I have had with the Soviet Ambassador,

> I believe at this time that the Soviet Union shares that concern of many other nations in the world about the extension of the war in Vietnam, its continuing; they recognize that if it continues over a long period of time the possibility of escalation increases and I believe the Soviet Union would like to use what influence it could, appropriately to help bring the war to a conclusion.

That the Russians had nevertheless undertaken to sponsor the North Vietnamese was explained as an unfortunate but entirely understandable consequence of the Soviet rivalry with Peking; it was not to be construed as a challenge or an act of hostility toward the United States. The Soviet Union, the public was led to believe, had only reluctantly become involved in the war in Southeast Asia. Mr. Harriman introduced this adroit analysis on August 8, 1965:

> The North Vietnamese are a fellow Communist country. The great competition that Moscow faces is for the leadership of the Communist international movement, and they are attempting to appear as vigorous in their support of international revolution as Peking. . . .

Secretary Rusk on July 22, 1966, observed that the Russians were "trapped as we are" by the ideological conflict with China. In a television interview on December 19, 1967, President Johnson remarked:

> Now, we can understand the Soviet Union's inhibitions and the problems they have as long as Vietnam is taking place. They are called upon to support their communist brother, and they are supporting him in a limited way with some equipment.

On March 4, 1969, Richard Nixon noted that

> the Soviet Union is in a very delicate and sensitive position as far as Vietnam is concerned . . . here you have Communist China aiding North Vietnam, you also have the Soviet Union aiding North Vietnam, each vying for power in the Communist world.

Washington had by the summer of 1965 made it clear that it no longer chose to regard the Soviet Union as its enemy in Indochina. On June 3 President Johnson stated, "There is no American interest in conflict with the Soviet people anywhere." In Bonn, on July 24, W. Averell Harriman was more specific: "The conflict in Vietnam is not with the Soviet Union."

The choice did not imply that long-term Soviet objectives were not inimical to the United States. But it did reflect the fact that the United States was willing to accept the apparent modifications in Soviet doctrine and mellowing of its attitude as a reality, and to admit that at given places and at given times there could be an identity of Russian and American interests. This concession and trust was extraordinary when contrasted with the intransigence and suspicion which only eleven years before had officially prevailed. "Soviet policy is like a powerful stream," John Foster Dulles had warned in 1954,

> the surface of which is sometimes nettled, the surface of which is sometimes calm, but . . . we cannot judge the force and direction of the current merely by looking at surface manifestations.
>
> The important thing . . . is that we should proceed in our own way, steadily building our own strength and our own unity, upon which our strength depends. There [are] . . . three great dangers to be avoided:
>
> 1) That we might by the surface calm of the Soviet stream be lulled into a false sense of security, 2) that by the rough appearance of the Soviet stream we might be frightened into a state of paralysis, or 3) be provoked into ill-considered and divisive action.

CHINA

When American officials in the years from 1950 to 1954 spoke of the turmoil in Asia, they linked the conflict in Korea with that in Indochina. They described the connections not only in terms of ideology, but also in terms of nationality. Both were part of the free world struggle against communism. Both were confrontations, as well, between the West and China.

The first suggestion that the Chinese were the common denominator of the wars in the Far East came during a combined session of the Senate Armed Services and Foreign Relations Committees on May 12, 1951. Asked whether he believed the fighting in Indochina had "a fairly direct strategic relationship" to the fighting in Korea, Secretary of Defense George Marshall responded:

> I think it has a very direct relationship and I think the operations in Korea in the destruction that has been effected on Communist China's supposedly picked troops has quite probably restrained action by the Communist Chinese forces on the Indo-Chinese frontier.

Two and a half years later, on September 2, 1953, Mr. Dulles stated without qualification what Mr. Marshall had clearly implied:

> We do not make the mistake of treating Korea as an isolated affair. The Korean War forms one part of the world-wide effort of communism to conquer freedom. More immediately it is part of that effort in Asia. A single Chinese Communist aggressive front extends from Korea in the North to Indochina in the South. . . . There is a risk that, as in Korea, Red China might send its own army into Indochina.

The fear of a Chinese plunge into Vietnam was not entirely without foundation. As early as August 9, 1950, John F. Melby, an American diplomat studying the situation in Asia for President Truman, warned that Peking posed a "real threat" to the future independence of Indochina. On March 20, 1951, Dean Acheson reported to the House Foreign Affairs Committee that there were Chinese nationals "involved" in the fighting. By August 11, 1952, John Allison, the assistant secretary of state for far eastern affairs, estimated that China had sent 10,000 men to provide technical and political advice to the Vietminh.

In the months before the collapse of the French garrison at Dienbienphu, such help was intensified and the Chinese verged perilously upon direct intervention. On March 29, 1954, Mr. Dulles asserted that China was aiding the D.R.V. "by all means short of open invasion." The following week, on April 5, he observed, "They are not perhaps openly and flagrantly committing aggression, but they save themselves from the charge only by technicalities." That same day he testified to the House Foreign Affairs Committee on the nature and scope of Peking's involvement:

> The rulers of Communist China train and equip in China the troops of their puppet Ho Chi Minh. They supply these troops with large amounts of artillery and ammunition. They supply

military and technical guidance in the staff section of Ho Chi Minh's command, at the division level and in specialized units such as the signal and engineering corps, artillary units, and transportation.

A State Department report, released simultaneously, supplied the details:

1. A Chinese Communist general, Li-Chen Hou, is stationed at the Dienbienphu headquarters of General [Vo Nguyen] Giap, the Vietminh commander.
2. Under him there are nearly a score of Chinese Communist technical military advisers at the headquarters of General Giap. Also there are numerous other Chinese Communist military advisers at division level.
3. There are special telephone lines, installed, maintained and operated by Chinese personnel.
4. There are a considerable number of 37-mm. anti-aircraft guns radar-controlled at Dienbienphu, which are shooting through the clouds to bring down French aircraft. These guns are operated by Chinese.
5. In support of the battle there are approximately 1,000 supply trucks, of which about one half have arrived since March 1, all driven by Chinese Army personnel.

The imminent attack never materialized, however.

Over the next decade, China provided support to the second generation of Communist forces challenging the authority of the Republic of Vietnam. Secretary McNamara on May 11, 1962, told of the discovery in South Vietnam of "munitions which were manufactured in Communist China." On May 21, 1964, Ambassador Stevenson described to the United Nations the capture of "recoilless rifles, rocket launchers, carbines, and ammunition of Chinese Communist" origin. The State Department indicated on December 28, 1965, that Chinese workers were engaged in repairing rail communications and roads in North Vietnam. The Pentagon on April 28, 1966, disclosed that about twenty thousand such laborers had by then been dispatched by Peking.

China's commitment during these years, however, at no time approached the level of active combat participation which it had reached during the spring of 1954. Nor did Washington expect that it would. China, officials maintained, wanted a victory in Vietnam, but not at the expense of Chinese lives. Deputy Defense Secretary Cyrus Vance said on October 7, 1965, that Peking would cynically urge Hanoi to fight on "whatever its cost in North Vietnamese blood; whatever its cost in North Vietnamese well-being." On July 12, 1966, President Johnson called China's policy in Southeast Asia a "policy of aggression by proxy." Secretary Rusk had commented during an interview the year before, on August 24, 1965, "There is a comment going around in the Communist world these days that Peking is prepared to fight to the last Vietnamese."[5]

This is not to say that the possibility of a war with China was never raised. Secretary McNamara confessed on September 5, 1965, "It would be irresponsible . . . to say that we run no risk of . . . such a war"; on February 20, 1966, George Ball said he could not "rule out the possibility of a Chinese involvement just as it occurred in Korea." But it was far more common for that possibility to be minimized, if not entirely discounted, than conceded.

Such optimism was especially prevalent at times when American activities were unusually provocative, at times when it seemed United States initiatives could spark a major war. On March 19, 1965, six weeks after the beginning of the aerial bombing of the North, Maxwell Taylor, the ambassador to South Vietnam, declared that "there are no indications of any sort" that China was preparing to enter the war; on April 2, he stated that the chances of Peking intervening were "very slight at the present time." The start of the B-52 raids against fuel depots in Hanoi and Haiphong on June 29, 1966, preceded by a day George Ball's assessment that there was "no serious possibility" of China's invading South Vietnam. On July 2, Presidential Assistant Walt W. Rostow said of the new campaign, "I don't believe it need lead to war with China." Three days later, when asked to evaluate the chance of an armed Chinese reprisal, Mr. Ball responded simply that there was "no evidence that it's likely to occur."

It was in China's attitude and not from any specific actions that the government found reason to regard her as a serious threat to the future of Southeast Asia. In the years after the settlement at Geneva, Peking had become the principal advocate of violence as an instrument of foreign policy; Vice President Nixon on May 31, 1960, had cited the Chinese "emphasis on the orthodox Communist philosophy of the need for force as an essential ingredient in world Communist tactics." It was taken as more than coincidence that neighboring Indochina was under siege and an object of conquest. Peking's polemics had critically influenced, perhaps inspired, and in a sense caused, the war in Vietnam.

The writings of Mao Tse-tung "on guerilla warfare have become classic references," Mr. McNamara observed on March 26, 1964, "The North Vietnamese have taken a leaf or two from Mao's book." Dean Rusk explained at a news conference on December 23, 1964, that "the theory of the problem [in Vietnam] rests in Peking. It rests in a militant approach to the spread of world revolution as seen from the Communist point of view." On February 18, 1965, the defense secretary testified that in Southeast Asia "the Chinese Communists are putting into practice their theory that any non-communist government of an emerging nation can be overthrown by externally supported, covert armed aggression."

In the first two weeks of October 1965, there was a barrage of statements denouncing China. It was inspired by a September 3 article written by Chinese Defense Minister Lin Piao which Washington interpreted as confirmation of its worst suspicions about the designs of Peking. Robert McNamara, on October 2, called it "a guide to Communist intentions and future actions, . . . a program of aggression, . . . a speech that ranks with Hitler's *Mein Kampf.*" On the fifth Secretary Rusk declared, "the overhanging problem of peace is the policy of Peking. It is Peking that has announced a policy of world militancy." At the same time, in Tokyo, Ambassador Reischauer argued that the Vietnamese conflict was a function of China's "might is right" political theory. On October 14 Secretary Rusk again centered attention on the Chinese "strategy of violence," and again accused China of being "the main barrier to peace in Southeast Asia."

The pattern went on into 1966. Arthur Goldberg on March 4, 1966, insisted that the difficulty in Asia was with China. He offered as evidence a passage from Chairman Mao's book, *Problems of War and Strategy:* "The seizure of power by armed forces, the settlement of an issue by war, is the central task and the highest form of Revolution." On July 9 Secretary Rusk talked of the encouragement Hanoi received from the intransigence and belligerence of Peking. Vice President Humphrey spoke on August 11 about the relation of China's "policy of aggressive expansion" to the conflict in Vietnam.

Then, in the last quarter of 1966, references critical of China declined suddenly.[6] This may have reflected a decision not to further rouse China's anger with passionate rhetoric while the warfare itself was rising to new levels of intensity. It may also have reflected an uncertainty about China's capacity to exert influence outside its borders when confronted with a growing rebellion within.

The relevance of China's "cultural revolution" to the fighting in Vietnam was never the subject of excessive commentary. Although twice during the summer[7,8] spokesmen touched on Peking's internal problems in the course of discussions on the war, in neither instance were their implications assessed. It was not, in fact, until after the turn of the year that the secretary of state and the president, in successive appearances, offered what was to be the only official evaluation of their significance.

Both men emphasized first that the situation remained complex and that any judgments were still largely speculative. But each went on in different ways to suggest that it could mean that there would be a decreasing impact by China upon North Vietnam. Dean Rusk on a panel interview on February 1, 1967, began by remarking that Hanoi was "strongly influenced by Peking and has been for some time"; then, commenting on the Chinese power struggle, he said, "It may be that events in China may give Hanoi somewhat more freedom of action than they might have felt they had a little earlier." Speaking at a news conference the next day, Mr. Johnson answered a question on China's troubles with a similar observation:

> I think that there's little I can add to what the general public knows about the events in China. I think that we all know that

there's—they're having very serious problems and I would not think that that would add anything to the strength of our adversaries in that area.

The relative absence of China as a figure in the rhetoric persisted until the fall of 1967.[6] Then, almost as suddenly as it had disappeared, it was revived, in menacing form. Dean Rusk told the press on October 12:

> Within the next decade or two there will be a billion Chinese on the mainland, armed with nuclear weapons, with no certainty about what their attitude toward the rest of Asia will be.
>
> Now the free nations of Asia will make up at least a billion people. They don't want China to overrun them on the basis of a doctrine of the world revolution. The militancy of China has isolated China even within the Communist world but they have not drawn back from it. . . .
>
> We are not picking out ourselves, we are not picking out Peking as some sort of special enemy. Peking has nominated itself by proclaiming a militant doctrine of world revolution, and doing something about it. This is not a theoretical debate; they are doing something about it.

For the next two weeks administration spokesmen talked steadily of the specter of China in Vietnam. On October 15 Vice President Humphrey asserted, "The threat to world peace is militant aggressive Asian Communism." On the seventeenth Undersecretary of State Nicholas Katzenbach repeated that Asians were "deeply concerned about their long-term security in the face of a militant, hostile, rigidly ideological Communist China." The same day Eugene Rostow, another State Department aide, predicted that if South Vietnam were lost, Chinese expansion would be further encouraged. Vice President Humphrey spoke on October 18 of "certain aggressive patterns of conduct of China"; on the twenty-third he outlined the "unbearable pressure from a nuclear armed Communist China" which would be brought to bear if South Vietnam were lost.

But the offensive ended abruptly eleven days after it had begun. Though the State Department undertook to "wholly repudiate"[9] it, Nicholas Katzenbach dismissed it as "sheer fantasy,"[10] and its utter "absurdity"[11] was pointed out by the president, the government was unable to counter the allegation that

Mr. Rusk had sought to inject the inflammatory notion of "Yellow Peril" into the debate on the war. Throughout the remainder of 1967 and all of 1968 there was little further mention of Peking's role in Vietnam.

There has always been an irrational element to the American phobia about China. It has derived from the complexities of Oriental culture and the sheer vastness in human and territorial terms of the Chinese state, and has been nurtured by the almost total lack of contact between East and West. It has given rise to an image of China as an omnipresence brooding over Asia, an image which both the politicians and the public share. "China is so large, looms so high," John Kennedy said on September 9, 1963. Robert McNamara at a hearing on January 29, 1964, referred to "the Communist giant to the north." On April 7, 1965, President Johnson told an audience at Johns Hopkins University of "the deepening shadow of Communist China."

These images never changed. Though at the end of the decade Washington shifted its focus away from China, the shift did not indicate any moderation in its attitude or lessening of its fear. Defense Secretary Laird, therefore, was merely reasserting the conventional wisdom, and offering a reminder, when he warned the Senate Armed Services Committee on March 19, 1969 that

> Communist China . . . still constitutes the most dangerous potential for threatening the peace in Asia. Its vast army and relatively large air and naval forces are now on the verge of being supplemented by an operational nuclear capability, giving Communist China the possibility of being one of our gravest national security problems in the 1970s.

NORTH VIETNAM

> A Provisional military demarcation line shall be fixed, on either side of which the forces of the two parties shall be grouped after their withdrawal, the forces of the People's Army of Vietnam to the north of the line and the forces of the French Union to the south.
>
> ARTICLE I, CHAPTER I
> GENEVA AGREEMENTS

The agreements reached at Geneva on July 21, 1954, recognized the military gains of the Vietminh in the North, and granted the D.R.V. control of the region above the seventeenth parallel. Though abused from the start, the settlement maintained an uneasy peace until late 1959, when intense guerilla activity broke out in the South.

From the outset the United States laid a primary responsibility for these disturbances upon the government of North Vietnam. Washington charged that the leaders in Hanoi were materially assisting the rebel forces. Secretary Rusk, in reviewing the situation for the press on May 4, 1961, noted that "a considerable number of the personnel and also some of the supplies undoubtedly have been coming in from the North." On October 18 he described the attacks in the South as "supported by cadres and by supplies moving in from the north."

In addition, it was early suggested that the political guidance of the rebels had originated in the North as well. In his May 4 review, Mr. Rusk explained the "upsurge of Communist guerilla activity" as having "apparently stemmed from a decision made in May, 1959, by the Central Committee of the Communist Party of North Vietnam which called for the reunification of Vietnam by all 'appropriate means.' "

Six months later, on November 1, W. Averell Harriman, sitting as the head of the U.S. delegation conferring on Laos, remarked in Geneva:

> it is a well known and proved fact that the guerillas who are fighting the government in South Vietnam, causing a great deal of human misery, have been supported by, built up by, if not directed by North Vietnam.

In December the suggestions became an unqualified assertion; on the eighth the State Department released a report offering documentary proof that "the elaborate campaign of subversion, terror, and armed infiltration" had been "carried out under the direction of the authorities in Hanoi."

For the next three years officials, regularly and with a minimum of stylistic variation, underscored that finding. At a briefing on March 1, 1962, Dean Rusk said that the Communist guerillas were "directed, trained, supplied and reinforced by

North Vietnam." President Kennedy referred on November 14
to "the assault from the inside . . . which is manipulated from
the north." On March 17, 1964, the White House stated, "The
supply of arms and cadres from the North has continued; careful and sophisticated control of Vietcong operations has been
apparent; and evidence that such control is centered in Hanoi
is clear and unmistakable." Undersecretary of State William P.
Bundy discussed, on September 28, the "Communist regime of
North Vietnam" and "the war it directs and supports in South
Vietnam."

In 1965 there was a significant change in emphasis.[12]
Though the Johnson Administration continued to cite the "support" and "control" rendered by North Vietnam, it began to
place increasing stress on the growing rate of "infiltration from
the north" and took note for the first time that spring[13] of the
presence of "North Vietnamese Army units" in combat in the
South; it adduced these facts as evidence of the deepening
involvement by Hanoi. Robert McNamara reported on April
26, 1965:

> The clandestine infiltration of personnel and matériel from
> North Vietnam into South Vietnam continues to play a vital role
> in providing the communist Vietcong with the leadership, the
> technical competence, with the weapons and with the ammuni-
> tion which they need to carry on their insurgency. . . . With the
> changing course, the changing nature and particularly, the in-
> tensification of infiltration both of arms and personnel into South
> Vietnam [Hanoi's action] has grown progressively more flagrant
> and more unconstrained. The latest step has been the covert
> infiltration of a regular combat unit of the North Vietnamese
> Army in South Vietnam.

At a news conference on June 16 he recalled:

> there is at least one regular North Vietnamese Army Batallion in
> South Vietnam, the Second Battalion of the 325th North Viet-
> namese Division. . . .
> Moreover, the Vietcong forces have recently been equipped
> through the infiltration of new weapons, modern weapons, from
> North Vietnam.

And again in August,[14] he repeated to a Senate subcommit-
tee that

in addition to the continued infiltration of increasing numbers of individuals and the acceleration of the flow of modern equipment and supplies, organized units of the North Vietnamese Army have been identified in South Vietnam.

Throughout the rest of the decade, officials devoted less and less attention to "support" and "control," focusing instead on the newer, more immediate aid. On February 18, 1966, Secretary Rusk testified to the Foreign Relations Committee that "beginning over a year ago . . . the greater number of men infiltrated into the South have been native born North Vietnamese" and indicated there was "evidence that nine regiments of regular North Vietnamese" had by then crossed the border. That September,[15] Arthur Goldberg revealed that "some seventeen identified regiments" were operating in the South. In December 1967,[16] the Pentagon estimated that 20,-000 North Vietnamese regulars were emplaced along the Cambodian frontier. President Johnson disclosed on July 31, 1968:

> The number of North Vietnamese soldiers now entering South Vietnam at the end of the Ho Chi Minh trail is now greater than at any other time in this war.
> We estimated that 30,000 North Vietnamese soldiers entered South Vietnam in July.

1965 also brought a multiplication of references to North Vietnam's "aggression" and ambition to "dominate the South." Mr. Rusk stated on February 25 that

> North Vietnam, in callous disregard of the agreements of 1954 and 1962 and of international law has directed and supplied the essential military personnel and arms for a systematic campaign of terror and guerilla action aimed at the overthrow of the Government of South Vietnam and at the imposition by force of a Communist regime.
> The evidence of North Vietnam's direct responsibility for this aggression has been repeatedly presented by the Government of Vietnam, the U.S. Government, and the International Control Commission.

Two days later the State Department officially diagnosed the war as an "Aggression from the North," a week and a half after that[17] denouncing the leaders in Hanoi for "trying to take over

South Vietnam by violence." Mr. Johnson contended in April,[18] "The basic cause of the conflict in Vietnam is the attack by North Vietnam on the independent nation of South Vietnam. The object of that attack is total conquest." That August,[19] Presidential Press Secretary Bill Moyers contended that "the quickest way to peace" was for "aggression from the North to cease."

These statements said in effect that Hanoi was a greater menace, posing a more direct threat to the security of South Vietnam than ever before, and reflected the harsher attitude which Washington began in 1965 to take toward the activities of North Vietnam. Their introduction, along with the accounts of the discovery of North Vietnamese regulars and the accelerating flow of war matériel across the demilitarized zone, paralleled the U.S. escalation and was related to it. The decision of February 8 to launch retaliatory air strikes against the North, that of July 28 to deploy 50,000 American soldiers rapidly in the South, and all the other decisions in the months between, were presented against the background of this increasing provocation and intransigence, and defended as the necessary response to it. The reviews of the growing rates of infiltration and the mounting concentrations of North Vietnamese troops tended to support the contention that the government in Hanoi had invited all that it had received. The talk of North Vietnam's "aggression" and her drive for "conquest" through "violence" went to the same point. There, however, the sense that Hanoi had gotten what it deserved derived not from the reasonable implications of statistical data, but from the immediate impact of loaded images, the connotations and associations of words like "aggression," "conquest," "violence." The appeal, fundamentally emotional, was bound to inflame without clearly defining the object of passion.

Such statements continued, reaching their peak in 1966. On January 22, Lyndon Johnson deplored the "hostility and aggressiveness in Hanoi and . . . [its] insistence on the abandonment of South Vietnam to Communist takeover." Mr. Stevenson insisted on February 1 that North Vietnam had "led, equipped and sustained the fighting in the South . . . for the purpose of imposing its will upon the people of South Vietnam by force." The next day the State Department expressed its opposition to "the attempt by North Vietnam to impose its will by force on South Vietnam." The president warned Hanoi on July 12, "as long as you persist in aggression, we will resist." On December 8 Secretary Rusk promised "the North Vietnamese are not going to be able to seize this country by force."

There was an abrupt decline in this imagery in 1967. It may have indicated a judgment by the administration that there were diminishing returns when emotive language like this was used over long periods of time. Or perhaps it represented an attempt to moderate the rhetoric in the hope that it would ease the process of face-to-face negotiations when it finally occurred. Whatever the reason, it ran counter to the general trend, which was to censure the North Vietnamese with increasing frequency—a trend that derived from the decreasing significance which the United States attributed to the Chinese and the Russians and the growing number of direct confrontations, both military and diplomatic, between Washington and Hanoi.

VIETMINH/VIETCONG

On March 20, 1952, Dean Acheson testified to the House Foreign Affairs Committee that "the bulk" of those opposing the Free French in Indochina were members of the Vietminh, and were Vietnamese, not foreign, nationals. This assessment, though never reconfirmed, was never denied. Yet throughout the years from 1950 to 1954 these rebels received scant attention from Washington. When officials did refer to them, it was to expose their leader Ho Chi Minh as a servant of outside Communist powers, and thereby repudiate their proclaimed goal of liberation.

On January 31, 1950, State Department spokeman Lincoln White told newsmen that while Ho Chi Minh "poses as a nationalist leader . . . what he is preaching is Indo-China for the Kremlin and not Indo-China for the Indo-Chinese." "He has," Mr. White added, "a long record under various aliases as a Moscow agent." Secretary Dulles, on March 29, 1954, developed this point further:

> Now Ho Chi Minh was indoctrinated in Moscow. He became an associate of Borodin when the Russian Borodin was sent to China to organize the Chinese Communist party. . . . After this association with Borodin, Ho Chi Minh transferred his activities to Indo-China.

On May 7, he repeated that Ho Chi Minh was "a Communist leader who was trained in Moscow and got his first revolutionary experience in China."

The counterparts to the Vietminh during the Vietnam War, the indigenous troops fighting within the borders of South Vietnam, were the Vietcong, and they received similar treatment. Their activities were described by the United States as a brutal and highly organized form of gangsterism and emerged as more of an annoyance than a menace. One of the first comments on their operations came in a report by State Department Press Officer Joseph Reap on the abduction of a South Vietnamese undersecretary of state. Released on October 3, 1961, it read:

> The Department views the kidnapping of Colonel Nam as another evidence of Communist contempt for the ICC and Communist reliance on terror as a method of operation. The Vietcong are now engaged in a campaign of terror and guerilla warfare in South Vietnam which is claiming 1500 lives every month.

Ambassador Lodge, denouncing a grenade attack which had injured eight Americans, said on May 3, 1964, "This is typical of the murderous methods used by the Vietcong and must appear utterly revolting to civilized people everywhere." On May 21, 1964, Adlai Stevenson presented a detailed account of their approach to warfare in a speech before the United Nations:

> Mr. President, Members of the Council, it is the people of the Republic of Vietnam who are the major victims of armed aggression. It is they who are fighting for their independence against violence. . . . It is they who suffer day and night from the terror of the so-called Vietcong.
> The prime targets of the Vietcong for kidnapping, for torture and for murder have been local officials, school teachers, medical workers, priests, agricultural specialists and any others whose position, profession or other talent qualified them for service to the people of Vietnam, plus, of course, the relatives and children of citizens loyal to their government.

WHO IS THE ENEMY?

WHO IS THE ENEMY? 37

The chosen military objectives of the Vietcong for gunfire, or arson, or pillage, have been hospitals, schoolhouses, agricultural stations and various improvement projects by which the Government of Vietnam for many years has been raising the living standards of the people.

The Government and the people of Vietnam have been struggling for survival—struggling for years—in a war which has been as wicked, as wanton and as dirty as any waged against an innocent and peaceful people in the whole cruel history of warfare.

It seems to me that there is something both grotesque and ironic in the fact that the victims of this incessant terror are the accused before this Council and are defending themselves in daylight, while terrorists perform their dark and dirty work by night throughout their land.

1964 was the first year in which there was any significant amount of discussion of the enemy, and the Vietcong was referred to then relatively more often than at any time thereafter, with a specific concentration on rebel combat activities that was never again equaled. In the period that followed not only was there less talk of Vietcong "subversion" and "terror," but a gradual and continuing increase in allusions to the Vietcong, or the National Liberation Front, as instruments of Hanoi.[20] The State Department, in its White Paper of February 1965,[21] said that all evidence showed

> that the key leadership of the Vietcong, the officers and much of the cadre, many of the technicians, political organizers, and propagandists have come from the North and operate under Hanoi's direction.

Eleven months later[22] Undersecretary Ball called the front, "purely and simply a ficticious organization created by Hanoi to reinforce a fiction." That April,[23] Vice President Humphrey declared to a gathering of the Associated Press:

> But you and I know that the National Liberation Front is exactly what its terminology says it is, a front. That is the only honest word. It is not national. It liberates no one. It is a front of Ho Chi Minh from Hanoi.

The same theme was struck again by Dean Rusk on February 1, 1967:

The leadership of the Vietcong in the South is made up of North Vietnamese generals, men that we know by name. One of them is a four star general who gives the political and military direction to the NLF, and we have this on a basis of a great deal of information.

In an interview in France in December 1968,[24] W. Averell Harriman, then chief U.S. negotiator at the Paris peace talks, described the Vietcong as "a creation of North Vietnam and an agent of Hanoi's aggression."

In each decade the local Vietminh and Vietcong were largely ignored by American officials, and when they were discussed it was frequently in order to dispute their independence and challenge their claims of autonomy. There was also, through the twenty years, extensive use of supranational, generic labels, such as "Communist" or "the other side," which merged together all who were involved at all in the hostilities. The combination of these patterns encouraged the inference that in each of these wars native forces were of minimal importance.

NOTES TO CHAPTER 2

1. McNamara, March 26, 1964.
2. Taylor, September 10, 1964.
3. State Department, October 3, 1966.
4. McNamara, February 1, 1968.
5. Eleven years earlier, on June 18, 1954, United Nations Ambassador Lodge offered a strikingly similar observation on the war in Korea. There, "apparently," he said, "the Soviet Union was willing to go on fighting to the last Chinese Communist."
6. In the first, second, and third quarters of 1966 denunciations of the Chinese were offered respectively in 14 percent, 18 percent and 12 percent of official statements. In the fourth quarter, the level dropped to 5 percent and did not exceed, or equal that figure until the October through December period of 1967, when it rose dramatically to 15 percent.
7. Ball, June 30, 1966.
8. Johnson, July 23, 1966.
9. State Department, October 16, 1967.
10. Katzenbach, October 17, 1967.
11. Johnson, October 25, 1967.
12. Shifts in the nature of the role the United States charged the North Vietnamese with playing in the South:

year	61	62	63	64	65	66	67	68	69
aid, support	2	2	1	12	4	4	0	1	0
direct control	3	3	1	13	13	7	4	5	0
infiltration	4	0	0	2	19	18	13	19	0
regular troops	0	0	0	0	16	14	14	23	5
takeover, seize	3	0	0	4	13	28	11	8	3
aggression	0	2	0	6	21	25	12	10	2
all North Vietnam	7	5	3	41	84	96	102	108	21

13. Diplomatic Corps, April 26, 1965.
14. McNamara, August 4, 1965.
15. Goldberg, September 22, 1966.
16. Defense Department, December 11, 1967.
17. State Department, March 9, 1965.
18. Johnson, April 8, 1965.
19. Moyers, August 6, 1965.
20. In 1964, 29 percent of the references to the Vietcong made mention of their military exercises—their guerilla tactics, terrorism, subversive campaigns—and there was no discussion at all of rebel submissiveness to the North Vietnamese. In 1965 the proportion dealing with violent action fell to 19 percent while that touching on their servitude to Hanoi increased to 7 percent. Over the next three years allusions to revolutionary fighting did not move above the 1965 level but those to Vietcong dependence continued to grow steadily: to 17 percent in 1966, 19 percent in 1967, and 29 percent in 1968.
21. State Department, February 27, 1965.
22. Ball, January 30, 1966.
23. Humphrey, April 25, 1966.
24. Harriman, December 17, 1968.

CHAPTER THREE

WHAT IS THE NATURE OF THE WAR?

Not an Internal Uprising

The Eisenhower Administration described the Indochina war as one of a spate of "Moscow-inspired and controlled revolutions."[1] Not only, it said, was Ho Chi Minh a Soviet agent,[2] having been schooled in Russia during the 1930s, but his forces were being trained[3] and receiving their material support—"the artillery, the ammunition, the equipment"[4]—from China, the newest Soviet ally.[5] Rebel dependence upon the Kremlin defined the so-called insurrection as a case of "open and covert invasion,"[6] and the conclusion was reinforced by official concentration upon "outside" powers rather than the indigenous Vietminh. Though Washington wholly conceded that the struggle may have started as "a war for independence," it stressed that it had long since been "taken over by international communism for its own purposes."[7] It was, therefore, hardly a revelation when the government[8] declared on April 20, 1954, that the Indochinese conflict was "just not a civil war."

The Johnson Administration similarly denied that the Vietnam War was an internal affair. It did this directly only infrequently. In 1964 Secretary McNamara claimed that the Southeast Asian crisis was not a function of "factional disputes"[9] and Adlai Stevenson charged that the other side deliberately "sought to pretend that the insurgency in South Vietnam is a civil war."[10] In 1965 a State Department White Paper insisted that "the war in Vietnam is not a spontaneous and local rebellion,"[11] an American delegate to the United Nations accused the Russians of laying down a "familiar smokescreen of propaganda"[12] when they called it a revolution, and the president explained, "it is not a civil war. It is sustained by power and resources from without. The very object of this tactic is to create the appearance of internal revolt."[13]

In 1966, a year in which the oratory reached new levels of intensity and desperation, the number of these statements rose to ten. At one extreme were the outright denials; there was Robert McNamara's resentment at "any implication that the war in Vietnam is in any sense a civil war"[14] and Hubert Humphrey's cynical "I hear that it is a civil war. I doubt that many believe that."[15] At the other were the partial and indirect concessions; Undersecretary Ball's acknowledgment that the situation had a "few of the attributes of an indigenous revolt,"[16] Secretary Rusk's, that there was a small "indigenous element."[17] In 1967 the ceiling again fell, remaining low in 1968.

Although officials rarely stated openly their conviction that there was no civil war in Southeast Asia, they implied as much in nearly every statement they made. As in the accounts ten years earlier, the war emerged as a result of foreign intrigue. The leaders in Hanoi, "spurred by Communist China"[18] and with the "moral and material support"[19] of the Soviet Union, "led, equipped and sustained the fighting"[20] in South Vietnam. Since 1959[21] when it "decided on conquest,"[22] the Democratic Republic had supervised the "training and infiltration of agents"[23] and provided "weapons and supplies";[24] later it "sent large forces of its own."[25] As for the Vietcong, the self-styled native movement based in the South, it had been "organized in Hanoi in 1960"[26] and continued to be "controlled, directed and masterminded from North Vietnam,"[27] "on a daily basis."[28] The war, with facets of "an insurgency . . . externally directed and supported"[29] and "overt external aggression,"[29] represented another critical confrontation with world communism.[30]

These explicit appraisals of the participants' roles were reflected by the rhetoric in other ways, ways which heightened the impression that the struggle was essentially international in character. Once again the local elements received far less attention than the foreign ones, although as in the decade before, it was the local elements who made up the main force of enemy strength. The Vietcong campaign of "terrorism, kidnapping and torture"[31] lacked the verbal dimension of the program of "aggression from the North,"[32] and it was in terms of aggression, rather than of guerilla warfare, that the hostilities were most often described.

Whether or not an armed dispute should be deemed a civil war is a complex question which depends not only on the identity of the combatants and their sources of support, but on the circumstances of the dispute's origin and the issues in conflict. The problem here is not, however, to assess the merits of the American answer, but rather to examine why having arrived at it, the government was so apparently intent upon convincing others that it was correct; why, aside from its validity, it was the most suitable response.

Part of the explanation rested undoubtedly with the doctrine of "nonintervention in civil disputes." Though international law remains vague on the matter of its application, the United States has traditionally endorsed the general prescription that internal disorders should be dealt with internally;[33] the principles of sovereignty and self-determination imply that each state has both the right and the responsibility to settle its own affairs. Having taken this position, it would have been both inconsistent and criminal for the United States to intervene in a Vietnam beset by domestic strife. Past posturing and legal constraints demanded that American assistance be granted under the color of repulsing an invasion.

Another part involved the dynamics of persuasion. In characterizing the war as a "war of aggression," officials rendered U.S. aid more readily understood as a political necessity. Supplying men and equipment to a government threatened by rebellion would have appeared as a brazen overextension of power, an arrogant attempt at policing the universe. Doing the same for a government endangered by an externally-based conspiracy was seemingly a more justifiable and fair engagement of American force.

Because of the small size of the sample it is difficult to establish with any certainty the attitude of the Kennedy Administration toward this issue. It can be said, however, that the civil aspects of the war were not so conveniently ignored, and less a source of ostensible embarrassment then than later on. As compared with the period following, there were not the repeated allegations of the complete domination of the National Liberation Front by the North nor any reports of open North Vietnamese involvement in the South. Over these three years spokemen described the conflict more in terms of guerilla tactics than as flagrant aggression and in 1963 gave, though marginally, more coverage to the activities of the Vietcong than to those of any of its northern allies. At a news conference during the summer of 1963[34] the president concluded a summary of Vietnam's turbulent history by specifically referring to the struggle as "the civil war" that had "gone on for ten years."

The absence of a concerted effort to deprecate the role of internal elements related to a lack of either jurisprudential or political pressures to mount one. American participation in 1963 was still limited enough for an attack on its lawfulness to be rather unlikely and premature; the credible promise that the participation would remain limited and that an end to the war was in sight reduced the need to dramatize the fighting or to galvanize the nation for heavy sacrifice.

NOT AN ISOLATED CONFRONTATION

President Truman, on September 14, 1951, called the battle in Indochina "the same fight for liberty" as that going on in Korea; eleven years later on April 11, 1962, in response to a reporter's question about the deaths of American advisers in Vietnam, President Kennedy commented that the U.S. mission there

presents a very hazardous operation, in the same sense that
World War II, World War I, Korea—a good many thousands and
hundreds of thousands of Americans died. So that these four
sergeants are in that long roll.

Neither of these statements is in itself of particular importance;
that is, neither was typical of, nor offered insight into, the official
positions of the Truman or Kennedy Administrations. They are
of interest, however, as forerunners of a line which, in later
years, was to be recited time and time again.

Faced with the task of explaining a remote and complicated
situation in Southeast Asia, Washington from 1964 on portrayed
that situation and the U.S. reaction to it as being consistent with,
and an outgrowth of, a postwar tradition of American interventions around the world. Ambassador Stevenson struck the comparison on May 21, 1964, at the United Nations:

> Aggression is aggression. Organized violence is organized vio-
> lence. Only the scale and scenery change. The point is the same
> in Vietnam today as it was in Greece in 1947 and in Korea in
> 1950.

The president reiterated this, expanding the list of referents, on
August 5, 1964:

> So to our friends of the Atlantic Alliance let me say this this
> morning: the challenge that we face in Southeast Asia today is
> the same challenge that we faced with courage and that we have
> met with strength in Greece and Turkey, in Berlin and Korea,
> and in Lebanon and Cuba.

He said to newsmen on July 9, 1965:

> We have lost in the neighborhood of some 300 men [in Vietnam]
> in the period since I have been President. We expect that it will
> get worse before it gets better. . . . [But] we have suffered 160,-
> 000 casualties since World War II . . . we did not allow Greece
> or Turkey or Iran or Formosa or Lebanon or others to fall to
> aggressors, and we don't plan to let up until the aggression
> ceases.

Four months earlier, on March 19, 1965, State Department
planner W. W. Rostow had told the German Society for Foreign
Policy that the problem of Communist encroachment was "just

as real" in Vietnam as it had been in Greece in 1947 or in Berlin in 1958.

The theme was sounded with regularity throughout 1966. The upsurge came as the consequences of the decisions to enlarge and deepen the U.S. role in Southeast Asia began to be more widely felt; in the five months from July to December, twice as many American had died in Indochina as in the six years previously. The emphasis on the relation between the new commitment and those undertaken elsewhere in the past was a simple and graphic way of conveying to the thousands of families who were for the first time being directly affected by the war the sense that their sons' sacrifices were of great importance and were not in vain.

The year opened with Mr. Johnson's State of the Union Message on January 12, which set the tone for the remaining twelve months:

> Tonight the cup of peril is full in Vietnam. That conflict is not an isolated episode, but another great event in the policy that we have followed with strong consistency since World War II . . . we gave our aid to Greece and Turkey, and we defended the freedom of Berlin . . . we have defended against Communist aggression in Korea under President Truman; in the Formosa Straits under President Eisenhower; in Cuba under President Kennedy and again in Vietnam.

Changing his focus somewhat, he made the same point on February 6, in a welcoming ceremony in Honolulu:

> were the Communist aggressors to win in Vietnam, they would know they can accomplish through so-called wars of national liberation what they could not accomplish through naked aggression in Korea—or insurgency in the Philippines, Greece and Malaya—or the threat of aggression in Turkey. . . .

On February 19 Vice President Humphrey asked how people who had endorsed government action in Berlin, Greece, Korea, and Cuba could "turn around and advise that you can forget Vietnam."

In the weeks prior to Memorial Day there was an especial, and understandable, preoccupation with placing Vietnam and the losses taken there in this broader context; between May

1965 and May 1966, the number of deaths had increased nearly tenfold from 385 to 3,466. In a speech at Princeton University on May 11, the president noted that

> not one single country where America has helped mount a major effort to resist aggression, from France, to Greece, to Korea, to Vietnam—not one single country where we have helped—today has a government servile to outside interests.

Seven days later he observed at a Democratic fund-raising dinner in Chicago:

> Our policy in Vietnam is a national policy. . . . In carrying out that policy we have taken casualties in Berlin and Korea and now in Vietnam. We have had 160,000 American casualties from World War II up until Vietnam.

On May 24, Secretary Rusk stated, "It is as important to defeat this type of aggression in Southeast Asia now as it was to defeat it in Greece 19 years ago." He went on to review American efforts in preserving world order since 1945:

> We supported Iran when its integrity and independence were threatened.
> When Greece and Turkey were threatened we assisted them. . . .
> When free Berlin was threatened, we organized an airlift which enabled it to live—without war. . . .
> We played a major role in repelling the Communist aggression against the Republic of Korea. . . . Since the end of the Second World War our Armed Forces have suffered more than 165,000 casualties in the defense of freedom.

In an official proclamation on May 26, Mr. Johnson promised that the United States would persevere in Southeast Asia, declaring, "In two World Wars and in Korea brave Americans gave their lives that men might live and prosper in freedom. We shall not forsake their sacrifice." Four days thereafter, at the Arlington Amphitheater, he recalled the names of the soldiers who had been the first killed in operations in Greece, Berlin, Korea, Quemoy, Cuba, and Vietnam. "These men," he said, "represent all those Americans who have risked their lives—and lost them—in the peace building efforts that America has made since 1945."

In 1967 the administration still talked of Vietnam as part of a pattern of U.S. involvement, but far less frequently. It was once again the president who, on September 29, reminded:

> Since World War II this nation has met and has mastered many challenges—challenges in Greece and Turkey, in Berlin, in Korea, in Cuba.
>
> We met them because brave men were willing to risk their lives for their nation's security. And braver men have never lived than those who carry our colors tonight in Vietnam at this very hour.

On October 25 he spoke of "the remote fields and hills where Americans have died for freedom—in Vietnam, in Korea, and in the Philippines."

By 1968, the initiative had all but run its course.

In Greece and Turkey, in Berlin and Korea, in Formosa and Cuba, the United States had been successful in responding to what it regarded as a major test of American will. Each event was the analogue of the others, and all were analogous to Vietnam, to the extent that each could be represented as a confrontation definable in terms of the same issues—communism, aggression, and freedom. Washington suggested that the nature of the conflict in Southeast Asia was best revealed against this background of twenty years of Cold War, since examined in isolation, the peculiarities of Vietnamese politics and geography took on an exaggerated significance. It indicated that the threat and potential dangers were as great there as they had been anywhere since 1945. And it implied that just as history had shown those stands to have been correct, so the perspective of time would also vindicate the current policies as being an appropriate response to a challenge of "free world" resolve.

Not a White Man's War

From 1952 to 1954 official Washington warned that if the people of Indochina did not become more heavily involved in the fighting, there would be little chance of defeating the Communists. In testimony before the Senate Foreign Relations Committee on March 18, 1952, Secretary of State Dean Acheson reported that the situation in Southeast Asia was "very serious" and would continue to be so until the French were able to assemble a large and effective native army. Thirteen months later, on April 12, 1953, the new chief of the State Department, John Foster Dulles, told the Congress that the military phase of the war was "not so favorable as we might have expected" and urged the speedy development of an Indochinese force. President Eisenhower, in his budget message of January 21, 1954, wrote:

> Additional native forces must be trained and equipped to preserve the defensive strength in Indo-China. This assistance is required to enable those gallant forces to sustain an offensive that will provide the opportunity for victory.

On March 23, 1954, Secretary of Defense Charles E. Wilson, in an appearance before the newsreel cameras, declared, "Effective and aggressive training of Indochinese troops is essential if the war is to be brought to a successful conclusion."

The government never pretended, however, that the lagging manpower was anything more than a symptom of the more fundamental problem of lagging spirit. The need to increase battalion strength was regarded as second to the need to instill in the Indochinese people a sense of dedication and purpose. President Eisenhower observed at a press conference on February 3, 1954:

> All of us have known, in every situation like you have here, that the heart and soul of the population really becomes the biggest factor of success or failure. By that I mean that if the Vietnamese want to be free, if they believe that through this kind of war they will be free, then you could have a probable success.

Speaking more generally, he commented on April 7:

> For many years, in talking to different countries, different governments, I have tried to insist on this principle: No outside country can come in and be really helpful unless it is doing something that the local people want.

On June 10 he set forth the implications of this theory for an American intervention in Indochina:

the United States can not alone by its military might achieve the policies that we have to pursue. There has to be—and I go back again to what I have been saying incessantly—it has to be the proper psychological, political bases for these things, or merely to go wage a battle somewhere is perfectly useless, costly and useless.

Though the United States never openly criticized its French ally, President Eisenhower's analysis of the situation in Indochina was at least implicitly an indictment of France's disregard of the aspirations of the local people. Her excessive reliance on European strength and expertise and her reluctance to grant full and immediate independence reinforced the impression that France was waging a "white man's " war on Asian soil; it greatly undercut the possibility of an enthusiastic and effective native participation.

In the years from 1960 to 1963, therefore, Washington stressed its determination to play a secondary role in the defense of South Vietnam. In a letter to President Diem, sent on October 25, 1960, Mr. Eisenhower said that though the United States would continue to furnish aid, the major responsibility for protecting that country's freedom would fall upon the Vietnamese themselves. The assistant secretary of state, W. Averell Harriman, testified at a congressional hearing on February 13, 1962, that there were "no present plans for the commitment of American combat forces," emphasizing to the committee, "It is their war." Though in the months that followed the United States began to increase its logistical training and transport operations, George Ball insisted in an address before the Economic Club of Detroit on April 30, 1962, that "we are not fighting the war . . . we are not running the war." Speaking at the Waldorf Astoria in New York a year later, on April 22, 1963, Mr. Rusk underscored the fact that it was the Vietnamese who were engaged in battle; the American involvement he described as being purely "limited and supporting."

In May 1963, the Diem regime began systematically to harass the Buddhist opposition. Its campaign of repression, which lasted through June and July, climaxed with a raid conducted by the secret police against the pagodas on August 21. Saigon's behavior was disillusioning to Americans, some of whom had regarded Mr. Diem as an exemplary figure, a leader of great stature;[35] it also demonstrated the futility of any attempt by a foreign power to assume the burden of Vietnamese destiny. The events of that summer led President Kennedy to observe, as his predecessor had nine years earlier, how critical nonmilitary conditions were in determining the outcome of a war. He told Walter Cronkite during a CBS television interview on September 2:

> We are prepared to continue to assist them, but I don't think that the war can be won unless the people support the effort and, in my opinion, in the last two months, the Government has gotten out of touch with the people.

Dean Rusk reiterated to newsmen on November 8, a week after Mr. Diem was overthrown and assassinated, that

> the reception, the support of the people themselves will be vital in this type of guerilla warfare. The attitude of the people becomes absolutely crucial. As I think it was Mao-Tse-Tung said: "If the guerillas are operating within a friendly population, every bush is an ally."

Throughout 1964, the Johnson Administration continued to contend that the solution of the problems in South Vietnam properly and necessarily rested with the government in Saigon. Robert McNamara, appearing before the House Armed Services Committee on January 29, said:

> we must recognize that the United States advisory effort cannot assure ultimate success. This is a Vietnamese war, and in the final analysis it must be fought and won by Vietnamese. To leave our advisers there beyond the time they are truly needed would delay the development of Vietnam's initiative. . . . I don't think we as a nation should assume the primary responsibility for the war in South Vietnam.

Nine days later, on February 7, Secretary Rusk commented to reporters:

> I think the resources and the capabilities are there to get this job done on the present basis of assistance to the Vietnamese so that they can handle this problem primarily with their own effort.

At a speech at the University of California in Los Angeles on February 22, Mr. Johnson reaffirmed that "the contest in which South Vietnam is now engaged is first and foremost a contest to be won by the Government and people of that country," and he repeated frequently[36] thereafter that the United States sought only to help the Vietnamese help themselves; he declared to the American Bar Association on August 12 that he had rejected the counsel of those who "call upon us to supply the American boys to do the job that Asian boys should do." On May 3 William Bundy, the assistant secretary of state for foreign affairs, had underlined how the operation there fundamentally "has to be a South Vietnamese thing."

In 1965, 1,369 Americans were killed in Southeast Asia. In 1966, another 5,008 died; in 1967, an additional 9,419. During those three years officials were increasingly less apt to characterize the United States as "helping," "assisting," or "supporting," that is, increasingly less apt to use words which implied that it was performing a limited role. They also ceased to insist that it was, and ought to be, a Vietnamese war. But on occasion, often when others raised the issue, they steadfastly maintained that the people of Vietnam were assuming the primary responsibility, and denied that the United States had changed either its course or its plans.

President Johnson remarked on March 25, 1965, that "the main burden of resistance has fallen on the people and soldiers of South Vietnam. We Americans have lost hundreds of our own men there and we mourn them. But the free Vietnamese have lost tens of thousands." In the course of the Senate Foreign Relations Committee hearings on the war on February 18, 1966, this exchange was recorded between Senator Clifford Case and Dean Rusk:

> *Senator Clifford P. Case:* How far can we go if we want to answer this question in escalating the number of American troops without turning this into an American war as opposed to a war of the Vietnamese?
> *Secretary of State Dean Rusk:* We are rather a long way from that point at the present time, Senator. I indicated that out of 25 battalions or larger scale operations in progress yesterday, that 20 of those were South Vietnamese. There are almost 700,000

South Vietnamese under arms in all categories, military and paramilitary. They are taking the bulk of the fighting, they are taking the bulk of the casualties, and many aspects of this struggle are peculiarly for them rather than for us, particularly the bringing of guerilla cadres out of the villages and things of that sort. I think we are at a considerable distance of this becoming our war in any sense exclusive of the South Vietnamese or in which they would be ultimately the junior partner. They are the major partner here in the fighting, and the foreseeable future, as I can see in the months ahead of us, that I think will remain the situation.

On December 19, 1967, during a television interview, Mr. Johnson defended his policies as being consistent with his campaign rhetoric of three years before. He recalled that in 1964

We made clear that the South Vietnamese ought to pledge every resource they had, that we would never supplant them, but we would supplement them to the extent necessary.

We did not plan to go into Asia and to fight an Asian war that Asians ought to be fighting for themselves. But if Asians were fighting for themselves and were using all the resources that they had in South Vietnam, there was no pledge, no commitment and no implication that we would not supplement them and support them as we are now doing.

In 1968 the phase of spiraling American escalation abruptly ended with the order to curtail the bombing raids against North Vietnam. In revealing that order on March 30 the president insisted that "the United States presence in South Vietnam has always rested on this basic belief: The main burden of preserving their freedom must be carried out by them—by the South Vietnamese themselves." He emphasized:

We and our allies can only help to provide a shield behind which the people of South Vietnam can survive and can grow and develop. On their efforts—on their determination and resourcefulness—the outcome will ultimately depend.

Against this background Defense Secretary Clark Clifford announced on April 11 that the initiative which had never officially passed to the United States was being returned to South Vietnam; at his first news conference he informed the press that "the policy decision has been made to turn over

gradually the major effort to the South Vietnamese." Thereafter, a steady stream of statements described the progress of
the new program.

President Johnson reported on May 3:

> We have detected increased efforts there and among our other
> allies and certainly in this country to expedite our equipment so
> that they may be able to effectively carry a larger share of the
> burden. As you know, they have taken certain actions in connec-
> tion with their own draft—drafting 19 year olds and drafting 18
> year olds.

On July 14 Mr. Clifford disclosed in Saigon that "we plan to give
weapons to A.R.V.N. forces—all of the A.R.V.N. forces—even at
the expense of our forces." W.W. Rostow, Mr. Johnson's special
assistant for national security affairs, predicted on January 4,
1969:

> If they are steady and we are steady, the United States can
> gradually fall back, not to isolation from Asia, but to a junior
> partnership role as they take more and more of their own destiny
> in their own hands.

On April 3 Defense Secretary Melvin Laird, speaking on behalf
of the Nixon Administration, assured the public that "we're
moving to Vietnamize the war as rapidly as we can."

For twenty years American spokesmen discussed the necessity of relying on the people of Indochina to defeat the Communists; to do otherwise, it was explained, would hamper the development of local initiative and weaken popular support. The
timing of these statements frequently seemed to be impelled by
outside circumstance. It may have been said to have been
"their war" in April 1954, because President Eisenhower was
annoyed at France's manifest insensitivity to nationalistic feelings; in September 1963, because President Kennedy was dis-
enchanted with Mr. Diem's oppressive and authoritarian tactics; in August 1964, because President Johnson sought to
contrast his position with the military adventurism advocated
by the Republican candidate, Barry Goldwater; in March 1968,
because domestic criticism and Asian setbacks demanded a reexamination and curtailment of the U.S. role. On other occasions, especially during the period from 1965 to 1967, when

government decisions seemed to have violated the spoken principles, it appeared to reflect an institutional aversion to admitting inconsistency.

Nevertheless, the insistence on the need for native responsibility cannot be simply dismissed as an empty rhetorical convenience. The notion of self-reliance, to which it relates, is a central, peculiarly American value, derived from the romantic experiences of the late nineteenth and early twentieth centuries, and associated with the life of Teddy Roosevelt and the phrase "rugged individualism." Applied to international affairs, it deems a nation willing and determined to depend on itself worthier than one content to accept the favors of others. The United States publicly foreswore a dominant position in Southeast Asia because to approve it would have suggested that the Vietnamese cause was bankrupt, that not even those most immediately affected were inspired enough to die for their country in that cause. Moreover, it would have raised doubts about America's professed altruism and lent credit to the charge that the United States was involved in a self-righteous, moral crusade.

NOT A QUEST FOR EMPIRE

Franklin Roosevelt, on a number of occasions before the end of the Second World War, registered his support for Indochinese independence and strong disapproval of plans simply to return the colony to France and the prewar status quo. When in 1950 President Truman opted to oppose the D.R.V. and recognize the French-sponsored Republic of Vietnam, he was acting to permit a result his predecessor had wanted to prevent. His administration argued then that the decision represented no departure from principle. To regard the United States as having made any concessions to colonialism, Ambassador Jessup contended on February 3, "would be a misinterpretation" of the government's moves. Recognition, the State Department explained on February 7, was "consistent with our fundamental policy of giving support to the peaceful and democratic evolution of dependent peoples toward self-government and independence."

Nevertheless, officials did continually have to meet the charge that by association America had become a party to French imperialism in Southeast Asia. Sometimes they responded by merely redirecting it at the other side. On May 8, 1950, Secretary Acheson spoke of the danger that Indochina would be "dominated by Soviet imperialism," and on August 13 Phillip Jessup warned that "Communist imperialism" was seeking the capture of the Far East. In June 1954, Mr. Dulles denounced Marxist revolutionaries as "the new imperialist colonialists,"[37] while United Nations Representative Lodge talked about the need to defend small nations against "imperialistic Communism . . . the twentieth century colonialism of the Soviets."[38]

Often, however, the government sought to deal with the issues substantively. On these occasions it emphasized the large measure of autonomy that Paris had agreed to grant to Laos, Cambodia, and Vietnam, presenting these undertakings as virtual assurance that France had abandoned all pretensions of empire. Given such commitments, the excesses of French colonial rule could be dismissed as matters for the historian and no longer of concern to the contemporary statesman.

The Elysee Accords, passed by the National Assembly in early February 1950, stood as the first measurable step taken by this enlightened France in deference to Indochinese nationalism. Out of them the Republic of Vietnam had been born, possessed of a degree of administrative control over local domestic affairs, even if not over foreign policy. These were followed late that autumn by a declaration by Foreign Minister Letourneau reaffirming the French resolve ultimately to make Indochina completely independent. Hailed by Assistant Secretary of State Dean Rusk for having "assured" that Vietnamese aspirations would be realized,[39] it had yet to be acted upon by the summer of 1953. On the third of July, however, Paris issued a fresh pledge: to seek immediately "to perfect the independence and sovereignty" of the Associated States.

The new promise was fairly seized upon by the Eisenhower Republicans as evidence that the faith in France's sincerity of purpose had not been misplaced. On July 14 John Foster Dulles noted

with great satisfaction the proposal of the French Government
to open discussions with each of the Governments of Cambodia,
Laos and Vietnam with a view toward completing their sovereignty and independence.

Three days later he explained its implications more fully:

In the past, there has been some criticism of the French Republic
for failing to promise liberty and independence to the three
associated states of Indo-China, Vietnam, Laos and Cambodia.
. . . The basis for that criticism should now be removed. The
French Government has given assurance that it stands ready to
grant complete sovereignty and independence to the three associated states. Negotiations on this matter will start in the near
future.

He returned to the topic again in a speech to the United Nations
General Assembly in September.[40] "The pretext" for the Vietminh insurgency, he said, "until now, has been that the Associated States of Indo-China were mere colonies and that the
Communist war was designed to promote 'independence.' " He
continued:

It is no longer possible to support such a pretext. The French
Government, by its declaration of July 3, 1953, has announced
its intention of completing the process of transferring to the
Governments of the three Associated States all remaining powers as are needed to perfect their freedom, their liberty.

And throughout the period from September to June, Washington underlined what it read as the conclusions to be drawn
from the July assurances with subtle, subliminal commentary.
Secretary Dulles talked to the American Legion on September
2 of the sacrifices which France had made in defense of "an area
which is no longer a French colony but where independence is
now in the making," and referred to "the liberty of the new and
independent states of Cambodia, Laos and Vietnam" at the end
of the month.[41] In his January 7 message on the state of the
union, the president recommended an increase in assistance in
order to "bring closer the day when the Associated States may
enjoy the independence already assured by France." That
May,[42] Mr. Smith expressed the hope for a settlement at Geneva that would provide the "opportunity for Cambodia, Laos
and Vietnam to enjoy their independence."

Contrary to these optimistic indications, however, even by the late spring 1954, independence was not a reality in Vietnam. Though on February 23 Walter Smith had reported that Vietnamese and French representatives would meet in Paris "to draw up a treaty which will complete Vietnamese independence," Secretary Dulles was still, on June 10, urging the French to "make good on their July 3, 1953, declaration of intention to grant complete independence." In fact, it was not until July 23, three days after a cease fire had been effected, that Mr. Dulles was able to reveal to the press that final "instructions had been given to the French representative in Vietnam to complete by July 30 precise projects for the transfer of authority which will give reality to the independence which France had promised."

The emergence of a sovereign state of Vietnam, imminent for so long, marked the beginning of the steady decline of French influence in Southeast Asia; the announcement in late September that the United States would no longer channel its assistance to Indochina through France followed by the decision in mid-November that America would take over the training of the South Vietnamese army were merely early signs of the shift away from Paris. Although willing to assume these responsibilities, the government was wary of inheriting along with them the reputation of an imperial master. Much had been accomplished by the fall of 1954 "toward laying the ghost of Western colonialism,"[43] and Washington was anxious not to do anything to reverse that progress. Therefore, from the start it was made clear that the United States would not involve itself or in any way intermeddle in the internal politics of Saigon.

The power struggle which erupted in the spring of 1955 between Bao Dai and Ngo Dinh Diem provided officials with a perfect and immediate opportunity to launch this policy of imposed self-restraint. Asked on May 6 whether the State Department had advocated a particular administrative solution to end the impasse, spokesman Lincoln White replied that "it is up to the Vietnamese to resolve this problem." Six days later John Foster Dulles told France's Foreign Minister Edgar Faure that Washington did not have Mr. Diem "in its pocket" and could not control his actions. On the seventeenth he elaborated:

we had to accept the fact that Vietnam is now a free nation—at least so that one half of it is and its not got a puppet government, and its not got a government we can give orders to and tell what we wanted to do or what we wanted to refrain from doing.

. . . You can only hold free Vietnam with a government that . . . doesn't take orders from anybody outside, whether it be from Paris or Cannes, for that matter, or from Washington.

Each succeeding event of similar moment was punctuated by the same studied protests that America had no role to play in Vietnam's domestic affairs. President Kennedy on June 26, 1963, politely termed "inappropriate" a request by Cambodian Prince Sihanouk that the United States move in to mediate the growing dispute between the Diem Government and the Buddhists. That September[44] the American Embassy described as "nonsense" a news article on an alleged CIA plot to depose the regime in Saigon. Commenting on a severe outbreak of violence by student and religious groups opposing President Nguyen Khanh, Robert McCloskey, the State Department press officer, said on August 26, 1964, that the official position was to give advice "when it is solicited" and not to impose a settlement; "riots," he had explained earlier in the week,[45] were "an internal matter for the Vietnamese Government." During April 1966, in the midst of another series of antigovernment demonstrations, the State Department again assured that it would "continue to regard the political problem in South Vietnam as one which the South Vietnamese must resolve"[46] and declared that American advisers removed from the contending sides would be returned only "when their presence there would not run the risk of involving them in the political struggle going on."[47] On May 21, the issue of control still unsettled, President Johnson stressed to newsmen, "we are not in Vietnam to dictate what form of government they should have."

Similar pledges and warnings were made in the months that followed. The impending selection of a constituent assembly caused Ambassador Lodge to advise employees of the U.S. Mission on September 4 to "conduct themselves so as to preclude the belief of any interference or involvement [on their part] in the election procedures." On June 30, 1967, as the first presidential campaign was beginning in South Vietnam, Robert

McCloskey emphasized that America "neither supports nor opposes any candidate." He added, "The United States consistently has taken the position that selection of candidates and the final choice for high office must be made by the South Vietnamese themselves." The same day, at the White House, press secretary George Christian declined to evaluate the effect of Premier Ky's withdrawal from the race for the presidency, deeming it "inappropriate . . . to express opinions regarding individual candidates or their activities." Throughout the spring and summer of 1968, as charges were brought against Truong Dinh Dzu for having advocated the formation of a coalition the year before, the American Embassy refused repeatedly to comment on the situation on the grounds that it was a "purely internal matter"[48] for the Republic of Vietnam.

There are several ways in which these statements and postures might be interpreted. Often they seemed to be attempts to deflect attention from the powerful and private diplomatic pressures being exerted in Saigon—diplomacy directed at preventing domestic disorder from unduly hindering Vietnamese ability to prosecute the war. Sometimes they appeared as convenient excuses for evading discussion of incidents which were embarrassing to the United States because they exposed the authorities in South Vietnam as corrupt, repressive, or inefficient.

They were, however, more than just ploys. Their content, far from being irrelevant, was enormously significant, a significance made obvious in the self-conscious repudiations of all intention of imposing a "Pax Americana" upon Indochina[49] or of playing the "global gendarme."[50] Society in South Vietnam, Vice President Humphrey insisted on October 30, 1967, need not be built "according to American standards. We don't want anything stamped 'Made in the U.S.A.' We want it stamped 'Made in Vietnam by the Vietnamese people.' " A decade earlier, on September 19, 1956, Dwight Eisenhower cited the Republic of Vietnam as a nation singularly "free" from any "mark of colonial domination." The effort was to convince the world that South Vietnam was not—and was in no danger of becoming—an oriental province of the United States, that Washington's impact upon Saigon was limited. It represented one part of a defense against the claim that American imperialism had become the central issue of the war in Southeast Asia.

The other part was to protest the selflessness of American aims. The United States, officials maintained, had no national objectives and sought to gain no influence in Vietnam. This theme, which was to gain prominence during the middle of the 1960s, was first suggested in May of 1954; General Walter Bedell Smith, addressing the delegates of the Geneva conference, affirmed that in southern Asia: "The United States, for its part, has no imperialistic designs. It seeks no special advantages for its citizens."[51] With somewhat more specificity, President Kennedy issued a similar disclaimer on September 25, 1961: "The United States seeks for itself no base, no territory, no special position in this area of any kind." In March of 1962,[52] Secretary Rusk told the press, "we have no desire for bases or other United States' military advantages." The next year on November 19, at another such briefing, he repeated that "as far as the United States is concerned, we do not have and have never had, any special United States' interest in terms of military bases or anything of that sort."

In 1964, as the administration spoke more and more about the war, these protests grew in number. On March 26, Robert McNamara, in sweeping fashion, denied there were any "designs whatever on the resources or territory of the area. Our national interests do not require that South Vietnam serve as a Western base or as a member of a Western alliance." United Nations Representative Stevenson was equally unequivocal on May 21: "First, the United States has no—and I repeat no—national military objectives anywhere in Southeast Asia." At a political rally in Minneapolis on June 28, President Johnson foreswore any desire for "conquest" or "dominion"; he said in a message to the Congress on August 5 that the United States had "no military, political, or territorial objectives" in South Vietnam.

1965 brought in both relative and absolute terms a further increase in such rhetoric. Coincident with the period of American escalation, it was seemingly a response to the cynical conclusion that a country does not engage in a foreign war and suffer the loss of men and treasure unless there are substantial and direct interests to protect; it was an attempt to discourage the inference that the change in U.S. tactics, manifest in the resort to armed force, indicated any change in underlying goals. Four times in a period of a week and a half after the February announcement of retaliatory raids on the North, the government made its point. On the seventeenth Mr. Johnson declared, "We have no ambition for ourselves. We seek no dominion. We seek no conquest." That evening the vice president disavowed an interest in Asian "domain." Dean Rusk opened his news conference on the twenty-fifth with a quotation from a presidential address: "In that region there is nothing we covet, nothing we seek, no territory, no military position, no political ambitions." In a White Paper released on February 27, the State Department repeated, "The United States seeks no territory, no military bases, no favored position."

And it continued to make the point with regularity in the months thereafter. Much as he had been quoted on February 25, President Johnson reiterated to newsmen on March 13, "In that region there is nothing that we covet. There is nothing we seek. There is no territory or no military position or no political ambition"; he was more concise on June 1: "We seek neither conquest nor domination." That July[53] Hubert Humphrey pledged, "We seek no territory. We seek no dominion." Secretary McNamara testified in August[54] that there was "no need for permanent military bases in Vietnam or for special privileges of any kind." On October 1, Mr. Goldberg denied that America's assistance was motivated by any desire for political or economic gain.

1965 was the year in which such statements were at a maximum. Though in late January and early February 1966, there was a period of unusual concentration as the government's formal position was clarified and submitted to the United Nations Security Council, by March a decline which intensified as the decade wore on had begun.[55] The reversal was not without explanation. Washington had sought throughout the year to assure its public at home, its allies, and the emerging neutral nations of the world, that the war in Vietnam was not, as the Communists had alleged, part of a campaign to create American dependencies in Asia. It had therefore vigorously, and without reservation, renounced any claims for itself of any sort. Having delivered so many such renunciations, Washington may have felt that persisting in them at the same frequency was more likely to arouse than allay suspicion. Thereafter, new stress was laid on the U.S. determination to insure South Vietnam's right to decide its future, and North Vietnam's program of aggression aimed at subverting that right.

Up until the end of 1965 the administration had expressed a lack of interest, variously, in securing "territory" or "bases," "economic" or "political" control, "conquest" or "domain," "alliance," "military rights," or "extraordinary privileges," in South Vietnam. Though this range did not narrow appreciably a year later, a focus, which had been absent before, did emerge, setting 1966 apart from preceding years.[56] Looking backward, the point of transition was marked by a letter sent by Ambassador Goldberg to Secretary General U Thant on January 4, in which he set forth in detail the official U.S. policy in Southeast Asia. In the course of this summary the ambassador had written, "the United States desires no ... bases in South Vietnam." It was this particular denial which he and others so consistently delivered from then until 1969. On July 12, 1966, President Johnson said, "We are not trying to establish permanent bases in South Vietnam. And we are not trying to gain one inch of new territory." Secretary Rusk told reporters on February 7, 1967, "We have made it clear that we want no bases in Southeast Asia and do not wish to retain United States' troops in Vietnam after peace is assured." On October 2, 1968, W. Averell Harriman reminded the Communist representatives at the Paris peace talks, "We have specifically stated many times that we have no designs for any permanent base or any special influence in South Vietnam." Mr. Nixon repeated to nationwide television audiences on May 14, 1969, "We seek no bases in Vietnam. We seek no military ties."

There was good reason for the sudden preoccupation with bases. In 1965, as the United States greatly expanded its commitment to the war, increasing the volume of material aid and dispatching for the first time sizable numbers of combat troops, it embarked upon an ambitious building program, the aim of which was the rapid construction of military installations at which the equipment might be stored and the men stationed. The results of this effort were the vast complexes which rose throughout the country. These massive and permanent additions to the landscape stood as a prominent symbol of the new Western presence in Asia. They were apt to be seized upon by critics, both in the United States and elsewhere, as fresh signs of the progressive American imposition upon the people of South Vietnam. Therefore, they had to be thoroughly and continually disowned as necessary but only temporary leaseholds which would be vacated and returned to Saigon as soon as the fighting was stopped.

Though this emphasis after 1966 had not been there before, it should not be assumed that the message out of Washington had in this interval changed fundamentally. The difference was, on the whole, more a matter of form than of substance. Certainly the randomness and variety of the period from 1961 to 1965 had given way to a structure and predictability in the later years. It was no longer the case that a speech would on one day disclaim ambitions for "bases, territory, and long term alliances," on another for "military, political or economic advantages," and on a third for "conquest or special position." It was now almost always, "We seek no bases or continuing military presence," or "We seek no bases or domain," or simply, "We seek no bases." However, the particular formula of words had never been of especial importance. Economic preferences, military bases, politial influence, and the rest were incidents of the exercise of hegemony. While each defined only one more or less inclusive aspect of foreign control, they were each figures for the totality of rights, power, and privileges enjoyed by nations with imperial possessions. The repudiation of military bases was, therefore, functionally equivalent to the repudiation of economic preferences or political influence: a figurative way of repudiating anything and everything connected with empire.

From 1953 to 1954 officials spoke of the "free and independent" status of the three Associated States, in part to rebut the contention that "French colonialism" was central to the war in Indochina. When twelve years later they talked of America's disinterest in "territory, alliance, and bases," it was to deny that decade's charge that the Vietnam War was a war of "American imperialism." Though the disavowals were responsive to the accusations made by the enemy, the accusations themselves were seldom, if ever, mentioned. Though the issues raised were issues of "colonialism" and "imperialism," these words were used with studied infrequency; Arthur Goldberg's declaration of September 22, 1966, "We do not seek to establish an American empire . . . in Asia," was striking precisely because it was a departure from the general pattern; equally unusual was the president's "We do not practice colonialism" statement of the following year.[57] By not acknowledging that its motives had been impugned, Washington lent neither publicity nor unwitting credit to the imputations. By avoiding the vocabulary of its critics, it lessened the chances that its position would be identified with their criticism and regarded as a defense against it rather than an affirmative stand.

When, one hundred years ago, soldiers, missionaries, and adventurers descended upon Asia and Africa, European statesmen defended their invasions as "civilizing missions"; to "take up the white man's burden," it was said, was a solemn responsibility owed by the advanced Western cultures to those more deprived and less fortunate. What followed were decades of abuse and exploitation carried out in the name of compassion and Christian virtue.

America sought for twenty years to dissociate itself from this tradition. It did so to an extent certainly because it thought the tradition wrong and misguided; it had brought more suffering than comfort and years of selfish and self-righteous foreign rule. But there was another factor as well. The international community had too often and too unanimously expressed its opposition to colonialism for its expressions to be ignored. President Johnson referred to both concerns, to the ethics and the expediency, when he explained his policies to the AFL-CIO in December 1965:[58]

> Every day someone asks, "Why are we in Vietnam?" And every day I want to answer: . . .
>   Not for reasons of empire: our own sense of others' rights and the harsh judgment of history do not speak well of either the morality or the logic of imperial ambitions.

NOTES TO CHAPTER 3

1. Nixon, June 27, 1954.
2. White, January 31, 1950.
3. Dulles, March 29, 1954.
4. Dulles, April 5, 1954.
5. State Department, April 17, 1954.
6. Smith, May 10, 1954.
7. Dulles, May 7, 1954.
8. Nixon, April 20, 1954.
9. McNamara, March 26, 1964.
10. Stevenson, May 21, 1964.
11. State Department, February 27, 1965.
12. Plimpton, April 5, 1965.
13. Johnson, May 5, 1965.
14. McNamara, April 20, 1966.
15. Humphrey, April 25, 1966.
16. Ball, October 12, 1966.
17. Rusk, October 13, 1966.
18. Johnson, July 28, 1965.
19. Rusk, June 27, 1966.
20. Goldberg, February 1, 1966.
21. Johnson, June 30, 1966.
22. Johnson, January 12, 1966.
23. Johnson, April 8, 1965.
24. State Department, December 13, 1966.
25. Rusk, March 11, 1968.
26. Rusk, January 26, 1966.
27. Johnson, June 17, 1965.
28. Rusk, October 12, 1967.
29. McNamara, February 1, 1968.
30. McNamara, February 18, 1965.
31. Lodge, April 26, 1967.
32. Katzenbach, October 17, 1967.
33. If the Vietnam War "was a civil war, the United States' attitude had traditionally been that there was a duty upon other states not to intervene in such a struggle." D.W. Grieg, *International Law* (London: Butterworths, 1970), p. 696.
34. Kennedy, July 17, 1963.
35. On May 13, 1957, General Eisenhower hailed Mr. Diem as embodying "the highest qualities of heroism and statesmanship"; almost precisely four years later, on May 12, 1961, Vice President Johnson described the Asian premier as the "Churchill of today."
36. Johnson, April 21, June 2, June 23, July 24, and December 23, 1964.
37. Dulles, June 10, 1954.
38. Lodge, June 19, 1954.
39. Rusk, November 27, 1950.
40. Dulles, September 17, 1953.
41. Dulles, September 30, 1953.
42. Smith, May 10, 1954.
43. Dulles, November 29, 1954.

44. Diplomatic Corps, September 2, 1963.
45. McCloskey, August 24, 1964.
46. State Department, April 5, 1966.
47. State Department, April 6, 1966.
48. Diplomatic Corps, June 14 and July 23, 1968.
49. Rusk, January 23, 1966; November 14, 1967.
50. Humphrey, July 12 and September 26, 1968.
51. Smith, May 9, 1954.
52. Rusk, March 1, 1962.
53. Humphrey, July 12, 1965.
54. McNamara, August 4, 1965.
55. Of the twenty denials of desire for advantage issued in 1966, eight or 40 percent of them were delivered during the first two months of that year.
56. Analysis of statements foreswearing interest in imperial gains in terms of the particular aspect of imperialism cited

year	54	60	61	62	63	64	65	66	67	68	69
bases	0	0	1	1	1	3	6	16	7	5	1
territory	1	0	1	0	0	3	7	5	0	1	0
military advantage	0	0	0	1	0	5	5	6	2	2	0
alliance	0	0	0	0	0	2	2	7	1	1	1
conquest	0	0	0	0	0	2	2	2	0	0	0
domain	0	0	0	0	0	1	4	2	1	0	0
economic benefit	0	0	0	0	0	1	3	2	0	0	0
political favor	0	0	0	0	0	2	2	0	0	0	0
special position	1	0	1	0	0	0	3	1	0	1	0
empire, colonies	1	0	0	0	0	0	2	4	1	1	0
all anti-imperial	2	0	1	1	1	8	21	20	7	6	1

57. Johnson, November 1, 1967.
58. Johnson, December 9, 1965.

CHAPTER FOUR

WHY MUST WE STRUGGLE?

GOALS

War is an essentially negative instrument of foreign policy, demanding the sacrifice of human life and the destruction of personal and national property. Because it is so inherently and undeniably wasteful, warring governments seek to deflect attention from the immediate and severe realities and train it upon ultimate, constructive goals. The ruin is carried out in the name of some stirring cause or noble ideal, for liberty or progress, for security or international peace.

Choice

Throughout the 1950s, and especially in 1954, Washington described its purpose in Indochina as the protection of Vietnamese freedom. On April 10, 1954, Secretary Dulles discussed

the need to assure that negotiations at Geneva "will not lead to
a loss of freedom in Southeast Asia, but will preserve that freedom in peace and justice"; on the fifteenth he spoke of allied
"determination to preserve . . . freedom in the area"; on the
twentieth he pledged to "strive to achieve . . . peace on honorable terms consistent with the independence of Vietnam, Laos
and Cambodia." A month later,[1] outlining the preconditions for
U.S. intervention, he stated emphatically, "We are only going
to go in for defense of liberty and independence and freedom."

The most moving testimonial to these values was, however,
given by Mr. Eisenhower. In a May 7 letter to Emperor Bao Dai
conveying the nation's sorrow at the losses taken by the Indochinese army at Dienbienphu, he wrote:

> their heroic resistance to the evil forces of Communist aggres-
> sion has given inspiration to all who support the cause of free-
> dom.
>
> These brave men made their sacrifice in order that individual
> freedom and national independence for the people of Vietnam
> should not be lost to Communist enslavement.

During the Kennedy years when war again erupted in
Southeast Asia, the government similarly characterized it as a
fight to assure the survival of liberty. Vice President Johnson
told local dignitaries in May 1961,[2] at the start of a visit to
Saigon, that the object of his mission was to "find better ways
to preserve the independence" of South Vietnam. Undersecretary George Ball, speaking in the early summer of 1962,[3] referred to the conflict as "the struggle to maintain a free and
independent nation"; on July 17, 1963, John Kennedy called it
a "struggle to maintain national independence"; the previous
February[4] Ambassador Nolting had labeled it simply a "struggle for freedom."

The pattern did not change in 1964. President Johnson
talked on April 14 of the U.S. interest in making its aid "as
effective as possible to preserve their freedom." He spoke in
July[5] of the longstanding commitment to "the freedom and the
independence of South Vietnam." In one of a series of statements reaffirming that commitment issued during the August
Tonkin affair,[6] he asserted that "the United States will continue

its basic policy of assisting the free nations of the area to defend their freedom." Ambassador Stevenson underlined the assertion in addressing the United Nations on August 5: "the United States cannot be diverted by military attack from its obligations to help its friends establish and protect their independence."

In 1965 the United States became more heavily and intimately involved in Southeast Asia and defined with more precision the nature of the freedom for which it fought. The two events, escalation and redefinition, were directly related. The American government, having assumed the role of a major participant in Vietnam, became more specific about its aims in response to pressures to justify both the increased burden placed upon its own people and the greater price being exacted from the enemy. As it did more in terms of war, the United States was bound to demonstrate that it was very clear about what it eventually sought in terms of peace. "Freedom" did not disappear from the official vocabulary and remained a significant rhetorical element through 1968. After 1965, however, a less ambiguous synonym gained currency; after 1965 spokesmen discussed the need to insure the countries of Indochina the right to choose their own course.

The theme itself had not been invented by the Johnson Administration. At Geneva, in July[7] 1954, General Smith stated the nation's "traditional position that peoples are entitled to determine their own future"; seven years later,[8] in Washington, President Kennedy maintained, "our ambition is to permit the Vietnamese people to control their destiny." Nor had the Johnson Administration avoided this formula before 1965. Adlai Stevenson, in a speech on May 21, 1964, said U.S. policy in Southeast Asia was to enable the inhabitants of the region to "go about their own independent business in whatever associations they may freely choose for themselves without interference from the outside." That September[9] Ambassador Taylor reported to the press that support for the South Vietnamese had been granted "for the purpose of allowing them to determine their own future as a free non-Communist state."

But until 1965 this goal had been cited infrequently: six times in 1954, once in 1961 and in 1962, twice in 1963, three times in 1964. Thereafter it appeared regularly and as a pivotal concern. The guarantee of South Vietnam's freedom to select and shape its destiny became the principal, explicit goal of American involvement.

In his defense message, delivered on January 18, 1965, President Johnson explained that the U.S. "purpose" was to "assist the Vietnamese to live in peace, free to choose both their own way of life and their own foreign policy." "Our one desire," he emphasized on March 13, "and our one determination is that the people of Southeast Asia be left in peace to work out their own destinies in their own ways." He repeated in April,[10] "Our objective in Vietnam remains the same: an independent South Vietnam, tied to no alliance, free to shape its associations and relations with all other nations." That August[11] he urged, "Let's allow these people a choice."

The line was not, however, the president's monopoly. General Taylor, reviewing the situation for newsmen on February 13, remarked:

> We continue, I would say, to pursue those vital objectives and goals we have set up for our effort in South Vietnam; namely we are still seeking and will expect to continue to seek indefinitely, until final success, a South Vietnam free to determine its own future without Communist interference.

On April 25 Secretary Rusk expressed the wholehearted support of the United States of "the rights of each nation to shape its own course," adding that it was "the purpose of the United States to support the right of every nation in Southeast Asia to lead a free and independent existence." At a Pentagon briefing in June,[12] Robert McNamara was more elaborate and dogmatic on the point:

> The ultimate goal of our country . . . in Southeast Asia is to help maintain free and independent nations there in which the people can develop politically and socially according to patterns of their own choosing and with the objective of becoming responsible members of the world family of nations.
> That's our objective. That's our only objective.

On July 30 Arthur Goldberg stressed the American resolve to help the people of Vietnam "in defending their independence, their sovereignty and their right to choose their own Government and make their own decisions." Deputy Ambassador Johnson contended that September[13] that the fundamental issue in Southeast Asia was "whether peoples and countries will be permitted to develop in their own way without outside interference."

In describing the U.S. mission in Asia as insuring the independence of South Vietnam, the government was appealing to the magnanimity of the American people, challenging them to accept a war as a crusade for freedom. To advance this selfless cause as the purpose of its intervention was consistent with the claim that the government had no national objectives in Southeast Asia. Often coupled with the renunciations of interest in territorial, military, or economic advantage, it represented another element in rebuttal to the charge that the Vietnam adventure was a perfidious exercise in American imperialism, for an imperial power sought to control destinies, not free them.

It was consistent as well with the wartime positions of other administrations. Woodrow Wilson at the start of the First World War and Franklin Roosevelt during the Second had each designated the establishment of popular, national governments a basic peace aim. In 1914 the Fourteen Points advocated the holding of plebiscites to decide the future course in the states of the former Austro-Hungarian and Ottoman Empires; in 1941 the Atlantic Charter proclaimed that the United States would support only those political changes desired by the peoples concerned.

The association with these historic declarations was strengthened in 1966. That year officials substituted for the injunctions that South Vietnam be given the chance to choose its own way or develop its own destiny or construct its own institutions, the less precise, but more simple and effective, demand for "self-determination," a demand made in other circumstances by both Presidents Wilson and Roosevelt. The expression, which before had been heard only occasionally, was in 1966 invoked no fewer than sixteen times. The American draft resolution on the war, submitted to the United Nations on January 31, recognized "the right of all peoples, including those in Vietnam, to self-determination." Vice President Humphrey told a Saigon audience on February[14] that the "common purpose" of the allies was "to build a society based on the principles of political freedom, [and] self-determination." In the autumn,[15] outlining "affirmatively and succinctly what our aims are," Arthur Goldberg stated, "We seek to assure for the people of South Vietnam the same right of self-determination . . . that the United Nations Charter affirms for all." Mr. Johnson, in a Melbourne address in late October,[16] talked of "the American boys, almost half a million of them" who had "left their homes" and gone "to the rice paddies of Vietnam to help that little nation of thirteen or fourteen million try to have the right of self-determination." On December 14, assessing his visit to European and North African capitals, Ambassador Harriman maintained that United States assistance to Southeast Asia was appreciated by those whom he had seen, and that most of the world's statesmen understood "that we are fighting . . . for Vietnamese self-determination."

These comments supplemented the fuller, already familiar statements of national purpose which proliferated. Repeated on thirty-eight occasions during 1966, they were concentrated in the months of January, February, June, and October,[17] for not unaccountable reasons. In January, the United States conducted a global peace offensive and put the Vietnam question before the United Nations Security Council. In February, Mr. Johnson met with the Saigon leadership in Hawaii and the Senate Foreign Relations Committee held investigative hearings on administration policy. In June, Washington ordered the commencement of aerial raids on petroleum facilities in Hanoi and Haiphong. In October the president traveled to Asia and conferred with the allies at Manila on the progress of the war. At each of these times there was a necessity for the government to clarify its policies, to respond to or anticipate the claims of its critics both within the country and without.

On January 1, 1966, after a diplomatic tour of the Far East, Hubert Humphrey declared, "We are [in Southeast Asia] guarding the right of people to make a choice." In a letter to Secretary General U Thant, released on the fifth, Mr. Goldberg noted "that the future political structure in South Vietnam should be determined by the South Vietnamese people themselves through democratic processes." On January 28 the secretary of state testified to Senate committeemen, "We believe that the South Vietnamese are entitled to make their own decisions without having them through force of arms by North Vietnam or anyone else."

"The United States is pledged," Mr. Johnson stated on February 8 at the conclusion of his Honolulu talks, to the ideal "of government by the consent of the governed." In remarks at a Medal of Honor Ceremony in April,[18] he summarized America's "basic principles": "That South Vietnam, however young and frail, has the right to develop as a nation, free from the interference of any other power, no matter how mighty or strong." Later that spring,[19] speaking at the Arlington National Cemetery, he said, "In Vietnam the United States is committed to a decent and limited purpose: . . . to let the people of Vietnam to decide in peace their own political future."

On June 29, in announcing the bombing of oil storage depots in the North, Robert McNamara also emphasized that America's "objectives" were "limited." "They are," he insisted, "solely" those of "permitting the South Vietnamese people to have an opportunity to shape their own destiny, to select and choose the political and economic institutions under which they propose to live." A message from Arthur Goldberg, made public the next day, made the same point, in much the same language:

> Our sole objective is to . . . permit the people, the opportunity to shape their own destiny—free of coercion—by choosing the political and economic institutions under which they wish to live.

In August,[20] the vice president listed as a major "objective in Vietnam" the restoration of peace "so its citizens can decide their own course." On September 8 Dean Rusk repeated the stipulation that any final solution to the war must "assure free choice for the people of Vietnam." And in a series of statements delivered during his Asian journey at the end of October, the president underlined the theme over and over again. The United States was determined to help "those fifteen million people to shape their own destiny";[21] to fight "to give the Vietnamese people a chance to build the kind of nation they want";[22] to enable them "to shape their own destiny, free of aggression from without and terror from within";[23] to insure "a free choice for the people of that country."[24]

In 1967, at a much lower but still significant level of intensity, officials continued to chant this liturgy in both its expanded and abbreviated forms. On February 9, Mr. Rusk lectured newsmen:

> Our objective in Vietnam is and always has been a limited one. A South Vietnam able to determine its own future without external interference. I need hardly repeat that this and this alone is our objective.

"We're in South Vietnam today," Lyndon Johnson argued that June[25] "because we want to allow a little nation self-determination." In August[26] Secretary McNamara reaffirmed America's "limited purposes": "We are fighting there only to assure the people of South Vietnam the right to choose their own political and economic institutions." Appearing before the General Assembly on September 21, Mr. Goldberg declared:

> it remains our view that the people of South Vietnam should have the right to work out their own political future by peaceful means, in accordance with the principle of self-determination, and without external interference.

There had always been the implication that providing the Vietnamese with the chance to decide their destiny was not only the principal aim of America's efforts, but had caused those efforts to be undertaken in the first place. In late September,[27] however, a San Antonio speech utterly confounded any such inference. The president began it familiarly enough:

> [Vietnam] is the arena where Communist expansionism is most aggressively at work in the world today, where it is crossing international frontiers . . . where it is killing and kidnapping, where it is ruthlessly attempting to bend free people to its will.
>
> And into this mixture of subversion and war, of terror and hope, America has entered with its material power and with its moral commitment.
>
> Why?
>
> . . . We cherish self-determination for all peoples—yes.

But, he went on to say, that would not explain why Americans were being sent to die in Southeast Asia. Self-determination remained a condition for an eventual peace, a nonnegotiable condition perhaps, but it could no longer be considered to be the major rationale for intervention.

A slight relative increase in these statements of purpose was registered in 1968, a spate coming in the spring when preliminary negotiations with the enemy started in Paris. At the opening session, held on May 13, W. Averell Harriman, chief of the American delegation, rehearsed the well-known and basic terms:

> The objectives of the United States are strictly limited. . . . We believe that the countries of Southeast Asia should be free to determine their own internal affairs and their international position as the people of those countries see fit.

On the fifteenth he stressed again the need of "letting the internal affairs of South Vietnam be settled by the South Vietnamese themselves," adding the clarification, "without outside interference or coercion."

During the summer months Hubert Humphrey, by then the main contender for the Democratic presidential nomination, assumed the burden of reiteration. On June 20 he underscored that any acceptable agreement would have "to protect the right of peoples to design their own lives, [and] to create their own institutions of government and social structure." "I want a political settlement," he wrote on July 12, "which will permit the people of South Vietnam to shape their own futures." He spoke on the twentieth of "our stand" in Vietnam "to permit the development of self-determination."

In September[28] Mr. Harriman warned the representatives of North Vietnam that a solution would not come until their side agreed "to permit the South Vietnamese people to make their own future in their own way, free from external force and violence." In October[29] the United Nations was reminded by Secretary of State Rusk of the nation's desire "to assure that the people of South Vietnam can decide their own destiny free of force." In November[30] Walt Rostow focused on the resolve of the leadership in Saigon to achieve a peace "in which South Vietnam could determine its own political future."

The change of administrations in January was not accompanied by any change in position. In his Inaugural Address on January 21, Mr. Nixon proclaimed:

> The peace we seek—the peace we seek to win—is not victory over any other people, but the peace that comes with healing in its wings; with compassion for those who have suffered; with understanding for those who have opposed us; with the opportunity for all the people of this earth to choose their own destiny.

On the twenty-fifth the new U.S. negotiator in Paris, Henry Cabot Lodge, rephrased the passage in less soaring, more familiar prose:

> The United States goal can be stated simply: to preserve the right of the South Vietnamese people to determine their own future without outside interference or coercion.

That May[31] Secretary William Rogers said that the decision as to the future of South Vietnam must arise in a way that "permits the people of South Vietnam their own free choice."

Self-determination, the right of a country to shape its own course, is a formal principle. It describes how a government should be chosen, not what the nature of that government—its economic, social, or political philosophy—should be. It represents a process rather than an outcome.

That process was defined with increasing precision throughout the decade. Between 1960 and 1964 there was primarily the ambiguous talk of "protecting,"[32] "maintaining,"[33] "preserving,"[34] and "defending freedom."[35] By January 1965,[36] "freedom" was clearly equated with political independence and effectively distinguished from civil rights. The stress in the initial statements was on the removal of enemy pressures threatening the state, with little discussion of how a Vietnamese government ought to be formed; officials just insisted vaguely that South Vietnam be allowed to "build its own institutions,"[37] that the people be permitted to "shape their own destinies,"[38] "settle their own future,"[39] "guide their own country in their own way."[40] In July,[41] however, Washington specified that this national development be conducted within an electoral framework and that recommendation too become a fixed element in the program. Dean Rusk urged "a democratic solution" the next January.[42] That February the White House called for "free elections"[43] and Mr. Johnson spoke of "a stable democratic government."[44] Vice President Humphrey insisted on "genuinely free elections" in March.[45] On December 19, 1967, the president added a final stipulation, that the polling be carried out in a "one-man-one-vote" system. Over succeeding months this last detail was repeated by others: Ambassador Harriman proposed an agreement "on the basis of one man, one vote" on May 18 in Paris; Mr. Rusk cited the aim of achieving "self-determination under a one man one vote arrangement" on August 20 in Washington; Hubert Humphrey endorsed "totally free elections in which one man and one vote" a week after that, on August 27, in Chicago.

A necessary consequence of being committed to a process and not an outcome was that the favored process could permit an unfavorable outcome, and the United States had periodically to reassure its audiences that it was aware of this possibility but was nevertheless sincere about what it said: that it would accept whatever government the Vietnamese themselves freely chose. "We are for free elections," Presidential Press Secretary Bill Moyers made clear on February 22, 1966, "with all of us abiding by the consequences of those elections, whatever they may be." A day later Lyndon Johnson pledged:

> we will insist for ourselves on what we require from Hanoi: respect for the principle of government by the consent of the governed. We stand for self-determination, for free elections, and we will honor their result.

Mr. McNamara, asked by a reporter that April[46] whether the United States sought "to establish a democratic state or an American type state in South Vietnam," replied that the nation's "goal [was] to allow those people to choose the form of political institutions under which they prefer to live." "I suppose," he continued, "you could conceive of them choosing some form other than a democratic form. If they did, we would adhere to that choice." In August 1968,[47] the vice president reaffirmed his belief "in the free processes of a free election and a free choice"; he went on, "if the people of South Vietnam wish to elect a government that includes within it forces and in-

dividuals that I do not approve of, that's their right." The following spring[48] Secretary Rogers told Senators that once it was

> certain that the voting process was an honest and fair process
> . . . [and] after the people in the South had made the decision
> we'd be bound by it. We wouldn't have any veto power. We
> don't want any veto power.

Though there may have been doubt about whether Washington would accept, or even permit, fully open elections in
Vietnam, there is no question that in so declaring it was taking
a stand wholly consistent with the premises upon which U.S.
involvement had been based. American spokesmen always
maintained that they opposed Communists not because they
were Marxists, men committed to an alien politicoeconomic
doctrine, but because they practiced aggression, because they
resorted to strategies of violence in order to impose their
dogma upon others. The operative objection was to the methods by which these men gained power, not the policies they
implemented once that power had been achieved. The "hope"
in Vietnam, Adlai Stevenson had written in 1965,[49] was to "establish the fact that changes in Asia are not to be precipitated
by outside force. . . This is the point of the conflict." To commit
themselves unequivocally to the goal of self-determination, to
the process of orderly and peaceful change, was the necessary
and logical position for those who shared that vision.

Better Life

Providing the people of Vietnam with an opportunity to
work out their destinies was the major but not, however, the
only affirmative U.S. objective in Southeast Asia. The government talked sometimes, too, of enhancing Vietnamese security
and often, when undertaking diplomatic and military initiatives, of securing Vietnamese peace. It talked as well of improving the quality of Vietnamese life.

This last line first appeared in the 1950s. The Democrats,
who introduced it, focused mainly on material progress. Secretary of State Acheson noted on January 20, 1950, America's
desire to promote "prosperity in Vietnam"; in his March,
1952,[50] message on the Mutual Security Program Mr. Truman

recommended that assistance be extended to Indochina in order to "enable the peoples of Asia to conquer the old, deepseated and agonizing economic problems and to share in the benefits of an expanding world economy." The Republicans, by contrast, tended to stress more metaphysical aspirations. President Eisenhower wrote on May 7, 1954, that the heroic defense of Dienbienphu would "forever stand" as the symbol of the free world's "dedication to the dignity of the human being." That July[51] John Foster Dulles cited "the goals of human justice, welfare and dignity" for which the country had fought in Vietnam and to which it would always be devoted.

There was nothing novel, therefore, when during the next decade, confronted with its own Indochinese crisis, the Kennedy Administration also gave attention to nonmilitary considerations. Upon his return from South Vietnam on June 9, 1961, Vice President Johnson advised that the United States work with Asian peoples to "improve their health, their housing and their standard of living so they will have something to fight for." In a letter to President Diem that October,[52] Mr. Kennedy underscored American determination to "build a better life through economic growth," and Dean Rusk referred to that assurance, the promise to "build a better growth," at a press conference in November.[53] On September 14, 1963, the State Department expressed the hope that the regime in Saigon was "moving to take constructive measures . . . to achieve a better future for the Vietnamese people."

In 1964 the Johnson Administration, too, indicated its concern about social welfare. The Department of State in mid-February[54] proclaimed its resolve "to work to achieve the time when Vietnam is at peace and its people are able to lead their lives in . . . prosperity." That March[55] Ambassador Lodge strongly urged Vietnamese province chiefs

> to create a civilized community where the people have security and can sleep at night, where the children can be educated, where their health can be cared for, where they are kept informed, where they can own their own land.

On August 5, listing his objectives for Southeast Asia, the president included, "That they devote their talents to bettering the lives of their peoples by working against poverty and disease and ignorance." There were, however, a total of only five such references over the whole year.

Then, in 1965, the "other" war became an issue of importance. On March 20 President Johnson declared: "The real goal of all of us in Southeast Asia must be the peaceful progress of the people of that area." Elaborating on the idea at Johns Hopkins in April,[56] he spoke of the common desire of everyone living in the region for "food for their hunger, health for their bodies, a chance to learn, progress for their country and an end to the bondage of material misery," and pledged that the United States would contribute to the realization of these desires with a "billion dollar American investment." He announced at a briefing on June 1 that the legislation for the initial $89 million would be submitted to Congress that afternoon, the first installment in a program "to create the conditions of hope and progress which are really the only lasting guarantees of peace and stability." "The sixteen million people of South Vietnam," he reminded reporters,

> survive on an average income of $100 per year. More than sixty per cent of the people have never learned to read or write. When disease strikes, medical care is often impossible to find. . . .
> This poverty and this neglect take their inevitable toll in human life. The life expectancy there is only 35 years.

He concluded, pledging, these "common enemies of man in South Vietnam . . . we are committed to defeat" in order to win "the wider war for the freedom and progress of all men." In a *Newsweek* interview granted the next month[57] he was hardly any less ambitious. "We are," he said, "going to make life better and more enjoyable and more significant for all the three billion people of the world."

In 1966 "social betterment" fully emerged as a fundamental American goal. Official designation came in early February as the leaders of Washington and Saigon met in Hawaii. Welcoming the Vietnamese president on February 6, Mr. Johnson cited their joint resolution "to build a decent society for the people of South Vietnam . . . to win victory over hunger, disease and despair." He promised at a session the next day that his nation would help "wage the other great effort in the South to make a dream of a better life a reality." On February 8, in the "Declaration of Honolulu," that promise was set forth formally:

> Just as the United States is pledged to play its part in the world-wide attack upon hunger, ignorance and disease, so in Vietnam it will give special support to the work of the people of that country to build even while they fight.
>
> We have helped and we will help them to stabilize the economy, to increase the production of food, to spread the light of education, to stamp out disease.

Over the next two and a half weeks this commitment was repeated relentlessly in the most intense verbal concentration of the war.[58]

Returning to Los Angeles immediately after the conference,[59] the president stressed the necessity of not only defeating aggression, but winning "the struggle against social injustice; against hunger, disease and ignorance; against political apathy and indifference." On February 11 he complained to newsmen: "A lot of our folks have felt that it is just a military effort [being made in Asia]. We don't think it should be that and we don't want it to be that." He went on:

> We have social objectives. One of our main goals is to defeat social misery. . . .
>
> . . . [We sought at the recent Pacific meeting] to place more emphasis in this field . . . [and we are] trying to get other people to put proper emphasis on it, too.

Four days later he suggested a spring review "to assure continuing forward movement in our war on social misery." "[O]ur basic purpose," he maintained on the seventeenth "[is] the building of a better society," adding

> Until the people of the villages and farms of that unhappy country know that they personally count, that they are cared about, that their future is their own—only then will we know that real victory is possible.

Throughout the period Vice President Humphrey reinforced these points. He vowed on February 9 that America's military operation would "be matched by a vigorous war against the age-old enemies of disease, hunger and social and economic deprivation." He underscored on both the twelfth and the twenty-fourth the importance of fulfilling the aims of the "social revolution." "We reaffirm our intention," he said on February 25, "to sustain the struggle . . . against the forces of poverty, illiteracy, famine and disease."

During the balance of the year, both men continued to advertise the cause with regularity. In March[60] the president ordered the dispatch of a task force to plan "an intensified attack on hunger, disease and ignorance" and thereby "give new promise and new purpose to the lives of the Vietnamese people." In April[61] the vice president called for a victory against "poverty, disease and despair." In May[62] the president pledged to persist in the battle to defeat "social misery" in South Vietnam.

Mr. Humphrey talked on June 8 of the "war against misery and despair." "We are engaged today," he commented on August 25, "in an unparalleled effort to erase poverty, hunger, ignorance and injustice in America. We are equally engaged in Southeast Asia in a struggle against the same enemies." On September 24 he stated, "The real war in Vietnam is the war against poverty, illiteracy and disease."

In October there was another presidential barrage. Mr. Johnson recalled on the thirteenth the actions of the United States to "try to build a stronger and more socially conscious and better economic base in South Vietnam for the poor people of that area." A week later[63] he urged the government in Hanoi to cease its attacks and join in "a war for human dignity, a war for health and enlightenment, a war for your children and generations of children to come." He said on the twenty-third that the Manila review, scheduled to begin the next day, would "mainly" focus upon "the ways we can help the South Vietnamese improve their economy and the life of all their citizens." On October 25 the conferring allies declared anew their "resolve" and "purpose" to seek to "conquer hunger, illiteracy, and disease."

In 1966 Washington sought to capture the nation's imagination and support by adapting the objectives of the Great Society to the war in Vietnam. The provision of educational service, medical assistance, more food and clothing, better housing would, it was maintained, give the people of Southeast Asia

something to fight for. The idea of marshalling American ener-
gies for ends so indisputably good, and thereby challenging the
Communist monopoly on change and reform, was inspired.
Moreover, the sudden emphasis on such dynamic and constructive measures, the elimination of virtually all the eternal problems of mankind, deflected attention from—or at least provided
a perspective against which to view—the equally dynamic campaign of destruction being carried out against the Vietcong and
the North Vietnamese.

Yet for the United States to expand its social and economic
mission so greatly when its military operations were expanding
as well was to confuse rather than clarify the issues, and also
placed an inordinate demand on American generosity. The program was certainly dramatic and ambitious, but was finally too
dramatic and too ambitious ever to win popular acclaim. It was
very expensive, extremely long-range, and in terms of ultimate
success highly speculative. Possibly for these reasons, after
November 1966, the Johnson Doctrine for revolutionizing life
in Asia was almost never stated again.

DISASTERS

The defense of America's policy in Indochina was couched
not only in terms of realizing the goals of "self-determination"
and "social betterment," but of obstructing communism and
resisting aggression, of preventing the unacceptable and far-
reaching repercussions which, it was said, would surely follow
if the enemy were to be victorious in Southeast Asia. The horrors which officials over a period of twenty years paraded before
the public were formidable. According to the government, a
success for the aggressors would fuel their desire for further
conquest and therefore greatly increase the chance of an even
larger, more destructive war; it would also enhance the stature
of those nations which had counseled the use of force as the
most effective means of securing rapid political change. The loss
of Vietnam would lead to the eventual collapse of the neighboring region, the serial outbreak of violence in underdeveloped
areas, and the gravitation of weaker states into the Communist
orbit. Such events would pose a direct and grave threat, not

only to the survival of the region, but to the security of the United States and the entire free world.

These dire predictions were not developed through argument, but were dramatically presented as more or less foregone conclusions, obvious results given the principle of "falling dominoes," the experiences of Munich, the nature of "peoples' wars." All rested apparently on a single premise: no battle could any longer be viewed in isolation, insulated from the great ideological struggle which divided the world; the outcome of every contest had broad implications, going beyond those immediately discernible, which would affect the subtle balance of power upon which global stability depended.

There were other assumptions as well. "Communists are all alike"—whether controlled by the Soviet Union or nominally independent, all were dedicated to the triumph of international socialism. "Aggressors are all alike"—as in the 1930s, so in the 1960s, to yield to them stimulated their ambitions for more dominion and control. "All backward and small countries are alike"—in Asia, in Africa, in Latin America, their destinies and allegiances were shaped by events in Washington, Moscow, and Peking.

Three more formal points should be noted. First, each of these themes presented negative justification for U.S. action. Each said the United States had to help because *not* to do so would invite unendurable consequences. Second, each operated as a self-fulfilling prophecy. Each assumed the necessity of holding Vietnam, made it a symbol of American determination, and thereby rendered enormous the psychological effects of a victory or defeat which might otherwise have gone virtually unnoticed. Third, none could be totally refuted. Each could be attacked for having logical flaws or for being excessively simplistic, but as with all forecasts, it was impossible to guarantee that any one of them was absolutely wrong.

The Domino Principle

Almost from the beginning of its involvement, the United States related the struggle in Indochina to the survival of the surrounding region. Donald R. Heath, minister to the Associated States, declared on a television program on February 4, 1951, that French and Vietnamese troops were "holding the pass against the spread of communism in Southeast Asia." On September 23, 1951, the State Department released a communiqué saying that "the successful defense of Indo-China is of great importance to the defense of Southeast Asia." In a message to Congress on the Mutual Security Program on March 7, 1952, President Truman called Indochina a point of "critical strategic importance to the free world." On June 18, 1952, Secretary of State Acheson referred to "the free world's bulwark in Indo-China." Two months later, on August 11, John M. Allison, the assistant secretary of state for Far Eastern affairs, described the fighting in Indochina as the key to future developments in that part of the world.

The Eisenhower Administration continued to take this line; that is, it made the same point that the security of Indochina and Southeast Asia were intertwined. But whereas the Democrats had spoken in vague, often hyperbolic generalities, the Republicans offered detail. "[I]f Indo-China should be lost," Secretary Dulles warned a joint meeting of Senate and House Committees, on May 5, 1953, "there would be a chain reaction throughout the Far East and Southeast Asia." Appearing before the same group of congressmen the next day, he elaborated. The collapse of Indochina, he said, would increase the pressures on adjacent Thailand, and if Thailand were then to be overtaken, the position of Burma would be "extremely acute" and that of Indonesia, "shaken." Were that entire "rice bowl" to go, Japan, which required the area for trade, would be forced to turn increasingly to Communist China in order to exist, and would gradually become an economic satellite of Peking. President Eisenhower reported to the Forty-fifth Annual Governor's Conference in Seattle on August 4:

> If Indo-China goes, several things happen right away. The peninsula, the last little bit of land hanging down there, would be scarcely defensible. . . . India would be outflanked. Burma would be in no position for defense. . . . All of that position around there is very ominous to the United States because finally if we lost all that how would the free world hold the rich empire of Indonesia.

On April 5, 1954, Mr. Dulles testified to the House Foreign Affairs Committee that the struggle against the Vietminh carried "a grave threat not only to Vietnam, Laos, and Cambodia, but also to such friendly neighboring countries as Malaya, Thailand, Indonesia, the Philippines, Australia and New Zealand."

Two days later Mr. Eisenhower codified all that had gone before. During a briefing for the press, at which he was asked to comment on the strategic importance of Indochina to the free world, he introduced the "falling domino principle."

> You have a row of dominoes set up, and you knock over the first one, and what will happen to the last one is the certainty that it will go over very quickly, so you could have the beginning of a disintegration that would have the most profound influences.

Applying this model, he outlined the "possible sequence of events" were the French Union Forces to be defeated: initially, "the loss of Indo-China, of Burma, of Thailand, of the peninsula, of Indonesia following." Then, he continued:

> the geographical position achieved thereby does many things.
>   It turns the so-called island defensive chain of Japan, Formosa, of the Philippines, and to the southward, it moves in to threaten Australia and New Zealand.
>   It takes away in its economic aspects that region that Japan must have as a trading area or Japan, in turn, will have only one place in the world to go, and that is towards China and Manchuria or toward the Communist areas in order to live.[64]

Throughout the rest of April and into the early part of May, officials alluded repeatedly to that April 7 reply. On April 11 Undersecretary Walter Bedell Smith stated that a Communist victory in Indochina would instantly threaten Burma, Thailand, the Malay Peninsula, and Indonesia, and eventually imperil the Philippines, Australia, and New Zealand. Vice President Nixon told a partisan crowd on April 20 that were Indochina to fall, "the whole of Southeast Asia would be put in jeopardy" and "Japan which must trade with the area would be put in jeopardy," also. On April 26 the president, changing his metaphor, compared Indochina to "a sort of cork in the bottle, the bottle being the great area that includes Indonesia, Burma, Thailand, all of the surrounding areas of Asia. . . ." The "great area," he said, was one with which the newly formed democratic type of Government in Japan must trade. If it is denied the opportunity to trade with that area, how can Japan with its 85,000,000 people ever develop into a civilization that we would consider dependable. . . .

In a radio-television address to the nation on May 7, the secretary of state reviewed these lines once again:

Now let us turn to the problem of Southeast Asia. In that great peninsula and the islands in the south, live nearly 200,000,000 people in eight states—Burma, the Free States of Indo-China, called Laos, Cambodia and Thailand and the states of Malaya and Indonesia. Communist conquest of this area would seriously imperil the free world position in the Western Pacific. It would, among other things, endanger the Philippines, Australia and New Zealand. . . . And it would deprive Japan of an important foreign market and source of food and raw materials.

This concentration on the huge implications of an enemy success coincided with an intense period of private maneuvering, during which Washington tried to secure Allied approval of a plan for a "united action" in Southeast Asia; the objective of the verbal offensive was to create a climate favorable to accepting the risk inherent in such a plan by publicizing the enormity of the stakes involved. The diplomatic initiative failed, however, to attract Anglo-French support, and the Vietminh captured the symbolic garrison of Dienbienphu in early May after a long siege; Indochina seemed by mid-spring on the verge of collapse.

On May 11, what had previously been advertised as an irreversible disaster became a problem of manageable proportions. At a State Department news session, these exchanges were recorded:

Q. Do you think, Mr. Secretary, that the Southeast Asia area can be held without Indo-China?
A. I do. The situation in that area, as we found it, was that it was subject to the so-called "domino theory."
Q. You mean that if one went another would go?
A. We are trying to change it so that would not be the case. That is the whole theory of collective security.
You generally have a whole series of countries that can be picked up one by one. . . . As the nations come together then the "domino theory," so-called, ceases to apply. And what we are

trying to do is to create a situation in Southeast Asia where the domino theory will not apply.

And while I see it has been said that I felt that Southeast Asia could be secured even without perhaps Vietnam, Laos, and Cambodia, I do not want for a minute to underestimate the importance of those countries. . . .

. . . But I do not want to give the impression either that if events that we could not control and which we do not anticipate lead to their being lost, that we would consider the whole situation hopeless. . . .

The day after, Mr. Eisenhower completely concurred:

Q. Mr. President, a couple of weeks—since we seem to be going into the past—a few weeks ago you told us of your theory of dominoes in Indo-China, the neck of the bottle.

Since the fall of Dienbienphu there has been a certain amount of talk of doing without Indo-China. Would you tell us your Administration's position: is it still indispensable to the defense of Southeast Asia?

A. Well of course, as I—again I forget whether it was before this body—I had talked about the cork and the bottle—well, it is very important, and the great idea of setting up an organism [sic] is so as to defeat the domino result.

When each standing alone, one falls, it has the effect on the next, and finally the whole row is down. You are trying, through a unifying influence to build that row of dominoes so they can stand the fall of one, if necessary.

As a rhetorical device, the domino principle was a dramatic way of demonstrating that an apparently peripheral contest could, strategically, be of pivotal significance. An all or nothing proposition—either the first domino was saved or all were doomed—it had the virtue of being both simple and graphic. Its utility, however, was limited; it remained useful only so long as that first domino could be shored up. Once that moment passed, it was impolitic and self-defeating to mention it again. When on May 11, confronted with a deteriorating battlefield situation and allied intransigence, Secretary Dulles conceded that Indochina was important but not absolutely essential to the defense of Southeast Asia, it was evident that for the Eisenhower Administration, that moment had come and gone.

The domino principle is too crude and mechanical to be considered either a helpful or valid doctrine of geopolitics; that is, it cannot be accepted that the fall of one country would inevitably lead to the fall of others nearby. It was on these grounds, the skillful and deliberately fostered impression of its inevitability, that the principle was in later years attacked and held up as representative of the primitive world view of the 1950s. Yet a close reading of the statements of that period reveals that, strong impressions notwithstanding, officials spoke not in terms of "certainties," but of "probabilities," of "threats," of "ifs" and "mights." Moreover, however unwittingly or parenthetically it may have been done, they did acknowledge that only if other, independent conditions were met would the loss of Indochina be the prelude to an irreversible chain of loss throughout Southeast Asia. Only if it were also assumed that after the first loss

1. "Communist forces . . . would . . . resume the pattern of aggression against the other free peoples in that area."[65]
2. "The neighboring countries remained weak and divided."[66]
3. "We [in the United States] would give up in despair."[67]

Therefore, while it is perhaps fair to charge these men with manipulating the public, it is something else again to accuse them of political naïveté. The domino principle was not at bottom an attempt to explain or to offer a theory of international dynamics; it was, rather, more an effort to rally support for a potentially dangerous foreign adventure.

The reversals suffered by the French Union in March, April, and May of 1954 dictated the shape of the agreement reached in Geneva that July. Though the United States was critical of its terms, it treated it less as the apocalypse than as an unfortunate setback. On July 23 John Foster Dulles emphasized that vigilance and resolve could "prevent the loss in North Vietnam from leading to the extension of communism throughout Southeast Asia and the Southwest Pacific." On January 17, 1956, he told newsmen that events had

> proved that the losses which were taken by that armistice can be
> limited and do not necessarily involve what was one time feared
> —that is, the loss of the whole Indo-China peninsula.

But the specter of a major calamity, lifted late in the spring of 1954, descended again in 1959. At a Founder's Day Address at Gettysburg College on April 14, President Eisenhower said:

> Strategically, South Vietnam's capture by the Communists
> would bring their power several hundred miles into a hitherto
> free region. The remaining countries in Southeast Asia would be
> menaced by a great flanking movement. . . . The loss of South
> Vietnam would set in motion a crumbling process that could, as
> it progressed, have grave consequences for freedom.

The "crumbling process" of 1959 was the analogue of the "falling dominoes" of 1954. "South Vietnam" had been substituted
for all of Indochina. An image of gradual disintegration had
taken the place of one of immediate collapse. "Grave consequences" stood where first Burma, Thailand, the peninsula,
Indonesia, then the Pacific Islands—Japan, Formosa, the Philippines, Australia, and New Zealand—had stood before. The message, however, was the same: if the enemy were not stopped at
the start it would become increasingly less likely that he could
be stopped anywhere else along the way.

The alarm sounded by Mr. Eisenhower was curiously
premature. In the summer of 1959[68] his secretary of state still
refused to relate the rising tide of violence to "the spread of
Communism in South Vietnam," and attributed it instead to
"terrorist organizations" which had been operating in that
country "for some time." Nevertheless, it is a significant bench-
mark: the first statement of a theme which was to become
central to the defense of the second decade of American involvement in Vietnam.

That theme, as it emerged over the years, was presented in
several forms. There was W. Averell Harriman's pregnant reference to South Vietnam as "the key" to the whole peninsula
in February 1962,[69] and Lyndon Johnson's oblique comment
that "what we're doing in South Vietnam has a very important
bearing on the whole sector of that part of the world," in August
1965.[70] There were the general prophesies of doom:

> In my opinion, for us to withdraw from that effort would mean
> a collapse, not only of South Vietnam, but of Southeast Asia.
>
> JOHN F. KENNEDY, JULY 17, 1963

> [To withdraw from Vietnam] would mean . . . grievous losses to
> the free world in Southeast and Southern Asia.
>
> DEAN RUSK, MAY 22, 1964

Had the men not been introduced, the Vietcong and North Vietnam would have won . . . and all of Southeast Asia would be in turmoil.

ROBERT S. MCNAMARA, MAY 11, 1966

[The U.S. decision to help Saigon rested on an unwillingness to accept the] Communist takeover of Southeast Asia that would clearly follow [had it remained idle].

WALT W. ROSTOW, DECEMBER 4, 1968

There was Ambassador Lodge's unequivocal claim that "the well-advertised domino theory applies here [to Vietnam],"[71] and other, detailed analyses to the same effect:

After Communist success in South Vietnam, the remainder of Southeast Asia would very shortly thereafter go neutralist, possibly eventually Communist. Burma would be affected, India also. Indonesia would soon line up with the Communists. We could be pushed out of the Western Pacific to Honolulu. That would be the short term effect over the next few years.

MAXWELL TAYLOR, SEPTEMBER 10, 1964

If South Vietnam falls "the rest of Southeast Asia will be in grave danger of progressively disappearing behind the bamboo curtain and other Asian countries like India and even in time Australia and your own [Japan] will in time be threatened.

WILLIAM P. BUNDY, SEPTEMBER 29, 1964

There were more striking variations as well. One, introduced in the summer of 1966, was in essence the converse of the standard Eisenhower "cork in the bottle" line. Beginning with the assumption that leaving Vietnam would gravely imperil the surrounding areas, officials contended that by staying the United States had provided the security for the neighboring states which had made possible the progress that they had recorded. American determination on the battlefield was helping to build a stable and prosperous "new" Asia. This dividend, it was to be inferred, made the investment in war worthwhile.

In ceremonies welcoming Australian Prime Minister Holt to the Captiol on June 29, 1966, President Johnson stated, "Shielded by the courage of the Vietnamese and their allies, many Asian countries are driving forward with real success in their economic and social development." The next day, speaking in Omaha, he expanded:

> Shielded by the courage of the South Vietnamese, the peoples of free Asia today are driving toward economic and social development in a new spirit of regional cooperation. All you have to do is look at that map and you will see independence growing and thriving in blood and blooming. . . .
>
> Our fighting in Vietnam, therefore, is buying time not only for South Vietnam but it's buying time for a new and a vital and a growing Asia to emerge and to develop additional strength.

He added the specifics in mid-July:[72]

> One country after another has achieved rates of economic growth beyond the most optimistic hopes of a few years ago.
>
> Indonesia has pulled back from the brink of Communism and economic collapse.
>
> India and Pakistan—600 million strong—have ended a tragic conflict and returned to the immense works of peace. . . .
>
> Nine Pacific nations—allies and neutrals, white and colored —came together on their own initiative to form an Asian and Pacific Council.
>
> New and constructive groupings for political and economic cooperation are under discussion in Southeast Asia.
>
> The multibillion-dollar Asian Development Bank is moving forward in Manila with the participation of 31 nations.
>
> And the development of the lower Mekong River basin is going forward despite the war. . . . This is the new Asia that is taking shape behind our defense of South Vietnam. Because we have been firm . . . others have taken heart.

Embarking upon a seventeen day Far Eastern tour that fall,[73] Mr. Johnson remarked, "Behind the terrible costs of combat and hostility a new Asia is gradually coming into its own"; he wrote upon his return[74] that the people he had encountered appreciated that

> by our firm stand in Vietnam and in Southeast Asia, we are buying time for all the nations of that region to face their own problems realistically and to begin to build their own future together as a region.

Another tack was taken in the autumn of 1967. For a brief time the administration cited the opinion of Asian authorities who, like their counterparts in the United States, foresaw a disastrous "neighborhood effect" if the Communists were to overtake South Vietnam. Mr. Johnson, in a speech given on September 29, in San Antonio, Texas, reported:

> The Prime Minister of Australia said: "We are there because while Communist aggression persists the whole of Southeast Asia is threatened. . . ."
> And the Prime Minister of Malaysia warned his people that if the United States pulled out of South Vietnam, it would go to the Communists, and after that it would be only a matter of time until they moved against neighboring states.

On October 18 Eugene V. Rostow of the State Department noted: "Responsible opinion throughout Southeast Asia believes that the outcome in Vietnam will determine the future alignment of the whole region." In an article published in the *New York Times Magazine* on November 12, Undersecretary William P. Bundy asked his readers "to recall the recent public statement of Prime Minister Lee Kuan Yew of Singapore that the outcome in Vietnam is the key to the future of South and Southeast Asia."

The views of such ostensibly eminent and knowledgeable local figures were meant to be taken as corroboration of often repeated American theory; administration pronouncements were not just necessary rationalizations for policy decisions but critical judgments shared by people who understood the situation from close proximity and in detail. This inference assumed an objectivity on the part of Asian leaders which was, however, lacking. Even if foreign officials did not privately subscribe to these estimates, it remained in their interest to support publicly the position of a government willing to undertake the defense of nearby territory. Put another way: there were reasons of potential economic, political, and military advantage for currying U. S. favor rather than incurring its wrath, and these reasons could well have motivated statesmen to speak when and as they did.

There was a third departure, statistically of little importance, but still of great interest. Each of these discussions started routinely with a dismissal of the "domino theory" for being either too subtle or not subtle enough, and went on to offer another argument to justify the conclusion that, nonetheless, a serious Communist threat existed throughout Southeast Asia. George Ball[75] explained the danger as a function of South Vietnam's unique geographical situation:

> One does not have to accept fully the automatic operation of the so-called domino theory to recognize the strategic significance of South Vietnam. It forms one shore of the South China Sea, which is the gateway to Malaya and Indonesia. It controls the mouth of the Mekong River, which is the coronary artery of Southeast Asia. If the Vietnamese people are to lose the struggle to maintain a free and independent nation, it would be a loss of tragic significance to the free world interests in the whole of Asia and the South Pacific.

Secretary Rusk found the peril in the presence of enemy units scattered throughout the peninsula. He admitted to newsmen in October 1967,[76] "I have never subscribed to the domino theory; it's much too esoteric." However, he added:

> There are North Vietnamese armed forces in Laos being opposed by Laotian forces. There are North Vietnamese trained guerillas operating in northeast Thailand. There are Communist dissident elements in Burma who are being aided, encouraged and helped from outside Burma across the Chinese frontier. There was a major Communist effort in 1965 to pull off a coup d'etat against Indonesia. You don't need the domino theory. Look at their proclaimed doctrine and look at what they're doing about it.

He repeated much the same evidence to the Platform Committee of the Democratic Party ten months later, on August 20, 1968:

> We do not need to debate on a highly theoretical basis, something called a "domino theory" in Southeast Asia. Peace in Southeast Asia is not just the problem of a massive intrusion by North Vietnam forces into South Vietnam. Tens of thousands of North Vietnamese forces are operating today in Laos contrary to the accords of 1962. North Vietnam agents and trained guerillas are operating today in Northern Thailand. Prince Sihanouk of Cambodia has charged Hanoi and Peking with supporting and stimulating the Red Khmer in Cambodia. Similar problems exist in Burma and eastern India, in northern Malaysia and Indonesia.

These last two statements complement those made by John Foster Dulles in May 1954, almost fifteen years before. He then had said that Southeast Asia could be held even if Vietnam were lost. Dean Rusk now implied Southeast Asia could be lost, even if Vietnam were held; for he gave no indication that the regular forces, the cadres, the sympathizers emplaced from Indonesia to India, already engaged in revolutionary activities, would cease to function if the regime in Saigon managed to survive. In demonstrating that administration concern for the safety of the whole of Southeast Asia was not fanciful, Mr. Rusk undercut the rationale upon which America's participation in Vietnamese affairs had since the early 1950s been publicly based: that what happened in Vietnam would determine what happened to the remainder of the region, that the stakes were more than "just the future of a small country."[77]

The Munich Analogy

Chain reactions, uncorked bottles submerged in water, falling dominoes—all were familiar, natural phenomena from the physical world appropriated as images for what officials over twenty years propounded as the dynamic relationship between control of Indochina and stability in Southeast Asia. These metaphors suggested, with more clarity than accuracy, the territorial repercussions which would follow from a Communist takeover in Vietnam. Such regional losses were, however, only one of the purported consequences of an allied defeat. Another was the outbreak of a major war.

This possibility was at first raised obliquely. The government contended that the period from 1930 to 1940 had established that in the face of a determined adversary a policy of appeasement and irresolution was fatal. For that decade, dramatized in the September 1938 attempt to assuage Adolf Hitler at Munich, had taught that aggressors regarded diplomatic compromise as capitulation, that they responded only to firmness and demonstrations of counterforce, that their dreams became more grandiose and their behavior less restrained with each success. Because it was assumed that "aggressors"—whether committed to

Fascism or Marxism—were of a kind, these lessons said that to ignore or minimize the threat which existed in Indochina would also be to encourage the enemy to press on with added fury elsewhere.

Such results did not automatically signal holocaust. However, the memories of the 1930s were not easily severed from events of the years thereafter; that is, if the North Vietnamese or Chinese or Russians were, as Washington claimed, to react to victory in Vietnam as the Germans had to victory in Czechoslovakia, then at least implicit in their comparison was the specter of a third world war.

Both Mr. Eisenhower and Mr. Dulles had struck the analogy in April 1954. The president, seeking to impress upon Prime Minister Churchill the seriousness of the situation in Indochina, had written on the fourth that if that area were not preserved

> the ultimate effect on our and your global strategic position . . . could be disastrous. . . . We failed to halt Hirohito, Mussolini, and Hitler by not acting in unity and in time. That marked the beginning of many years of stark tragedy and desperate peril. May it not be that our nations have learned something from that lesson?

The next week[78] the secretary of state told Anthony Eden that the drive launched by the Vietnamese was, in its significance, "analogous to the Japanese invasion of Manchuria in 1931 and to Hitler's reoccupation of the Rhineland." Each of these passages was, however, part of a wholly private exchange.

It was not until 1964 that such ideas were put forward publicly, the initial veiled allusion coming in an address by Defense Secretary McNamara on March 26. After dismissing suggestions that the United States agree to the neutralization of Vietnam, he said, "we have learned that 'peace at any price' is not practical in the long run, and the cost of defending freedom must be borne if we are to have it at all." Two months later, on May 22, Mr. Rusk similarly criticized the advocacy of withdrawal, predicting that it would "bring us much closer to a major conflagration." He added, "Surely we have learned in the course of the last thirty-five years, that a course of aggression means war and that the place to stop it is at its beginning." After the reported second attack on American destroyers in the Gulf of Tonkin on August 5 Mr. Johnson warned:

> Aggression—deliberate, willful and systematic aggression—has unleashed its face to the entire world. The world remembers, the world must never forget, that aggression unchallenged is aggression unleashed. We of the United States have not forgotten. That is why we have answered this aggression with action.

In 1965 there was a slight proportional and numerically significant increase in the use of this theme, and the previously vague references to the experiences of the past became more focused and specific. The secretary of state recalled in March[79] that pre-World War II aggressors had become even more ambitious when they were not checked, and the vice president recited in July the record of failures compiled by the appeasers.[80] The president told newsmen on April 27:

> Defeat in South Vietnam . . . would encourage and spur on those who seek to conquer all free nations that are within their reach. . . . This is the clearest lesson of our time. From Munich until today, we have learned that to yield to aggression brings only greater threats and brings even more destructive war. To stand firm is the only guarantee of a lasting peace.

At a speech at a "Jefferson Day" dinner on June 3, he urged the nation not to delude itself "by the belief that peace can be secured by submissiveness or that peace can be extended by expediency." Throughout the 1930s, he continued,

> we propelled ourselves—and all mankind—toward tragedy, not by divisiveness, but by vacillation, not by determination and resolution, but by irresolution, not by action, but by inaction. . . .
>
> The failure of the free men of the 1930s was a failure not of the "sword," but rather a failure of the "soul"—and there must be no such failure in this decade . . . the world shall not walk again the road to darkness that led mankind into the valley of war thirty years ago.

On July 28 he counseled against abandoning South Vietnam, because such a surrender would not bring peace:

> . . . we learned from Hitler at Munich that success only feeds the
> appetite of aggression. The battle would be renewed in one
> country and then another country, bringing with it perhaps even
> larger war and crueller conflict as we have learned from the
> lessons of history.

There was little statistical variation in 1966. On January 5,
Dean Rusk said that the "harsh aggression . . . in process in
Southeast Asia" was reminiscent of missed challenges "when
Japanese militarists went into Manchuria in 1931, when Mus-
solini went into Ethiopia, when Hitler started on his course of
action." He elaborated on May 24:

> The clearest lesson of the 1930s and '40s is that aggression feeds
> on aggression. I am aware that Mao and Ho Chi Minh are not
> Hitler and Mussolini. But we should not forget what we have
> learned about the anatomy and physiology of aggression. We
> ought to know better than to ignore the aggressor's openly pro-
> claimed intentions or to fall victim to the notion that he will stop
> if you let him have just one more bite or speak to him a little
> more gently.

He noted again on August 22 how between the First and Second World Wars many had dismissed Japanese aggression in
Manchuria as unimportant, reassuring themselves with the misguided hope that "maybe if the aggressors get just another bite
they'll be happy," emphasizing they had been "treated pretty
poorly in the past." He denounced their attitude as "the cynicism" and "the neglect that led to World War II." On June 3 he
had declared simply and dramatically that "if we lose the lessons of World War II the survival of man is literally involved."

And other officials took the same tack. In remarks at an
industry dinner on January 17, 1966, United Nations Representative Goldberg explained administration policy as a reaction to an "awesome lesson of history" which indicated that the
"cannibalistic appetite of the aggressor" is endless, continually
gaining in "momentum and scope." Answering questions at a
Democratic National Committee meeting on April 20, Vice
President Humphrey said he did "not apologize" at all for
United States actions in Vietnam: "What we are doing is right.
We have learned that aggression unchecked is aggression un-
leashed." On June 16, appearing before national legislative

leaders, President Johnson defined American involvement as designed

> to serve notice on those who live in this world with us that gangsterism and aggression and force are not to be rewarded. We were hesitant to take that stand in World War II when Hitler went through Poland. We thought we could sit that one out. We had a lot of the fathers of that time who said it was not our concern. They carried umbrellas around saying that we had been to Europe to save democracy in World War I, that we shouldn't get involved in World War II.

It was this message that he brought with him on his fall journey to the Far East: six times in the thirteen days from October 21 to November 2,[81] he justified the U. S. position as a function of these historical lessons. He put it unequivocally at a reception in Melbourne on the day he arrived:

> as the aggressor marched in the Low Countries in the late thirties, that ultimately wound up in World War II, there are aggressors prowling tonight on the march again.
> Their aggression shall not succeed. . . . [Our boys] are going to stay there until this aggression is checked before it blooms into World War III.

On October 25 his message reappeared in more temperate language in the final declaration of the Manila conferees: "Accepting the hard-won lessons of history that successful aggression anywhere endangers the peace, we are determined . . . that aggression in the region of Asia and the Pacific shall not succeed." To the National Assembly in Seoul, on November 2, he repeated:

> we acted [in Southeast Asia] to stop the aggression . . . because we knew that such aggression feeds on itself. We had watched one country after another fall in the 1930s to Nazi aggression in Europe and militarist imperialism in Asia.

Nor was there any change in 1967. Secretary of State Rusk told a gathering in Scarsdale, New York, on May 7 that the government's stand was "in response to the lesson of World War II." Undersecretary of State Nicholas Katzenbach observed at a commencement assembly at Smith College on June 4, "Those who lived through the prelude and aftermath of World War II

cannot help but be deeply skeptical about the capacity of idealism and vision alone to withstand calculated aggression and
force." On November 17, in a spirited and literary defense of
his position, Mr. Johnson said:

> if you saw a little child in this room that was trying to waddle
> across the floor and some big bully came along and grabbed it by
> the hair and started stomping it, I think you'd do something
> about it. And I think we thought we made a mistake when we
> saw Hitler moving across the landscape of Europe and the
> concessions that were made by men carrying umbrellas at that
> time, I think in retrospect we thought that was a mistake.

In 1968, as the prospects for peace seemed to improve with
the opening of talks in Paris, the figures from the late 1930s
were injected less and less frequently into the rhetoric. When
they were, they tended to be presented in a more moderate
manner. Reflective of this was a statement by the president on
March 18: "wanting peace," he remarked, "praying for peace
and desiring peace, as Chamberlain found out, doesn't always
give you peace." Another was made at one of his final press
conferences on December 27:

> But what really counts is whether we can keep people from
> dying, whether we can get our men home. Just running out is not
> going to do it, because we have found out, as Mr. Chamberlain
> did, and a good many times in our history, that unless things are
> settled honorably, they are not settled. You pay more dearly later
> if you appease.

Whether they referred specifically to Neville Chamberlain
and Adolf Hitler, to Munich, to 1938, or broadly to "the learning," "the lessons," "the memories" of the recent past, because
of the context, the impact of these passages was the same: to
cause people to retrieve, even if momentarily and fragmen-
tarily, the experiences which had precipitated the Second
World War. These experiences gave definition and vivid form
to the dangers of acquiescence to men of ambition and violence. Their relevance could, though it never was, have been
argued on two grounds: first, that the West had dismissed
Czechoslovakia, as much of it tended to dismiss Vietnam, as a
noncritical area, a place of little strategic importance; second,
that the Nazis, as the Communists, were irrevocably and wholly

committed to a program of eventual world domination. Such similarities were verbally mediated by the practice of describing the enemy's activities in Southeast Asia as "aggression"; the description, which had been applied as well to the advances of the Wehrmacht across Europe, was a point of literal identity further linking the two periods.

Interspersed among these analogies, pregnant with their intimations of disaster, were a series of statements which made the same point, that to ignore aggression would only increase the danger of a larger war. Unlike the analogies, however, these statements were explicit about the ultimate risk of conflict. They were often written in the terms of cost-benefit analysis; much as in the 1950s, the denial of assistance to France was rejected as a course "penny wise and pound foolish,"[82] so in the 1960s the option of withdrawal was disapproved as likely to produce far greater expenses later on. It was not only remembered horrors, but sound economics, which made postponement and vacillation bad policy.

Lyndon Johnson, far more than anyone else in the government, adopted this line. He declared on May 17, 1966:

> if we fail in frustrating this aggression the war that would surely come in Asia would produce casualties not in the 1700s, but in the hundreds of thousands and perhaps in millions.
>
> Your Government, therefore, under your President is determined to resist this aggression at the minimum cost to our people and to our allies and to the world.

On September 5, he characterized the war as a small engagement, joined "to keep from fighting larger wars." The following January[83] in his speech on the state of the union he explained it that way again:

> We have chosen to fight a limited war, in Vietnam, in an attempt to prevent a larger war—a war that's almost certain to follow, I believe, if the Communists succeeded in overrunning and taking over South Vietnam by aggression and by force. I believe, and I am supported by some authority, that if they are not checked now the world can expect to pay a greater price to check them later on.

That autumn he gave it especial emphasis. On September 22, 1967, he stated that it was clearly "worth paying the price" demanded to make Southeast Asia secure: "I say that the price of Communist conquest. . . , of risking a third World War by our failure to stand in Vietnam, is a far heavier price to pay." At a fund raising dinner on October 7, he told party regulars that "softening or renouncing the struggle in Vietnam" would mean "increasing the chances of a major war—not this year, but in the years ahead." Addressing a group of Jewish labor leaders on November 9, he predicted that a loss in Vietnam could mean forfeiting "our hope for world stability. We may risk a far more terrible war in the future because we didn't see this one through." He advised members of the AFL-CIO on December 12 that the war would not be ended by solutions that "call for surrender or for cutting and running now." "Those fantasies," he warned, "hold the nightmare of World War II, and a much larger war tomorrow."

Though he repeated it less regularly, he had not abandoned this theme in 1968. On March 31, he praised American soldiers serving in Southeast Asia for "helping the entire world avoid far greater conflicts, far wider wars, far more destruction, than this one." In a talk before the American Legion on September 10, he maintained that if he

> had not drawn the line against aggression in Vietnam . . . some American President, some day, would have to draw the line somewhere else.
> And I ask you at how much greater cost? How many millions of young Americans would be lost in the larger war that would surely and inevitably come?

In October,[84] adopting the language of accountancy, Clark Clifford reported:

> I know that the President feels that the sacrifices made in Vietnam constituted a very worthy one. It is an appropriate investment because by so doing we have prevented a much larger effort later on which could have been infinitely more expensive in both lives and treasure.

The following May 1969,[85] Richard Nixon, as his predecessor had, contended that to abandon South Vietnam "would bring peace now, but it would enormously increase the danger of a bigger war later."

It is difficult to try to relate the collapse of Southeast Asia, foreshadowed by the domino principle, with the outbreak of general war, suggested by the retrospectives to the late 1930s. Were these alternative outcomes? Once Vietnam was gone, the West would have to decide whether to allow the rest of the region to go by default or accept the international calamity which armed resistance would provoke. Were they concurrent outcomes? Once Vietnam was gone, the enemy would be encouraged to move into the territories nearby; as his influence in the area widened and his ambitions increased the West would then act militarily to protect the remaining peninsular holdings. Or were they serial outcomes? Once Vietnam was gone, the neighboring region would quickly disintegrate, and the intolerable situation created thereby would compel the West to resist further disintegration of its Pacific defenses with massive force.

The last of these scenarios comes in fact closest to the vision the government appeared to entertain. Mr. Johnson warned in an address in September 1967:[86]

> your American President cannot tell you with certainty that a Southeast Asia dominated by Communist power would bring a third world war much closer to terrible reality. One could hope that this would not be so.
> But all that we have learned in this tragic century strongly suggests to me it would be so.

Ten months before, on December 6, 1966, a somewhat more detailed presentation had been given by Ambassador Lodge. The fall of Vietnam, he said, would immediately place the Asian countries in the neighborhood under the effective control of the Chinese. In the second phase, he continued, "they start looking around at Australia and Japan, and I'm sure you can't imagine any threat to Australia and Japan that would not bring on World War III."

But even though logically the domino principle and Munich analogy were interconnected, or at least susceptible to interconnection, they functioned usually as independent points. Each was a different sort of simplification of a complex prophesy, each providing a particular perspective from which American actions could be rendered justifiable.

The Test Case Rationale

From 1964 to 1968 officials counseled the nation against forgetting its history. They maintained that the United States was compelled to assist the Republic of Vietnam as a reaction to what it had learned in the previous half-century about the psychology of aggression: that there were fundamental similarities between events in Europe before the Second World War and the current crises in Asia.

But they also advised that in its detail the Vietnamese situation presented a confusing and unfamiliar face, that in its form it was very unlike what had gone before. The new enemy, Mr. Johnson[87] cautioned, had "chosen a different terrain, a different people, and a different kind of war to satisfy his appetite." Secretary McNamara[88] characterized the fight as being fought in a "twilight zone" between combat and political subversion, the other side employing the tactics of sniping, ambush, raiding, extortion, and assassination; while Dean Rusk[89] spoke of it as an ominous exercise "of terror and sabotage, of stealth and subversion."

The Communists called these special wars, "wars of national liberation," and while the government lampooned the implication that a victory would serve the cause of freedom, it recognized the unorthodox strategy as posing a serious threat to the Western world. In a report filed in November 1961, General Maxwell Taylor had warned that these bombardments were a "dangerous Communist technique which bypasses our traditional political and military responses." Robert McNamara explained them in 1964[90] as a program for "in effect crawling under the nuclear and conventional defenses of the free world." Lyndon Johnson said on June 30, 1966, that their theory was "that in the long run a modern scientific and industrial nation such as ours is helpless to defend a smaller and weaker country against the imported terror of guerilla warfare." At times, then, Washington represented the enemy's Southeast Asian campaign as an attempt to develop a foolproof method of expansion.

And at times it justified American involvement as a response to that challenge. In March 1964,[91] in a comprehensive review of far eastern affairs, the secretary of defense introduced the theme that South Vietnam was "a test case for the new Communist strategy." Vice President Humphrey insisted on February 19, 1966, that a "pilot project of Communist strategy" was being conducted in the "test tube of Vietnam." In July,[92] the president outlined his positions as having evolved out of the need "to demonstrate that guerilla warfare, inspired by one nation against another, cannot succeed." That May,[93] Secretary Rusk had cited "what the Communists, in their familiar upside down language call 'wars of liberation,'" describing the attack on the Saigon Republic as "a critical test of that technique of aggression."

The argument that the enemy sought in Vietnam to prove the viability of its unconventional approaches to modern warfare and that this had dictated a U. S. intervention was never used extensively. It was only at one period, during the two and a half weeks from February 16 to March 4, 1966, that it received anything more than scant attention; then, as the Senate Foreign Relations Committee was hearing testimony on administration policy, each of the administration's five key spokesmen[94] focused on this issue of "liberation wars," possibly in an attempt to provide a more convincing and less stereotyped rationale for its increasingly criticized and controversial decisions.

Nor did the government define with any great degree of consistency or coherence what, accepting this argument, would follow from an allied defeat. Two results were, however, suggested. If the enemy's Vietnamese experiment succeeded: (1) China's stature in both Communist and neutral nations would be immeasurably enhanced, and (2) there would be other so-called popular uprisings breaking out serially around the world.

The first of these predictions was most closely associated with Robert McNamara, in statements he made between the spring of 1964 and the summer of 1965. It reflected his judgment that Peking enjoyed a special relationship with Hanoi, and that Maoist doctrine had, at least by the middle of the 1960s, come to exert the dominant influence upon the leadership of North Vietnam. Though Premier Khrushchev had in January 1961 initially discussed movements of liberation, he

departed from the line taken by Dean Rusk, which continued
to note Russia's advocacy as being significant. Soviet moral support was implicitly dismissed as expedient, gratuitous, and half-
hearted; it was the Chinese who spurred on the Democratic
Republic, and it was their particular version of war which was
being carried out in Southeast Asia; Vietnam was presented by
him as a crucial issue in the dispute between the moderates in
Moscow and the extremists in Peking. "Success in Vietnam," he
told the National Security Industrial Association in 1964,[95]
"would be regarded as vindication for China's views in the
world wide ideological struggle." On February 18, 1965, appearing before the House Armed Services Committee, he was
more specific:

> A Communist success in South Vietnam would be claimed as
> proof positive that the Chinese Communist position was correct
> and they will have made a giant step forward for control of the
> world Communist movement. Such a success would also greatly
> increase the prestige of China among the non-aligned nations
> and strengthen the position of their following everywhere.

During the summer[96] he repeated that testimony almost word
for word at a hearing of the Senate panel on appropriations:

> a Communist success in South Vietnam would be taken as posi-
> tive proof that the Chinese Communists' position is correct and
> they will have made a giant step forward in their efforts to seize
> control of the world Communist movement.

The contention that Peking would be the main beneficiary
of a victory in Indochina was not, however, strictly confined
either to Mr. McNamara or the period from 1964 to 1965. It had
been clearly foreshadowed by President Kennedy in September 1963. In a televised interview on the ninth, he had remarked, "if South Vietnam went, it would . . . give the impression that the wave of the future in Southeast Asia was with
China and the Communists." And five and a half years later,
with somewhat less clarity, it was revived by President Richard
Nixon:

> Another reason for not withdrawing unilaterally [from South
> Vietnam] stems from the debates within the Communist world

between those who argue for a policy of containment or confrontation with the United States and those who argue against it. If Hanoi were to succeed in taking over South Vietnam by force it would greatly strengthen those leaders who scorn negotiation, who advocate aggression and who minimize the risk of confrontation with the United States.

The other suggestion—that the capture of South Vietnam would be the prelude to revolutionary contagion—was made by a broader range of officials and expressed in a far wider variety of forms. Assistant Secretary of State William Bundy, talking of peoples' wars to a Tokyo audience in September 1964,[97] said, "If the Communists succeed in Vietnam they will use the same technique with growing frequency elsewhere in Asia, Africa and Latin America." On April 19, 1965, his deputy, Leonard Unger, predicted that a failure to take a firm stand in Southeast Asia against that "war of liberation" could lead "to similar struggles in other Asian nations." That December[98] Ambassador Goldberg ominously labeled such struggles "the greatest threat to peace" in the world. Mr. Johnson declared the next February:[99]

> If the takeover of Vietnam can be achieved by a highly organized Communist force employing violence against the civilian population, it can be achieved in another country, at another time. . . .
> If this "war of liberation" triumphs, who will be "liberated" next?

Six months thereafter, in a speech before the American Legion in August,[100] he restated those fears and revealed their basis:

> Make no mistake about the character of this war. Our adversaries have done us at least one great service. They have described this war for what it is in unmistakable terms. It is meant to be the opening salvo in a series of bombardments, or as they are called in Peking, "wars of liberation." And if it succeeds in South Vietnam, then, as Marshal Lin Piao says, and I quote him, "the people in other parts of the world will see that what the Vietnamese people can do they can do, too."

The test case rationale had territorial implications that were more extensive than those of the domino principle; the test case rationale portended the loss of three continents, while the domino principle forecast the collapse of only a subpart of one. The process it described was similar to, and complemented, that described through the Munich analogy: the Munich analogy taught that an enemy victory in Vietnam would stimulate the aggressors to march forward in an effort to seize other areas and would plunge Asia into a general war; the test case rationale proclaimed that a victory would, as well, spur subversive cadres on a campaign to undermine unstable countries from within. The force of the prophesy rested again on the assumption that the Southeast Asian outcome would have a decisive effect, in this case upon the future prospect of Communist-inspired guerilla rebellions.

As it had classed together the contiguous nations of southern Asia and the backward, largely rural sections of the world, the government also treated the "hundred little countries" as a homogeneous group. With some regularity from February 1965 to October 1966, Washington maintained that these smaller states had a definite stake in the turn of events in South Vietnam. The president emphasized to members of the news media on March 20, 1965, that the people of Indochina

> have the right to live side by side in peace and independence, and if this little country does not have that right, then the question is what will happen to the other hundred little countries who want to preserve that right.

That August[101] he urged an audience to remember that, while 114 states belonged to the United Nations, "all the big powers can be counted on the fingers of one hand." "If," he went on, "this little nation goes down the drain, ask yourselves, what is to happen to all the other little nations?" Secretary Rusk confided during a televised discussion in March 1966,[102] that seventy-five of the hundred small nations "support what we're doing in Vietnam. Many of them can't come forward publicly and give us support because they have similar problems of their own." But were the United States to frustrate the Communists in Southeast Asia, those "one hundred small countries around the world will breathe a sigh of relief and be glad it came out that way." Two months later, on May 17, at a fund raising dinner in Chicago, Mr. Johnson commented, "not just that one little country of fourteen million people, but more than one hundred little countries stand tonight and watch and wait," and he restated in June[103] that America was not only fighting for the rights of the South Vietnamese but "for a hundred nations' freedom and liberty." In mid-summer[104] Mr. Rusk assured the annual convention of the Veterans of Foreign Wars that if the United States were to prevail in Indochina, "a hundred small nations around the world will clap their hands."

A list of the hundred little countries was never released, so it was always obscure whether the littleness was a reference to land area, population, or effective political power. Nor was the dimension or exact nature of the threat posed ever defined, so the fundamental question of what relevance the war had to them remained forever unanswered. It would, therefore, not be unjustifiable to dispose of these passages as dramatic, but ultimately meaningless rhetorical excesses. Nevertheless, it is interesting to speculate upon how content might be poured into them.

The operation of the domino principle depended upon the fact that the fall of South Vietnam would strategically improve the enemy's position for further assaults in the region, upon the physical and geographic significance of such a loss. By contrast, the logic of the little countries' defense, like that of the test case rationale, was grounded in the symbolic importance of that occurrence. Both Communist insurgents and the heads of the hundred minor governments were closely observing the Southeast Asian war as an experiment, and each would draw far-reaching conclusions from its results. As dissident elements within preindustrial areas would hold the "liberation" of Vietnam as the signal for action, so the ruling bodies of weak, essentially defenseless nations would also regard that event as a signal, either to accommodate with or make concessions to those who could guarantee their security.

The movement of iron filings between the poles of a magnet suggests the dynamics of the process. The filings, the little states, gravitate to the pole, the rival centers of the capitalist and Marxist Worlds, which exerts the strongest pull. A victory by the North Vietnamese enemy would be a show of strength which would inexorably draw those leaders who feared for their

nation's safety into the orbit of Moscow or Peking, ostensibly
the source of revolutionary dangers and the point from which
these dangers could be controlled. The perspective here was
that of the potential victim, rather than of the possible belligerent. The inquiry made by each, however, was the same: could
the West, with its clear technological superiority, successfully
cope with a novel and primitive variation of limited warfare?

The National Interest

The possibility that the seizure of Indochina would eventually lead to the capture of all of Southeast Asia was from 1950
to 1954 the major rationale for U.S. support of French operations in Vietnam. The immediate implications of withholding
assistance were ominous: the threat that nearly two hundred
million Asians would become subject to Communist control.
Though officials devoted not inconsiderable attention to such
tragic human costs, on the whole, the emphasis was more self-
centered. The principal concern was the effect of the enormous
territorial losses on America. "The United States has a very vital
interest in the developments in this area," Secretary Dulles told
the nation in a televised report on February 24, 1954. Six
months earlier[105] the president had been more specific. The
impact of a Vietminh victory, he warned, "would be of a most
terrible significance to the United States of America, our
security, our power and ability to get certain things we need"
from Southeast Asia.

The economic importance of Southeast Asia had been recognized and lamented by Washington throughout the Second
World War; then, with Japanese troops in occupation in Burma,
Indochina, Malaya, and Indonesia, America found itself wanting in resources upon which its defense industries heavily depended. It was mentioned by President Truman in March
1952,[106] forming part of the justification for a renewed Mutual
Security Program appropriation for the area. But it did not
receive any sustained notice until the spring of 1954 when, as
the government sought to prepare the public for the possibility

of an allied intervention, it was presented as an issue of critical concern.

The region, John Foster Dulles pointed out on March 29, "is rich in many raw materials such as tin, rubber, oil, iron ore." On April 7, varying the detail, President Eisenhower observed:

> there were from this area, two of the items from this particular area that the world used, were tin and tungsten. They were very important. There were others, of course, and the rubber plantations, and so on.

On both the tenth and the fifteenth, Mr. Dulles repeated that the region possessed vast stores of "economic resources." The president on April 23 talked of "tin and tungsten and rubber and platinum and many other items used in our daily lives, [that] we do not produce." "We cannot," he added darkly, "live alone." Three days later, in an address to the United States Chamber of Commerce, he spoke elliptically of "the great products of the region, one of which we must have." Two weeks after that,[107] Secretary Dulles again noted the "extremely valuable assets in terms of oil, rubber and tin" with which the area was endowed.

There was never this intense a concentration on the military security aspect of the U.S. interest. Nor was the matter particularly well-explained when it was raised. The danger appeared to derive from two sets of circumstances. First, that the enemy in Indochina was more anti-American than anti-French: the rebels were Communists; Communists sought finally to destroy bourgeois society; the locus of that society was the United States. "International communism," Mr. Dulles maintained in September 1954,[108]

> thinks in terms of ultimately using its power against the United States. Therefore, we could honestly say, using the words that President Monroe used in proclaiming his doctrine, that Communist armed aggression in Southeast Asia would, in fact, endanger our peace.

Three months before, on June 10, he had cautioned:

> There is a danger that the Chinese Communists—in their feeling of power and in their hatred for the United States—may under-

take to try to capture the free world positions in the Western Pacific with a view to driving the United States back to California.

Second, that the peninsula and surrounding islands were ideally situated as communciation and staging areas, their geography making them a key in America's forward defenses. In July 1953,[109] the secretary of state said frankly that if Southeast Asia were overrun "our position in the Western Pacific could be put in jeopardy." The following March[110] he made clear why: the area lies "astride the most direct and best developed sea and air routes between the Pacific and South Asia. It has major naval and air bases."

Marxist theory and geostrategic realities thereby combined to transform the Indochina war from a minor, distant, jungle skirmish to a crisis "of great consequence"[111] to the safety of the United States.

The Johnson Administration seldom considered either the human or economic significance of the battle in Vietnam. It did, however, constantly refer to its bearing on national security. The images it adopted were designed to establish that the boys fighting on the remote battlefields of Asia were protecting the lives of their friends and families back home, that the assault in South Vietnam was being directed by fanatical men committed single-mindedly to the dismantling of the American system. On June 28, 1964, Henry Cabot Lodge, the outgoing ambassador to the Republic of Vietnam, left Saigon proclaiming, "The stakes here are great for you, for us, and for the world." In early July[112] his replacement, former General Maxwell D. Taylor, arrived and declared: "Here the security of the United States and the free world are at stake." That February[113] Dean Rusk cited legislative judgment that "peace and security in Southeast Asia" were "vital" to the "national interest."

Over the succeeding months and years it was the president who most frequently reaffirmed these lines. In a request for funds on May 4, 1965, he argued the case for U.S. intervention on grounds of "the necessities of American security." He said in New York on the eleventh, "We would rather men would quarrel with our action to insure peace, than curse us through all eternity for our inaction which might lose us both our peace and freedom." On June 1 he spoke of the conflict where "men are dying to preserve our freedom"; on July 28 he prophesied that to be driven out of Vietnam "would certainly imperil the security of the United States itself." He told an industrial council on December 2:

> No one of us—businessman, laboring man, Government employee—can ever forget what American fighting men are doing in Vietnam may well determine the shape and form of your future, your country's future.

That February[114] he warned that it was "vitally important to every American family that we stop the Communists in South Vietnam." In June[115] he pledged, "we shall not be diverted from doing what is necessary in the nation's interest," and in July[116] he complained that sometimes "we don't recognize the men that are dying for us." On March 10, 1967, he decorated the Third Aerospace Rescue and Recovery Group for "exceptional gallantry"; he reminded the attending press that such sacrifice was made "so that you might breathe freely and speak freely and utilize the First Amendment."

But though he talked regularly of the link between America's fate and the war in Asia, until the fall of 1967 its significance remained largely peripheral. Often noted parenthetically or perfunctorily as part of a patriotic appeal, it emerged as one issue—not the only one, and not the most important—in the evolution of a commitment to Vietnam. "Of course," Mr. Johnson conceded late in 1966,[117] "our policies are shaped with a proper regard for our security and welfare." He went on,

> but much of the energy of our efforts has come because we believe it is right that the strong should help the weak defend their freedom; that the wealthy should help the poor overcome their hunger; that nations, no matter how small, or fragile, or young, should be free from the coercion of others.

Such magnanimity and high purpose, enlightened in the abstract, was criticized as being neither an appropriate nor a straightforward justification for decisions which called for the laying down of American lives and the draining of American

treasure. It is "not enough," Richard Nixon advised a meeting
of industrialists on September 12, 1967, "to moralize about our
being there to defend democracy or guarantee freedom of
choice." "Candor" requires that the United States admit that its
forces are in Asia because "our vital national interest is at
stake."

This admission, the government could have rightly con-
tended, had been made periodically in the past. But it did not.
Instead, on September 29, a little more than two weeks after
Mr. Nixon's challenge—and as if in response to it—President
Johnson read this statement:

> Why . . . have [we] chosen to defend this Asian nation. . . ?
> We cherish freedom—yes. . . . We abhor the political murder
> of any state and the bodily murder of any people by gangsters
> of whatever ideology. And for twenty-seven years . . . we have
> sought to strengthen free people against domination by aggres-
> sive foreign powers.
> But the key to all that we have done is really our own
> security. At times of crisis, before asking Americans to fight and
> die to resist aggression in a foreign land, every American Presi-
> dent has finally had to answer this question:
> Is the aggression a threat not only to the immediate victim,
> but to the United States of America. . . ?

During the next half year, in the midst of increasingly res-
tive and vocal dissent, Washington underlined the point that
national interest was, and had always been, the critical impetus
behind American involvement in Vietnam. On October 15 the
vice president stressed:

> We are in Vietnam . . . because the United States of America has
> a stake in freedom.
> The threat to our own security is in Asia. And we are fighting
> there not only for the Vietnamese but for ourselves and the
> future of our country.

Lyndon Johnson lectured newsmen on November 17, "I think
that our aims in Vietnam have been very clear from the beginning . . . namely to protect the security of the United States."
In March 1968,[118] Hubert Humphrey urged "a ringing vote of
confidence for an American President who refuses to play the
politics of popularity when the peace and security of the United
States are in the balance." That spring,[119] announcing the par-

tial suspension of bombing and his own noncandidacy for office, that president declared:

> During the past four and a half years, it has been my fate and my responsibility to be Commander in Chief. I have lived daily and nightly with the cost of this war. . . .
>
> And throughout this entire long period I have been sustained by a single principle: that what we are doing in Vietnam is vital not only to the security of Southeast Asia but it is vital to the security of every American . . . the heart of our involvement in South Vietnam . . . has always been America's own security.

Explanations seldom followed these recurrent and provocative allusions, and it was only occasionally that officials discussed exactly how an Asian guerilla war bore on U.S. security. When they did, their discussions proved to be only elaborations of already familiar arguments, variations on well-known themes. The repeated warnings of the general disaster which would follow a Communist success—the domino-like collapse of the rest of southern Asia, the resumption of aggression on a post-Munich pattern, the multiplication of people's wars—were merely rephrased and expanded to comprehend the American mainland.

Four different perspectives were taken to describe the impact of the domino principle upon the United States. On March 26, 1964, Secretary McNamara emphasized, as John Foster Dulles had a decade before, the importance of the region's fortunate geographic situation:

> Southeast Asia has great strategic significance in the forward defense of the United States. Its location across east-west air and sea lanes flanks the Indian subcontinent on one side and Australia, New Zealand and the Philippines on the other and dominates the gateway between the Pacific and Indian Oceans.
>
> In Communist hands this area would pose a most serious threat to the security of the United States.

When, at a news conference in the autumn of 1967,[120] Dean Rusk was asked to explain why "our security is at stake," his response focused on the specter of an encroaching China:

> Now from a strategic point of view it is not very attractive to think of the world cut in two by Asian Communism reaching out through southeast Asia and Indonesia, which we know to be their

objective; and that . . . the free nations of Asia should be under the deadly and constant pressure of the authorities in Peking, so that their future is circumscribed by fear.

Now these are vitally important matters to us, who are both a Pacific and Atlantic power.

President Johnson, addressing the Veterans of Foreign Wars in August 1968,[121] merely enlarged the list of potential dominoes to make his point. "There are," he began, "some among us who appear to be searching for a formula which would get us out of Vietnam and Asia on any terms." He continued:

Laos, South Vietnam, Thailand, Malaysia, Singapore, Indonesia [would be lost and] pretty soon we could be back to the Philippines and even back to Honolulu.

I profoundly believe that this course would be disastrous to the interests of the United States.

The next month[122] Hubert Humphrey directed his attention to the classic theory of the balance of power:

I sincerely believe that our stand in Vietnam has surely been of some significant help to stability and security in that part of the world.

And that is vital to our national interest, because if all Asia were to go Communist, and fall prey to aggression, or at least all of Southeast Asia, the power balance in this world would be thrown out of kilter completely, and there's no way of predicting what the cost would be to this country in terms of its own defense.

In summary: the disintegration of Southeast Asia would jeopardize American safety because it would provide China with a favorable military position in the area at the expense of the United States, lead to subsequent enemy takeovers in the offshore islands, and radically alter the regional alignment of Communist and non-Communist nations.

There was neither the same originality nor scope to the commentary on the relevance of Munich. The analysis went no further than asserting that no one is secure when there is an aggressor on the prowl. "We all have so much to remember, so much to be thankful for," Lyndon Johnson remarked in Melbourne, on October 21, 1966,

And I hope it won't be necessary for another Hitler to gobble up the Low Countries and march through Poland. . . .

I hope it won't be necessary to have our fleet turned upside down at Pearl Harbor for ourselves finally to realize where our national interest lies.

Two days later he was more vague and foreboding:

Most of our people have learned the lesson of this century, that nations must not turn their backs on those whose freedom is imperiled by aggression. When they have done so, and the melancholy history of our time tells us that they have, it was not long before their own freedom faced the same mortal danger.

Arriving on Guam on March 20, 1967, he observed that the Second World War had "changed forever the world as we had known it." "It taught us lessons," he went on, "we shall never forget—most important that the peace of all the world is threatened when aggressors are encouraged to feed on any part of it." Early in 1968[123] he denounced Ho Chi Minh as another Adolf Hitler and warned that if the rebel leader were not confronted and stopped at the beginning, many hundred of thousands more Americans would be defending their country nearer home.

The most, and perhaps only, detailed treatment of the national implications of the test case rationale was supplied by Deputy Defense Secretary Cyrus Vance in an address on October 7, 1965. Basing his interpretation on a speech by Peking's Minister of Defense, he concluded that Communist China was intent on demonstrating, using Vietnam as its laboratory, that the victory of liberation movements in rural areas of the world could lead to the isolation and, finally, the seizure of the industrial giants. He reported:

Just as Communism in China, says Lin Piao, succeeded by capturing and then encircling and defeating the cities so the global Communist movement will ultimately succeed first by capturing Asia, Africa and Latin America thereby encircling North America and Western Europe and then decisively defeating the United States and its Western allies.

Within Asia, Africa, and Latin America through wars of national liberation, says Lin Piao, the United States will be surrounded, will be encircled.

And where is all this to begin, he asks. It has already begun, he replies. And the place in which it has begun is Vietnam. Vietnam, says Lin Piao, is now the focus of the revolutionary movement against the United States.

An extremely interesting, though utterly unique rendering of the threat to U.S. security was presented in a talk given by the president at Camp Stanley, South Korea, in November 1966.[124] Betraying alternately American arrogance and anxiety, he proclaimed:

We are going to have to stand and say, "Might doesn't make right."

There are three billion people in the world and we only have two hundred million of them. We are outnumbered fifteen to one. If might did make right they would sweep over the United States and take what we have. We have what they want.

We had better establish a rule . . . that no dictator, just because he has power, because he has might can snuff out freedom and liberty.

We have had to show it couldn't be done in Korea. . . . We are showing now it can't be done in Vietnam. . . . It is better to do it there than it is in Honolulu.

The nation's "interest" in Vietnam arose primarily out of the far-reaching geopolitical repercussions a Communist takeover could have. That event would, it was said, "see this world slip down the slippery slope,"[125] and have reverberations that might render the United States militarily more vulnerable and less safe within its borders.

There was, however, another source of "interest." It derived from the premise that the destinies of free peoples were inextricably bound up with one another, the notion that freedom was of one piece. This idea stood simultaneously as a repudiation of narrow isolationism, a commitment to international responsibility, and a reaffirmation of the poetic vision that "no man is an island." It implied a moral obligation on the part of those who lived in liberty to seek the liberation of those who did not and suggested that the mission would be of benefit to liberator and liberated both. The acceptance of a common fate for the "free world" meant that the erosion of freedom in one place influenced its stability everywhere else. It made it practical and honorable for the United States to defend Vietnam, for Vietnam under this romantic analysis was intrinsically important to America.

The postulate had been set out by both Republicans and Democrats in each decade of the war. On September 3, 1953, Secretary Dulles commented, "We are not indifferent to the welfare of other people, and oftentimes our own welfare is tied into that of others." "More closely than ever before," President Eisenhower stated the following January,[126] "American freedom is interlocked with the freedom of other peoples." Lyndon Johnson told members of the Associated Press at a luncheon in the spring of 1964,[127] "The independence of Asian nations is a link in our own freedom." At a dinner address in February 1966,[128] he remarked on "how inseparably bound together are America's freedom and the freedom of her friends around the world." "It is our conviction that peace, like freedom, is indivisible," he declared the next year.[129]

> Neither the New World of the Americas, nor the Old World of Europe, can hope to fulfill its dreams and ambitions until the ancient world of Asia has become a full and equal partner in the forward movement of man.
> This conviction lies at the very root of American policy in Vietnam.

Washington concluded, then, that to ignore the Vietnamese would not only be cynical, but self-defeating; Mr. Eisenhower put it plainly to reporters on July 21, 1954: "I think that when the freedom of a man in Vietnam . . . was taken from him, I think our freedom has lost a little." Conversely, to respond to the Vietnamese would be a course both generous and opportune. "We cannot assure liberty for ourselves unless others have it," John Foster Dulles maintained in February 1955.[130] "Freedom," he went on, "cannot survive in an environment hostile to freedom." In the years after 1964, that point was made again, in various ways, many times.

Robert McNamara claimed on March 26, 1964, "Our own security is strengthened by the determination of others to remain free." That December,[131] questioned by newsmen about the national interest in South Vietnam, Secretary Rusk explained:

> the American interest can be expressed in very simple terms. Where there is a country which is independent and secure and in a position to work out its own policy and be left alone by its neighbors, there is a country whose position is consistent with our understanding of our interests in the world. It's just as simple as that.

The president, speaking in Baltimore in April 1965,[132] insisted, "We fight because we must fight if we are to live in a world where every country can shape its own destiny. And only in such a world will our freedom be finally secure." He elaborated on the theme in his State of the Union Message the following January.[133]

> The touchstone of . . . [our Southeast Asian] policy is the interest of the United States—the welfare and the freedom of the United States. But nations sink when they see that interest only through a narrow glass. In a world that's grown small and dangerous, pursuit of narrow aims could bring decay and even disaster.
> An America that's mighty beyond description—yet living in a hostile or despairing world—would be neither safe nor free to build a civilization to liberate the spirit of man.

With unusual intensity and drama, he reminded a Capitol gathering on February 12, 1968, that

> Since Lincoln's time, the revolutionary dream of human dignity and equality for all has been spreading across the world.
> And so today, when Americans are asked to help Lincoln's ideas flourish in places far from these steps, we ask ourselves the hard and searching questions:
> Are these ideas still valid? Do they deserve a hearing elsewhere if free men so choose? Are we ourselves safer and stronger when they do get a hearing and when they flourish?
> If we answer those questions affirmatively . . . we are sometimes forced by an adversary to back our belief with steel—just as Lincoln did.

That March[134] Mr. Rusk testified to the Senate Foreign Relations Committee that "we have a basic commitment to freedom, for ourselves. And that requires an environment in the rest of the world where freedom can survive and flourish, as Dean Acheson put it." "Freedom—like aggression—is contagious," Secretary of Defense Clifford commented a month later.[135] "The more there is elsewhere, the greater the chance of safeguarding your own."

Freedom in the United States, the administration contended, required a free climate in the world in order to thrive and grow. The support of freedom abroad, therefore, was calculated to better insure its survival at home; enhancing the freedom of other peoples would also enhance the security of Americans.

But what did "freedom" mean in this context? Was it civil liberty, "equality for all" as the president phrased it, or was it independence in the realm of foreign affairs, what Secretary Rusk called a state's position to "work out its own policy"? And whether human rights or national autonomy, how and to what extent did it really affect U.S. interests? Would democratic-sovereign nations necessarily share America's perspective on international issues? Did it follow that they would establish relations with, or grant trade concessions to, or install the military apparatus of the United States? Was it certain that their leaders would never forcibly oppose the U.S. government's overseas initiatives and that they would refuse any role in an anti-American combination?

The answer to each question is "no"; no benefit flowed automatically from the flourishing of freedom. The most that could be said unequivocally was that the free governments were not per se allied in an ideological conspiracy directed against the United States, that free governments were generally non-Communist as well.

Non-Communist countries are countries which are not self-consciously modeled on the revolutionary program of Karl Marx. The classification signifies nothing whatever about the particular character or style of the regimes. They may be democratic or despotic, autonomous or servile. They are free only in the restricted sense that to be non-Communist is to be free from communism; whatever the prevailing mythology, both formal logic and experience demonstrate that even if every Communist takeover marked the beginning of internal repression and the end of national independence, its overthrow or absence would guarantee neither the restoration of civil liberty nor the return of sovereignty. Free governments are likely to be non-Communist, but there is no especial likelihood that non-Communist governments will be free.

It would, therefore, have been less misleading and ambiguous if officials had described America's interest in a secure, world environment as a function of opposing communism rather than of preserving freedom. But clarity and accuracy of expression are not the determinants of rhetoric; force, impact, effectiveness are. The talk of "interlocking destinies" and "indivisible humanity" may have been so much bombast, just words that upon analysis were utterly devoid of any meaningful content. But if such words could move people and touch their emotions, they would continue to be repeated however little substance they had.

PROMISES

Washington offered three sorts of reasons for its participation in Vietnam. The first set involved the articulation of goals for improving the quality of South Vietnamese life. Touching everything from the design of the educational system to the standard of health care, it focused mainly upon the demand that the people of that country have the right, through free elections, to select their own government.

The second rested upon the theory that a judicious application of limited pressure against Hanoi at present would postpone, if not preclude, the necessity of applying massive force over a wider area later on. The prediction was that a Communist victory in the peninsula would have consequences which, eventually, would prejudice the security of the United States.

Ultimately both reasons were grounded in a kind of utilitarianism. Though the direct appeal in the first case was to magnanimous impulses and in the second to an instinct for preservation, in effect both were defenses based upon the good that

American policy would do: for South Vietnam, by providing conditions for its economic, social, and political betterment; for the United States, by forestalling events whose repercussions would threaten its safety.

Justification 1 dealt primarily with the issue of self-determination; Justification 2, with the question of self-interest. Justification 3 revolved around the matter of self-respect. America, it said, entered Vietnam because it was bound to honor its commitments. Unlike 1 and 2, Justification 3 did not derive from principles of utility but from principles of obligation; it related not to what the nation hoped to achieve politically or prevent geostrategically in Southeast Asia, but to a neutral, wholly abstract belief that the pledge word should be upheld. The three, however, were interconnected.

The objective of insuring a democratic Vietnam and the obverse requirement of combatting Communist aggression explained why at the outset the United States had decided to make a stand in Asia. Having made that decision, it was then formalized through executive assurance, international agreement, and public declarations of support. These formal expressions were later alleged to have compelled America to assist the South Vietnamese and became themselves explanations for the deepening American involvement. As legal arguments for that assistance, they retained their force, regardless of whether or not democracy and communism remained preoccupying concerns.

It was late in 1961 that Washington first suggested that it was committed to help the republic in Saigon. At a briefing on November 29, President Kennedy commented that his order to call up the Army Reserves had been motivated by the "increased tensions in Vietnam." The purpose of the alert was "to indicate that the United States is serious about its commitments; that it means to meet its commitments." The allusion did not recur again until May 1963,[136] and then only parenthetically in a reference to the "commitment" to the "integrity of South Vietnam." The kind of obligation involved, its scope, its nature, it origin, it significance, were questions not only unanswered, but in the spring of 1963 still unasked.

The following winter, however, Lyndon Johnson adopted the uncertain image and immediately transformed it into a central theme. Speaking at the University of California at Los Angeles on February 21, 1964, he said:

> In South Vietnam terror and violence . . . press against the lives and liberties of a people who seek only to be left in peace . . . our country has been committed to the support of their freedom and that commitment we will continue to honor.

That May[137] he told members of Congress, "By our words and deeds . . . we are pledged before all the world to stand with the free people of Vietnam." By June that pledge had become pivotal. "Four basic themes," he noted to reporters on the second, "govern our policy in Southeast Asia." "First," he declared, "America keeps her word . . . we are bound by solemn commitments to help defend this area against Communist encroachment. We will keep this commitment." Three weeks later[138] he reiterated, "The policy of the United States toward Southeast Asia . . . [can be] summarized . . . in four simple propositions. 1. America keeps her word." On August 5, in the wake of the North Vietnamese attack of U.S. warships in the Gulf of Tonkin, he again reviewed the "four simple propositions" and for the third time listed, "One, America keeps her word." "Here as elsewhere," he went on, "we must and shall honor our commitments."

In 1965, at over twice the level of intensity, there was more of the same. The year opened[139] with a State of the Union Message that proclaimed, "We are [in Vietnam] . . . first, because a friendly nation has asked us for help against Communist aggression . . . we pledged our help . . . we will not break it now." On January 18 the president concluded a statement on national defense with a promise to "continue to honor our commitment in Vietnam." He insisted to newsmen in February[140] that he had "intended to make it abundantly clear that we had a commitment to help those people help themselves and we intended to abide by it."

From April to mid-May there was a barrage. Then, in the weeks after the initiation of continuous bombing against the

North and before the confirmation that American forces were engaged in active combat in the South, the recurrent refrain of commitment provided a background against which all that had happened, or would happen, appeared to be inevitable: the United States was morally and legally bound to safeguard Vietnam, it had no choice. "Why are we in South Vietnam?" "We are there because we have a promise to keep," Mr. Johnson maintained on April 7. In a letter to neutral leaders released the next day he contended that American assistance had been extended "in fulfillment of our longstanding commitments." On the tenth he remarked in Texas, "[Though we] love our peace and we hate war ... our course is charted always by the compass of honor." He added, "Where we have given our commitments to others, we shall keep them." That May[141] he vowed, "We will not abandon our commitment to Vietnam."

In the month and a half preceding the July 28 announcement of the dispatch of fifty thousand U.S. troops to southern Asia, there was another spate. Again, the effect was to create an atmosphere in which each subsequent step seemed unavoidable. On June 17, President Johnson defended the interdiction of North Vietnam as an action taken to convince the enemy that "we were there to keep our commitment and we were going to keep it." He stated at a news conference in early July,[142] "[In Vietnam] we committed our power and national honor." On the thirteenth he repeated that we expected to uphold "[our] commitment," and maintained:

> Our national honor is at stake. Our word is at stake. And it must be obvious to all Americans that they would not want the President of their country to follow any course that was inconsistent with our commitments or with our national honor.

During the autumn and winter it was principally Secretary Rusk who undertook to reinforce that line, the reaffirmations coming most often in the context of warnings to China. He talked on November 5 about how "very important" it was that "Peking not be misled about the determination of the American people and the American Government to meet our commitments," and he stressed on the eleventh that that "commitment" would be upheld. At the beginning of December,[143] he emphasized that the danger of "confrontation" lay with China, pledging, "We are going to meet our commitment in South Vietnam." On the thirtieth he again urged the Chinese to understand "that we have a commitment in South Vietnam" and would "make good on the commitment."

The next year Washington turned its attention to the principle of self determination; two years after that, in late 1967, it focused on the question of U.S. security. Though over that period the number of references declined, American integrity remained a critical issue until 1969. Its continuing importance was made plain whenever Washington was under pressure to defend its course; at these times, it was invariably turned to and underlined as central to the government's case.

Between January and February 1966, the government conducted a massive campaign to open negotiations with the enemy and explain its policies to the world; it also placed "Vietnam" formally on the United Nations agenda, and underwent intense and exhaustive hearings before the Senate Foreign Relations Committee. Asked on January 21 whether Communist refusal to begin talks would invite "hard steps" in retaliation, Dean Rusk responded only to say "our commitment to the safety and freedom of South Vietnam is deep"; he cautioned that the danger of escalation always existed "when an aggressor sets out to impose his will by force on someone else and those of us who have commitments are resolved to meet our commitments." When on the twenty-ninth the peace offensive closed and the bombing of the North was resumed, he rationalized the move as "necessary" to "meet our responsibilities to South Vietnam and the South Vietnamese forces." He stressed the profound "national responsibility which is both political and military" to insure that "our commitments to South Vietnam and the South Vietnamese forces are met."

At the end of June the United States expanded the scope of its attacks upon North Vietnam, authorizing air strikes against oil storage depots on the outskirts of Hanoi and Haiphong; immediately there were outcries of the risk of the indiscriminate murder of innocent civilians. The day of the initial raid,[144] Mr.

Johnson emphasized in an Omaha speech: "The word of the United States must remain a trust that men can live by and can live with and can depend upon." He pleaded that we must "keep our commitments" and thereby "let the rest of the world know that when America gives its word, America keeps its word." Two weeks later, on July 12, he declared, "we have committed ourselves to the defense of one small country. . . . We do not intend to let them down. Our word will be good." "We are not," he restated on the twenty-third, "going to break America's word."

In mid-February 1967 another initiative to start discussions with the enemy had ended in failure and in succeeding days the boundaries on the war widened. By March 10, for the first time, American gunners had fired across the demilitarized zone, American demolition teams had mined North Vietnamese waterways, and American pilots had strafed major iron and steel fabricating plants. On March 1, United Nations Ambassador Goldberg arrived in Saigon to "reaffirm our commitment to the Vietnamese people"; on the fifteenth the president recalled that two years before "we were forced to make a decision between major commitments in defense of South Vietnam or retreat"; Mr. Rusk promised at the end of the month,[145] "the United States shall meet it commitments in Vietnam. We will do our duty there."

During the fall, nearly seventy-five thousand people marched on the Pentagon to protest against official policy, that only the most visible sign of the growing public discontent. Mr. Johnson told reporters on the first of November, "We seek to do nothing except keep our commitment." At another briefing, on the seventeenth, he noted, "every country that I know in the [Indochina] area that is familiar with what's happening there thinks its absolutely essential that Uncle Sam keep her word." That December[146] he pledged, "I will honor and respect our sworn commitment to protect the security of southeast Asia."

The Tet offensive the following February challenged the optimism about progress in Vietnam and forced a reexamination and reappraisal of the premises upon which the American position was based. In March Senator Eugene McCarthy's impressive performance in the New Hampshire primary indicated that there was a current of popular disapproval of the war exceeding all previous estimates. In a passionate address on February 27, President Johnson charged his listeners to understand:

> There must be no betrayal of those who stand beside us.
> There must be no breaking of our trusted commitments. When we give our word we must mean what it says. America's word is America's bond.

He remarked to a businessman's group in mid-March,[147] "We must meet our commitments in the world and in Vietnam." "We have commitments," he reaffirmed on the thirty-first, "that we are going to keep."

In Western society, the keeping of promises is an attribute of what is described as honor. The philosopher, seeking to explain why this is so, might frame his answer by referring to the concepts of "rationality" and "free will." What distinguishes man from the lower species, he might say, is his ability to reason and choose. The promise, the expression to do or forego from doing something at a future time, is the embodiment at once of both reason and choice; that is, it involves both the weighing of circumstances and the rendering of decision, activities which the notions of "reason" and "choice" comprehend. The promise is, therefore, a particularly human act, separating man from more primitive beings. It is because this is so—because to make a promise defines one as a man—that whether it is kept or not is taken seriously and considered an indication of a person's higher worth; it is regarded as an appropriate basis for assessing character and judging virtue; in other words, it is essential to the question of honor.

To the politician, the connection between honor and promise-keeping is far less metaphysical, more a function of social morality and law: it is honorable to keep promises because the failure to keep them will detrimentally affect those who have relied on their worth. On March 26, 1964, Secretary McNamara pointed out that the people of South Vietnam had "taken the risks and made the sacrifices linked to the commitment to membership in the family of the free world." "They have done this," he continued,

> in the belief that we would back up our pledges to help defend them. It is not right or even expedient—nor is it in our nature —to abandon them when the going is difficult.

The next year[148] the president put it graphically and with even more force:

> we are in Vietnam to fulfill one of the most solemn pledges of the American nation. . . . Strengthened by that promise, the people of South Vietnam have fought for many long years. Thousands of them have died. Thousands more have been crippled and scarred by war. And we cannot now dishonor our word, or abandon our commitment, or leave those who believed us to the terror and repression that would follow.

Abandonment was especially ignominious when the promisor was so large and powerful and the promisee so small and utterly dependent.

In 1965, in the aftermath of the first announced American escalation of the war, the government issued a new warning: a failure by the United States to meet is obligations would not only signify bad faith but would imperil world stability. Global security, as well as national conscience, required that America's commitments be fulfilled.

The initial intimations of disaster came at a news conference in early April.[149] "We have a commitment to the people of South Vietnam," Mr. Johnson observed. "If we ignore that treaty, we might as well tear up all the treaties that we are party to." He elaborated somewhat on May 4: "The [enemy's] aim in Vietnam is not simply the conquest of the South, tragic as that would be. It is to show that the American commitment is worthless." That December[150] he was more specific; America had to make good on its word in Vietnam because "if it is not good in Vietnam, who can trust it in the heart of Europe."

Consistency in the pursuit of obligations had, according to Washington, a value in and of itself; it was important whatever the particular merits of a particular commitment. Only if a nation was prepared to fulfill all its undertakings could it assume that any of them would be believed. America had to stand firm in Vietnam if it would have others respect its assurances to stand anywhere else in the world. There was, however, more to it than that.

The full argument, in all its apocalyptic detail, became absolutely clear in 1966. On February 12 Mr. Rusk set down the major premise: "The integrity of the pledged word of the United States is the principal pillar of peace around the world." The minor premise was advanced by the president in May.[151] "If America's commitment is dishonored in South Vietnam, it is dishonored in forty other alliances or more that we have made." The immediate implications of such assumptions were outlined that August[152] by Deputy Undersecretary of State U. Alexis Johnson: if the United States left Southeast Asia without a proper settlement, her allies "will feel we have abandoned commitments we have made" to Indochina and her adversaries could miscalculate or discount the value of the rest. George Ball had reviewed the final consequences on January 30: American repudiation of its bond with the Republic of Vietnam would cause the "tearing and weakening [of] the entire structure on which the world's security depends." The U.S. pledge to South Vietnam had both general and generalizable significance. It had become a symbol for all American guarantees, guarantees to which global equilibrium was closely bound. Were, therefore, Washington to turn its back on Saigon, America's friends would lose heart, her enemies would be encouraged, and calamity would surely and inevitably follow.

It had all been summarized in a message to Congress at the start of the year:[153]

> We will stay [in Vietnam] because in Asia, and around the world are countries whose independence rests in large measure on confidence in America's word and in America's protection.
>
> To yield to force in Vietnam would weaken that confidence, would undermine the independence of many lands, and would whet the appetite of aggression. We would have to fight in one land and then we'd have to fight in another—or abandon much of Asia to the domination of Communists.

1966 marked the peak of these prophesies; from 1967 on they continued to be recited, but with progressively decreasing frequency—a trend which may have acknowledged the inadvisability of overstating such gloom and despair. Throughout the period, however, Mr. Rusk proved the constant Jeremiah, warning incessantly of the tragedy which would befall mankind if the national promise were not upheld. In a talk given to businessmen on May 1, 1967, he maintained that

> the integrity of . . . [our mutual security] alliances is at the heart of the maintenance of peace, and if it should be discovered that the pledge of the United States is meaningless, the structure of peace would crumble and we would be well on our way to a terrible catastrophe.

At a press briefing that October[154] he argued:

> those who would place in question the credibility of the pledged word of the United States under our mutual security treaties would subject this nation to mortal danger. If any who would be our adversary should suppose that our treaties are a bluff, or will be abandoned if the going gets tough, the result could be catastrophe for all mankind.

In March 1968,[155] in testimony before the Senate Foreign Relations Committee, he repeated his ominous forecast.

> I have tried to emphasize the overwhelming importance of the fidelity of the United States and the necessity for people to understand that at the end of the day we will meet our commitments . . . if there is ever any doubt on that subject, there is a catastrophic war ahead.

Fourteen months after that a new president appeared on television to defend the war. Though his wording was perceptibly different, the underlying message was recognizably the same. "A great nation," Richard Nixon stated on May 14, "cannot renege on its pledge. A great nation must be worthy of trust." He went on

> When it comes to maintaining peace, "prestige" is not an empty word. I am not speaking of false pride or bravado. They should have no place in our policy. I speak, rather, of the respect that one nation has for another's integrity in defending its principles and meeting its obligations.

> If we simply abandon our effort in Vietnam, the cause of peace might not survive the damage that would be done to other nations' confidence in our reliability.

The second strand of the commitment line, like the first exhorting honor, ultimately derived from the jurisprudential axiom *"pacta sunt servanda,"* that contracts should be kept; the upholding of agreements, promises, and treaties inspired trust and promoted expectations of "good faith" upon which social dealings depended and in the absence of which all human interaction would be reduced to chaos. In its catastrophic implications, the commitment theory was much like the test case rationale, the Munich analogy, and the domino principle—another specimen for the parade of horribles. In the manner of its presentation, however, it was quite special.

The other rhetoric was primarily descriptive: a North Vietnamese success would have an impact upon the fate of underdeveloped countries, the ambitions of the aggressor, the stability of Southeast Asia; it would encourage other revolutionary movements, increase the danger of a larger war, render Laos, Cambodia, Burma, Thailand, Malaya, and Indonesia more vulnerable to communism. What would happen was cited endlessly, but why or how it would come about—the mechanism and the dynamic of the process—was left largely to inference, deduction, and imagination.

The commitment theory, in contrast, was fully articulated, with all the assumptions and logical steps clearly defined. America's performance in Asia had become a trial of American credibility. If the United States were to desert, or compromise, or be defeated, its reputation as a great power would be gravely impaired. Detection of this weakness, this irresolution and infidelity would induce the enemy to surge with increased confidence in other areas, and despairing allies to accommodate or capitulate in his wake.

In its structure, this argument was an integration of elements highlighted in each of the other major themes. The idea that Vietnam was a focus of world attention, a showcase with experimental significance, was central to the test case rationale.

The notion that a loss by the free world would have the psychological effect of emboldening the aggressor, making his designs even more grandiose, was at the heart of the Munich analogy. The general point that the outcome in Indochina could have dramatic and far-reaching reverberations and climactic repercussions was the essence of the domino principle. The commitment theory, in a sense, was the explanatory model for all the other formulas; within its framework these other defenses could be better and more completely understood.

NOTES TO CHAPTER 4

1. Dulles, May 25, 1954.
2. Johnson, May 11, 1961.
3. Ball, July 22, 1962.
4. Nolting, February 12, 1963.
5. Johnson, July 24, 1964.
6. Johnson, August 5, 1964.
7. Smith, July 21, 1954.
8. Kennedy, November 29, 1961.
9. Taylor, September 9, 1964.
10. Johnson, April 17, 1965.
11. Johnson, August 3, 1965.
12. McNamara, June 16, 1965.
13. Johnson, September 15, 1965.
14. Humphrey, February 10, 1966.
15. Goldberg, September 22, 1966.
16. Johnson, October 21, 1966.
17. Eight times in January, five in February, seven in June, and five in October spokesmen referred to America's objective of guaranteeing a choice for the South Vietnamese; in no other month were there more than three such references.
18. Johnson, April 21, 1966.
19. Johnson, May 30, 1966.
20. Humphrey, August 20, 1966.
21. Johnson, October 17, 1966.
22. Johnson, October 26, 1966.
23. Johnson, October 18, 1966.
24. Johnson, October 22, 1966.
25. Johnson, June 27, 1967.
26. McNamara, August 25, 1967.
27. Johnson, September 29, 1967.
28. Harriman, September 25, 1968.
29. Rusk, October 2, 1968.

30. Rostow, November 14, 1968.
31. Rogers, May 14, 1969.
32. Johnson, April 20, 1964.
33. Nolting, January 12, 1962.
34. Kennedy, October 26, 1961.
35. Johnson, Jaunary 7, 1964.
36. Johnson, Janurary 18, 1965.
37. Johnson, June 1, 1965.
38. Johnson, May 4, 1965.
39. Johnson, March 25, 1965.
40. Johnson, April 7, 1965.
41. Johnson, July 28, 1965.
42. Rusk, January 23, 1966.
43. White House, February 21, 1966.
44. Johnson, February 26, 1966.
45. Humphrey, March 11, 1966.
46. McNamara, April 20, 1966.
47. Humphrey, August 1, 1968.
48. Rogers, March 27, 1969.
49. Stevenson, December 14, 1965 (released).
50. Truman, March 6, 1952.
51. Dulles, July 12, 1954.
52. Kennedy, October 26, 1961.
53. Rusk, November 17, 1961.
54. State Department, February 17, 1964.
55. Lodge, March 30, 1964.
56. Johnson, April 7, 1965.
57. Johnson, July 25, 1965.
58. Between February 8 and 26 the new theme was heralded on thirteen occasions, on an average, that is, of two days out of every three.
59. Johnson, February 8, 1966.
60. Johnson, March 6, 1966.
61. Humphrey, April 25, 1966.
62. Johnson, May 17, 1966.
63. Johnson, October 19, 1966.
64. When John Foster Dulles first talked about the effects of the extension of Communist control into Southeast Asia on January 23, 1953, he spoke of the impact that it would have upon India. He said at the time that if the Russians

    could get this peninsula of Indo-China, Siam [Thailand], Burma, Malaya, they would have what is called the rice bowl of Asia. That's the area from which the great peoples of Asia, great countries of Asia, such as Japan and India get, in large measure, their food.
    And you see if the Soviet Union had control of the rice bowl of Asia that would be another weapon which would tend to expand their control into Japan and India.

    Despite this early expression of concern, the president's later omission of India from his catalogue of catastrophe was not an incomprehensible shift. By the end of March, 1954, Prime Minister Nehru had openly declared his sympathy for the revolutionary Vietminh and had denounced the Free French armies as nothing but a colonial expeditionary force. His ministrations to the British not to get entangled on the side of these reactionaries, made the huge subcontinent seem expendable, if not already lost.

65. Dulles, March 29, 1954.
66. Dulles, May 7, 1954.
67. Dulles, May 11, 1954.
68. Herter, July 9, 1959.
69. Harriman, February 13, 1962.
70. Johnson, August 25, 1965.
71. Lodge, April 25, 1967.
72. Johnson, July 12, 1966.
73. Johnson, October 18, 1966.
74. Johnson, November 7, 1966.
75. Ball, July 22, 1962 (reprinted).
76. Rusk, October 12, 1967.
77. Johnson, August 14, 1966.
78. Dulles, April 11, 1954.
79. Rusk, March 4, 1965.
80. Humphrey, July 12, 1965.
81. Johnson, October 21 (twice), October 23, October 25, November 1, and November 2, 1966.
82. Dulles, April 12, 1953.
83. Johnson, January 10, 1967.
84. Clifford, October 25, 1968.
85. Nixon, May 14, 1969.
86. Johnson, September 29, 1967.
87. Johnson, December 9, 1965.
88. McNamara, February 17, 1962.
89. Rusk, February 18, 1966.
90. McNamara, March 26, 1964.
91. McNamara, March 26, 1964.
92. Johnson, July 12, 1966.
93. Rusk, May 24, 1966.
94. Johnson, February 16, 1966.
    Rusk, February 18, 1966.
    Humphrey, February 19, 1966.
    McNamara, February 23, 1966.
    Goldberg, March 4, 1966.
95. McNamara, March 26, 1964.
96. McNamara, August 4, 1965.
97. Bundy, September 29, 1964.
98. Goldberg, December 10, 1965.
99. Johnson, February 16, 1966.
100. Johnson, August 30, 1966.
101. Johnson, August 3, 1965.
102. Rusk, March 6, 1966.
103. Johnson, June 16, 1966.

104. Rusk, August 22, 1966.
105. Eisenhower, August 4, 1953.
106. Truman, March 6, 1952.
107. Dulles, May 11, 1954.
108. Dulles, September 15, 1954.
109. Dulles, July 17, 1953.
110. Dulles, March 29, 1954.
111. Dulles, May 5, 1953.
112. Taylor, July 2, 1964.
113. Rusk, February 25, 1965.
114. Johnson, February 6, 1966.
115. Johnson, June 18, 1966.
116. Johnson, July 5, 1966.
117. Johnson, October 21, 1966.
118. Humphrey, March 22, 1968.
119. Johnson, March 31, 1968.
120. Rusk, October 12, 1967.
121. Johnson, August 19, 1968.
122. Humphrey, September 26, 1968.
123. Johnson, March 1, 1968.
124. Johnson, November 1, 1966.
125. Rusk, February 16, 1966.
126. Eisenhower, January 7, 1954.
127. Johnson, April 20, 1964.
128. Johnson, February 23, 1966.
129. Johnson, April 10, 1967.
130. Dulles, February 22, 1955.
131. Rusk, December 23, 1964.
132. Johnson, April 7, 1965.
133. Johnson, January 12, 1966.
134. Rusk, March 11, 1968.
135. Clifford, April 22, 1968.
136. Kennedy, May 8, 1963.
137. Johnson, May 18, 1964.
138. Johnson, June 23, 1964.
139. Johnson, January 4, 1965.
140. Johnson, February 4, 1965.
141. Johnson, May 13, 1965.
142. Johnson, July 9, 1965.
143. Rusk, December 9, 1965.
144. Johnson, June 30, 1966.
145. Rusk, March 28, 1967.
146. Johnson, December 12, 1967.
147. Johnson, March 16, 1968.
148. Johnson, July 28, 1965.
149. Johnson, April 1, 1965.
150. Johnson, December 20, 1965.
151. Johnson, May 17, 1966.

152. Johnson, August 23, 1966.
153. Johnson, January 12, 1966.
154. Rusk, October 12, 1967.
155. Rusk, March 12, 1968.

CHAPTER FIVE

HOW DID AMERICA BECOME INVOLVED?

DOCUMENTS

Between the mid-summer and early fall of 1954, Washington, in three different forms, expressed its concern about the future of Southeast Asia. These expressions were conveyed in a letter sent in October, a treaty initialed three weeks earlier, in September, and a declaration issued a month and a half before that, in July. In the years which followed, to varying extents and in changing contexts, each was cited to explain the sources and justify the continuation of American involvement in the area; each was cited to support the repeated contention that the national honor was at stake in Vietnam.

The Eisenhower Letter

During the autumn of 1954, representatives of the United States and France met to discuss the future relationship between each of their governments and free Indochina. On September 29 they reported agreement that thenceforward "economic aid, budgetary support, and other assistance to each of the associated states will be direct to that state." The decision, along with a more detailed discussion of the possibilities of U.S. help, was transmitted by Mr. Eisenhower in a letter to the president of the Republic of Vietnam, Ngo Dinh Diem, dated October 1, 1954. It read:

Dear Mr. President:

I have been following with great interest the course of developments in Vietnam, particularly since the conclusion of the conference at Geneva. The implications of the agreement concerning Vietnam have caused grave concern regarding the future of a country temporarily divided by an artificial military grouping, weakened by a long and exhausting war and faced with enemies without and collaborators within.

Your recent request for aid to assist in the formidable project of the movement of several hundred thousand loyal Vietnamese citizens away from areas which are passing under a de facto rule and political ideology they abhor are being fulfilled. I am glad that the United States is able to assist in this humanitarian effort.

We have been exploring ways and means to permit our aid to Vietnam to be more effective and to make a greater contribution to the welfare and stability of the Government of Vietnam. I am, accordingly, instructing the American Ambassador to Vietnam to examine with you in your capacity as Chief of Government, how an intelligent program of American aid given directly to your Government can serve to assist Vietnam in its present hour of trial, provided that your Government is prepared to give assurances as to the standards of performance it would be able to maintain in the event such aid were supplied.

The purpose of this offer is to assist the Government of Vietnam in developing and maintaining a strong, viable state, capable of resisting attempted subversion or aggression through military means. The Government of the United States expects that this aid will be met by performance on the part of the Government of Vietnam in undertaking needed reforms. It hopes that such aid, combined with your own continuing efforts, will contribute effectively toward an independent Vietnam endowed with a strong government. Such a government would, I hope, be responsive to the nationalist aspirations of its people, so enlightened in purpose and effective in performance, that it will be respected both at home and abroad and discourage any who might wish to impose a foreign ideology on your free people.

The Eisenhower letter, released on October 25, went virtually unnoticed that year. A decade afterwards, however, it was discovered by the Johnson Administration. On March 26, 1964, in a review of America's long relation with Indochina, Secretary McNamara noted that President Eisenhower had early decided "to give direct American aid to the new Government [of Vietnam] to enable its survival" and quoted the passage from his offer to Mr. Diem in which Washington's "purpose" was defined: "to assist the Government of Vietnam in developing and maintaining a strong and viable state, capable of resisting attempted subversion or aggression through military means." Describing his own policy on April 21, Mr. Johnson compared it to that practiced in 1954,

> when then-President Eisenhower wrote the then President of South Vietnam and said, "We want to help you help yourselves. If you want to save your country and have freedom in your country, we want to help you do it."

Two month later the letter was produced as the "commitment" the United States had gone to South Vietnam to uphold. America's course in Southeast Asia, the president contended at a briefing on June 2, had been "begun by General Eisenhower, in a letter of October 25." After reading the document in its entirety to the assembled press, he went on to say:

> Now that was a good letter then, and it is a good letter now, and we feel the same way. . . . In the case of Vietnam, our commitment today is just the same as the commitment made by President Eisenhower to President Diem in 1954—a commitment to help these people defend themselves.

The following February[1] he observed that the "statement ten years ago by our President to the general effect that we would help the people of Vietnam help themselves" constituted "our basic commitment to Vietnam." That April[2] he referred to an Eisenhower "commitment" again, though attributing to it far less weight.

The Eisenhower letter was significant in two respects. First, it was evidence that the United States had made a pledge to Vietnam and therefore supported the claim that America's honor was at issue in southern Asia. Second, it was a document which proved that the government's Vietnamese policy was both longstanding and bipartisan in origin. For both reasons, it was mentioned by President Johnson during July as background for the decision, announced on the twenty-eighth, that the United States would undertake a greatly expanded combat role in the war; it was the original promise out of which American military intervention had necessarily and consequentially grown. "President Eisenhower made our first commitment there in '54," Mr. Johnson reminded newsmen on July 13. "We cannot just get out," he insisted to an interviewer two weeks later. "Eisenhower said we will come to their aid."

On August 17, as United States soldiers landed in Vietnam, Mr. Eisenhower was asked what his intentions had been in writing to Mr. Diem eleven years before. His answer effectively repudiated all that had been previously suggested by Washington:

> We said we would help that country. We were not talking about military programs, but foreign aid. . . . There was no commitment given in a military context. . . . At the time, we did not see the need for a major military effort in Vietnam.

On August 18, Press Secretary Bill Moyers stressed that the general's interpretation was in no sense at variance with that entertained at the White House. In the course of an unusually lengthy statement, he reported, "The President does not feel there is any difference with General Eisenhower and he thinks the purposes of the Johnson Administration are the same as those of the Eisenhower Administration." He added that Mr. Johnson assumed full responsibility for the current programs and actions and, disregarding earlier, clearly contrary declarations, described the 1954 letter as material only as a matter of "historical reference."

The following day, without withdrawing his prior comment, Mr. Eisenhower emphatically rejected the implication that he at all disagreed with the government's position in Southeast Asia: "I have said again and again that I support the President. . . . I have done everything I can to show I'm behind him." People should, he urged, realize "how different the circumstances [there] are today from a decade ago."

On August 23 the Johnson Administration issued a pamphlet

explaining the American commitment to Vietnam. The inclusion in it of the full text of the October 1954 offer made it clear why such great efforts had been taken the preceding week to avoid the impression of any misunderstanding on its relevance and meaning. Nevertheless, despite the denials of disagreement, despite the expressions of accord, the general's clarification had an apparent effect: after August, the Eisenhower letter was not cited again.

The SEATO Treaty

On October 1, 1954, President Eisenhower had written Ngo Dinh Diem proposing that the United States undertake a program of direct financial assistance to the Republic of Vietnam. The object of the program was to create, in the aftermath of a long war, a stable, secure, and responsive native government.

Six months earlier, when that war was marked by an increasing and increasingly effective enemy offensive, and there was real question whether that beleaguered republic would survive at all, a very different proposal had been made, a proposal in its essence military rather than economic, in its form, multinational rather than unilateral. It had been introduced, dramatically, in an address delivered on March 29, by John Foster Dulles. He advised news executives that evening that the possibility that a Communist victory in Indochina would presage the imposition of communism throughout the area was a "possibility that should not be passively accepted, but should be met with united action." Though there might, he acknowledged, be "serious risks" involved, they would be "far less than would face us a few years from now if we dare not be resolute today."

During the days which followed, Washington proved as vague about the nature of the recommended action as it was insistent upon the necessity that it be carried out against a background of unity. On March 31 the president replied with an abrupt, "Well, of course, the speech must stand for itself," to a reporter's request for a clarification of the pregnant language of the night before. "I would deprecate action of the United States alone.... The only thing I am talking about now is united action," Mr. Dulles emphasized on April 5, dismissing any speculation that he was equally disposed to an entirely American expedition. The vagueness about the plans reflected not only an unwillingness to disclose secret strategy to the enemy, but an uncertainty about their detail prior to consultation with the Allies. The insistence on allied consultation mirrored the refusal of the legislative leadership to endorse any operation which might, as Korea had, lay the major burden of an Asian war on the United States, and the reluctance of the executive branch to proceed without legislative sanction.

Throughout April 1954 therefore, the government sought to convince the British and French of the need to forge an immediate coalition to save Indochina. By the end of the month, however, it had received no more from London and Paris than the limited pledges that each would "examine the possibility" of establishing "a collective defense."[3,4]

In May and June, as peace negotiations began in Geneva and became deadlocked, and the fighting wore on endlessly in Vietnam, Washington reassured the public at home that it remained opposed to a wholly American rescue mission. On May 4 Defense Secretary Wilson described U.S. military participation as impossible in other than a multilateral framework. Three weeks later,[5] Secretary Dulles outlined the prerequisites for dispatching an American force: "We don't go in alone," he stressed. "We go in where the other nations which have an important stake in the region recognize the peril as we do." He reiterated in June:[6]

> The task of pacification, in our opinion, cannot be successfully met merely by unilateral armed intervention. Some other conditions need to be established. Throughout these Indo-China developments, the United States has held to a stable and consistent course and has made clear the conditions which, in its opinion, might justify intervention.
>
> These conditions were and are . . . (4) a joining in the collective effort of some of the other nations in the area; and (5) assurance that France will not itself withdraw from the battle until it is won.

Over the same period, officials shifted their attention from securing a temporary, emergency combination, to the eventual establishment of a permanent, regional alliance. In a May 7 radio-television address, the secretary of state declared:

> we are ready to take part with the other countries principally concerned in an examination of the possibility of establishing a collective defense within the framework of the Charter of the United Nations to seek the peace, security, and freedom of Southeast Asia and the Western Pacific.

On the tenth Walter Smith cited America's demonstrated "devotion to the principle of collective security and its willingness to help in the development of collective security arrangements in Southeast Asia." Toward the end of the month,[7] Mr. Eisenhower reaffirmed the government's longstanding advocacy of "collective arrangements for assuring the security of Southeast Asia."

On July 20 an agreement was reached at Geneva on a cease-fire in Indochina, and that afternoon Charles Wilson made it clear that in the event the hostilities were resumed America was still resolved not to act unless in concert with others. The next day the president noted that his administration was "actively pursuing discussions with other free nations with a view to the rapid organization of a collective defense in Southeast Asia." By July 23 Secretary Dulles was already speaking optimistically of their chances for success:

> The United States for over a year advocated united action in [Indochina] . . . but this proved not to be practical under the conditions which existed.
> We believe, however, that now it will be practical to bring about collective arrangements to promote the security of the free peoples of Southeast Asia.

On September 3, representatives from Australia, France, New Zealand, Pakistan, the Philippines, Thailand, the United Kingdom, and the United States convened in Manila for what Mr. Dulles described as "one of the most important conferences of our time."[8] Guided by a State Department draft, they produced within five days a Southeast Asia collective defense pact. It provided that

> The parties to this treaty . . .
> Intending to declare publicly and formally their sense of

unity, so that any potential aggressor will appreciate that the parties stand together in the area, and

Desiring further to coordinate their efforts for collective defense for the preservation of peace and security,

Therefore agree as follows: . . .

ARTICLE 4

1. Each party recognizes that aggression by means of armed attack in the treaty area against any of the parties or against any state or territory which the parties by unanimous agreement may hereafter designate would endanger its own peace and safety, and agree that it will in that event act to meet the common danger in accordance with its constitutional processes. Measures taken under this paragraph shall be immediately reported to the Security Council of the United Nations.

2. If, in the opinion of any of the parties, the inviolability or the integrity of the territory or the sovereignty or the political independence of any party in the treaty area or of any other state or territory to which the provisions of Paragraph I of this Article from time to time apply is threatened in any way other than by armed attack or is affected or threatened by any fact or situation which might endanger the peace of the area, the parties shall consult immediately in order to agree on the measures which would be taken for the common defense. . . .

The Protocol

The Parties to the Southeast Asia Collective Defense Treaty unanimously designate for the purposes of Article 4 of the treaty the states of Cambodia and Laos and the free territory under the jurisdiction of the state of Vietnam.

This treaty, as its terms were read throughout the 1950s, expressed three principles central to what then was American foreign policy. First the United States would not intervene unilaterally in a war in Asia. The Manila Pact represented the realization of the *ad hoc* coalition which had been vainly sought the spring before. It was a mechanism which had plainly evolved out of the repeatedly stated condition that unity and collaboration must precede the assumption by America of any significant responsibility overseas.

Second, the United States would involve the Congress as a full partner in decisions comprehending the application of military force. Under Article 4, Section 1 of the agreement, in case of an "armed attack" each party was obligated to defer to its "constitutional processes" before taking action. The same phrase had at least twice in 1954 appeared in presidential statements, defined each time as legislative authorization. "There is going to be no involvement of America in war [in Indochina]," Mr. Eisenhower pledged on March 10, "unless it is a result of the constitutional process that is placed upon Congress to declare it." In April[9] he reiterated that "we would not get into a war except through the constitutional process which of course involved a declaration of war by Congress." The understanding of congressional consent was, however, supported by more than such inferential analysis. In the course of the Senate debates on ratification in January 1955, the State Department interpreted Article 4 as requiring, in the face of a "common danger," that the question of whether and how to respond

> will be brought before the Congress by the President and the administration, and will be considered under our constitutional processes. We are not committed to the principle . . . that an attack on one is an attack on all, calling for immediate military action without further consideration by Congress.

Third, the United States would depend upon maximum flexibility and the element of surprise in protecting itself and its allies against potential aggressors. The "new look" in Republican defense strategy, unveiled in March 1954,[10] argued against America's building huge, stationary armies in Asia and in favor of the development of more versatile air and sea power. On September 15, in reviewing his mission to the Philippines, Secretary Dulles reported that this argument had been presented and adopted by the delegates there.

> We considered at Manila how to implement the treaty. One possibility was to create a joint military force. However, I explained that the United States' responsibilities were so vast and far-flung that we believed that we would serve best, not by earmarking forces for particular areas of the Far East, but by developing the deterrent of mobile striking power, plus strategically placed reserves.
> This viewpoint was accepted.

Two years later, in June 1956,[11] he recalled that acceptance:

> we agreed [at Manila and] . . . it was understood that we would not attempt to establish a force-in-being in SEATO. . . . We have

to depend primarily on an appropriate cooperation of local forces-in-being with the mobile striking power of the United States which is available in the Western Pacific.

The Southeast Asia Treaty was conceived as another part of America's global response to the Communist menace. It emerged in late 1954 to limit the loss which in early 1954 it had been proposed to prevent. It was neither as far-reaching nor as automatic as its Western European counterpart, NATO; that is, unlike the North Atlantic Treaty, it did not prescribe the maintenance of large scale ground troops in place, and it predicated military action on congressional assent. It purported to represent a community of nations with a shared interest in the security of the region, each member of that community being prepared to move with others in the event of armed aggression.

In the almost four years from the spring of 1961 until the late winter of 1965, officials alluded to SEATO in two contexts— they cited its formation as a historic point in the evolution of U.S. interest in and involvement with Southeast Asia, and they referred to the communiqués of its yearly meetings to underscore and justify American anxiety about the situation in Vietnam. On May 4, 1961, Secretary of State Rusk noted that "the members of the Southeast Asia Treaty Organization expressed their concern about the situation in Vietnam in our recent conference in Bangkok." President Kennedy reminded the press on February 14, 1962, of

the SEATO pact . . . signed in 1954—September 8—though Vietnam was not a signatory. It was a protocol state and, therefore, this pact, which was approved by the Senate with only, I think, two against it under Article IV, stated that the United States recognized that aggression by means of armed attack against Vietnam would threaten our peace and security.

In an address on April 20, 1964, before the Associated Press, President Johnson mentioned "the statement of the SEATO allies that Communist defeat is 'essential.' " Dean Rusk quoted more extensively from that same statement in a speech to the American Law Institute that May:[12]

At the meeting of the Council of the Southeast Asia Treaty Organization in Manila last month, seven of the eight members joined in declaring the defeat of the aggression against South Vietnam to be "essential not only to the security of the Republic of Vietnam, but to that of Southeast Asia."

On August 5 Mr. Johnson contended, "In 1954 we made our position clear toward Vietnam." He continued

> In September of that year the United States signed the Manila Pact on which our participation in SEATO is based. That pact recognized that aggression by means of armed attack on South Vietnam would endanger the peace and safety of the nations signing that solemn agreement.

Mr. Rusk spoke similarly at a news conference the following February:[13]

> The attitude of the United States towards threats to the peace in Southeast Asia has been made clear many times and in the most serious and formal ways:
> (A) By the ratification of the Manila Pact in February, 1955, which includes South Vietnam as a protocol state. This treaty was approved by a vote of 82 to 1.

Then, in March 1965, the treaty was presented in a third connection. On the twentieth, Mr. Johnson characterized it as that "which obligates us to the commitment we've made." Previously SEATO had been deemed relevant because its founding marked an early and solemn expression of American interest in that region and because its members shared American alarm about the mounting Communist pressures in the South. That day, the government saw relevance as well in its language, which it now said bound America to defend Vietnam.

The point is not that before this date no one recognized a SEATO commitment or its bearing on the war. In a major statement on Southeast Asia policy on June 2, 1964, the president took note of the fact that "like a number of other nations we are bound by solemn commitments to help defend this area against Communist encroachment." In another speech, on August 5, he was even more specific:

> Our commitments in that area . . . [are] defined in the Southeast Asia Collective Defense Treaty [which] . . . obligates the United States and other members to act in accordance with their Constitutional processes to meet Communist aggression.

But before March the administration never appeared to be saying that it was that commitment which compelled the United States to pursue its course in Vietnam; it declared that a treaty commitment to the area existed, but it did not represent it as an operative obligation. Thereafter, the contention that SEATO did dictate American action was clearly and consistently made.

On April 1 President Johnson advanced this interpretation for a second time, structuring his remarks in a way that indicated how new it still was:

> We have a commitment to the people of Vietnam. That commitment is not only the result of the commitment of President Eisenhower made in his letter, but that the Congress of the United States and the Senate made in its vote of 82 to 1 approving the SEATO treaty.

By May the novelty had worn off and he stated unequivocally in a message to Congress on the fourth:

> we are directly committed to the defense of South Vietnam. In 1954 we signed the Southeast Asia Collective Defense Treaty. That treaty committed us to act to meet aggression in South Vietnam.

During a press conference on July 15, he noted again that "the Senate has ratified the SEATO treaty by a vote of 82 to 1 pledging the United States to come to the aid of any nation upon their request who are parties of the treaty or protocol."

In 1966 officials talked much more frequently of SEATO in these revised terms. On February 4 the State Department said that the United States had become involved in Southeast Asia as a result of its treaty obligations. Mr. Rusk testified to the Senate Foreign Relations Committee later that month that[14]

> in joining SEATO the United States took a solemn treaty engagement of far-reaching effect. Article IV, paragraph 1, provides that "each party recognizes that aggression by means of armed attack would endanger its own peace and safety, and agrees that it will in that event act to meet the common danger in accordance with its constitutional processes."

He concluded by asserting that "this fundamental SEATO obligation" had "from the outset guided our actions in South Vietnam."[15] "This nation has had to intervene," Hubert Humphrey contended in April,[16] "not of our own volition," but "by treaty, by obligations and by commitment." That November[17] the president underlined that Southeast Asia was an "area where we have treaty commitments that we consider the solemn promise of all the people of the United States of America."

There was little relative change in the intensity of these assertions in the first three quarters of 1967, but they proliferated during the last part of the year as government policies were subjected to increasing criticism.[18] At a briefing on November 17, Mr. Johnson recalled to newsmen that "in 1954 under the leadership of President Eisenhower and Secretary Dulles we had a SEATO treaty." He went on:

> it was gone into very thoroughly by the Senate, and the men who presented the treaty then said this is dangerous. The time may come when we have to put up or shut up. . . . And the time came when we had to decide whether we meant what we said when we said our security was tied into their security and that we would stand in unison in the face of common danger.
>
> Now we're doing this.

He pledged on December 12:

> We will not now nullify the word of the Congress or the people as expressed in the SEATO Treaty that we would come and take our stand in the face of common danger and that treaty was ratified by a vote in the Senate of 82 to 1.

In an interview on the nineteenth he spoke about the help being given the Republic of Vietnam, help "we agreed to" many years before "in the SEATO Treaty."

In 1968 there was an abrupt decline in these references, particularly after April when, with the opening of negotiations to end the war, justifications for American entry became more and more superfluous. The theme was never abandoned, however. On September 10, in one of the last defenses of his position, President Johnson still talked of the line "drawn against aggression in Vietnam, in keeping with the treaty that we signed—the SEATO obligations."

In February 1965 in a major exercise of executive authority,

Lyndon Johnson ordered the continuous aerial bombardment of North Vietnam. That March, Washington introduced the idea that the SEATO pact was an obligation which had committed the United States to this protection of the South. The timing permitted the inference that international law arguments were just convenient rationalizations for exceedingly controversial, wholly discretionary presidential acts.

When years later the government explained that climactic period, it sought to dispel such cynicism. According to the official version, "aggression" in a formal and legal sense had begun in Southeast Asia by February 1965. That occurrence triggered the responsibility, defined in Article IV, Section 1 of the SEATO treaty, which obligated members to confront a "threat to the peace." In order to discharge that responsibility, the United States was forced to enlarge its role in the war. The treaty, therefore, had not only substantiated the American escalation, but had demanded it.

In a letter to Senator Henry Jackson, released in early 1967,[19] Mr. Johnson recounted this process in detail. Since 1954, he wrote, the North Vietnamese had been carrying out a program of illegal infiltration into the South.

> [Then] in 1964 they radically expanded this course of action. The trails became roads. Bands of infiltrators became regular military units.
>
> Neither of the co-chairmen of the Geneva conference. . . proved able to stop this violation; nor did the three members of the International Control Commission. . . .
>
> With this failure of the international machinery designed to enforce the Geneva agreements we were thrown back therefore on our treaty responsibilities. Under the SEATO treaty, presented to the Senate by President Eisenhower and ratified overwhelmingly, we had agreed that in the face of "armed attack in the treaty area" we would "act to meet the common danger."
>
> By February, 1965, it was unmistakably clear there was armed attack in the most literal sense: South Vietnam was almost lost to that armed attack. And in that month, on the recommendation of the National Security Council, I decided that we had to "meet the common danger" by bringing our air power to bear against the source of aggression.

This plausible and logically coherent review leaves two facts peculiarly unaccounted for. First, why at the time the air raids were announced were they not related in any way at all to the terms of the treaty? Second, and conversely, when Washington did finally refer to its obligations by treaty, why was it not in connection with that bombing or in a major address, but as a parenthetical news conference aside?

But even accepting the government's scenario, establishing that aggression had taken place did not prove that America had a duty under SEATO to intervene. That called for demonstrating as well that the treaty's binding force was not contingent upon the reactions of the other signatories to the attack. Though such a demonstration did undeniable violence to the corporate spirit in which the pact had been framed and involved an utter disregard of the history surrounding its creation, it accorded entirely with the language of Article IV, which deferred to the intentions of "Each Party." Washington's understanding of that provision, based on a literal reading, was declared in a statement issued on March 6, 1962, in the midst of the Laotian crisis:

> the United States intends to give full effect to its obligations under the [SEATO] treaty to act to meet the common danger in accordance with its constitutional processes. The Secretary of State reaffirmed that this obligation of the United States does not depend upon the prior agreement of all other parties to the treaty, since the treaty obligation is individual as well as collective.

Four years later, in February 1966,[20] Dean Rusk outlined in comprehensive fashion the implications of that declaration:

> The language of this treaty is worth careful attention. The obligation it imposes is not only joint but several. That is, not only collective, but individual. The finding that an armed attack has occurred does not have to be made by a collective determination before the obligation of each member becomes operative. Nor does the treaty require a collective decision on actions to be taken to meet the common danger. If the United States determines that an armed attack has occurred against any nation to whom the protection of the treaty applies, then it is obligated "to act to meet the common danger" without regard to the views or actions of any other treaty member.

A State Department brief on the legality of the war, published the next month,[21] repeated that the SEATO engagement did not depend upon a "collective decision" by the parties. On May 20, 1969, Secretary of State Rogers reaffirmed the March 1962 communiqúe and said that it remained the operative restatement of Article IV responsibilities.

While it maintained that it was legally committed to protect Vietnam, alone if necessary, the Johnson Administration was nonetheless sensitive to the charge that it was assuming an unconscionable burden in Asia, that it was being taken advantage of again, and attempted to rebut this assertion in various ways. Confronting the issue directly, Mr. Rusk reported on October 12, 1967, that "five [SEATO] signatories have engaged their forces alongside Korean and South Vietnamese troops." "Indeed," he added, "the proportion of non-United States forces in South Vietnam is greater than non-United States forces in Korea." Mr. Johnson stressed similarly on May 30, 1968, "The war is not being fought in Vietnam simply by Americans. It is being fought by the South Vietnamese, the Australians, the New Zealanders, the Koreans, the Thais and the Filipinos."

With slightly more subtlety the State Department distributed in March 1968[22] a list of thirty-seven nations who along with America were aiding Vietnam, among them:

> Argentina—5000 tons of wheat flour. Dominican Republic—An offer of cement. Italy—A surgical team and science scholarships. New Zealand—Combat forces being increased to about 360 men; economic assistance in medicine and education. Pakistan—Flood relief.

There was also a constant stream of allusions to the "allies" —their meetings, maneuvers, casualties, plans. Because of the associations of this word with battles of the past, it was meant to convey a sense that the struggle for Southeast Asia was being joined by a vast and dedicated coalition.

By the end of the decade a cruel paradox had become evident. The United States had, virtually unassisted, dispatched a huge land army to wage a war undeclared by Congress, in the name of a treaty designed to enshrine the principles of "united action," "mobile deterrence," and "constitutional due process."

The Geneva Declaration

A meeting of the foreign ministers of the United States, France, the United Kingdom, and the Soviet Union—John Foster Dulles, Georges Bidault, Anthony Eden and Vyacheslav Molotov—took place in Berlin between January 25 and February 18, 1954. They reached the following agreement:. . .that the problem of restoring peace in Indo-China shall also be discussed at the conference [of the Big Four at Geneva in the spring] to which representatives of the United States, France, the United Kingdon, the Union of Soviet Socialist Republics, the Chinese Peoples' Republic and other interested states will be invited.

Communiqúe, FEBRUARY 18, 1954

The Berlin accord on a Vietnam parley was not an occasion for official rejoicing. In March[23] Secretary Dulles made it clear to reporters that his own hopes for gaining peace were not bound up with the forthcoming discussions. Mr. Eisenhower was no more encouraging when on April 7 he was asked about the possibilities for their successful outcome: "I wouldn't class the chances as good, no, not one that the free world would consider adequate to the situation." Nor did the vice president lift any spirits on the sixteenth with his comment on the proven "futility of negotiations" with the Communists.

The reservations and apparent disinterest in diplomacy, striking when contrasted with the enthusiasm for a military solution, were no less obvious once the talks began; then pessimistic words were underscored in action. On May 5, two days before the opening of the Indochina phase of the conference, Mr. Dulles left Geneva and Undersecretary Smith assumed the leadership of the American delegation. By June 21, Mr. Smith had also departed and the U.S. Ambassador to Czechoslovakia, U. Alexis Johnson, had been designated the chief spokesman. At the end of the month,[24] as Mr. Johnson prepared for a July visit to Prague, the State Department felt compelled to deny speculation that he too was about to withdraw.

In downgrading American participation, Washington was being difficult, but hardly deceitful. From the outset it had made it plain that, as compared to Paris, its position in any discussion would be largely peripheral. Throughout the period it stressed that "a large measure of initiative"[25] rested with France which had a "special set of primary interests,"[26] that though the United States was a "friendly and interested nation"[27] it was "neither a belligerent nor a principal in the negotiations."[27] The rationale was suspect: while refusing a major conference role on the grounds that it was not directly concerned in the area, the government led the campaign for armed intervention, arguing Indochina's "transcendent importance"[28] to the free world; nonetheless, U.S. intentions were never in doubt.

The logic behind Washington's position—the real reason for opposing negotiations and supporting "united action"—was to be found in the assumptions which underlay the Cold War. According to this demonology, Communists, uncivilized and utterly unscrupulous, will trade empty promises against any and all hopes in order to further their goal of world domination. Conventional standards of international morality, principles of fairness and good faith, are meaningless to them. Given their primitive, Marxist world view, Western power, not diplomacy, is needed to meet their everpresent challenge to Western security and freedom. It is sheer force and the willingness to use it—and only that—which the enemy respects and, finally, understands. By 1954 the crusading evangelism of Joseph McCarthy had made such assumptions gospel in America, and hysteria and ideological intolerance became commonplace, even respectable. In such a climate, any compromise would have been branded a betrayal.

Having declared and publicly demonstrated that its responsibilities at Geneva were limited, there was little expectation that the Eisenhower Administration would sponsor the results those talks would produce. Any expectations there might have been were undermined by official pledges that America would "not be a party to any treaty that makes anybody a slave,"[29] that it would not "acknowledge the legitimacy of Communist control of any segment of Southeast Asia,"[30] for since the Vietminh had undisputed power in the North, some concessions were inevitable.

It was, therefore, no great surprise that the settlement,

which partitioned Vietnam at the seventeenth parallel, was not endorsed by the United States. America completely dissociated itself from the agreement, embodied in a declaration joined in by all the other attending parties, and issued instead its own noncommittal statement. Read by Walter Bedell Smith, it provided that

> The Government of the United States, being resolved to devote its efforts to the strengthening of peace in accordance with the principles and purposes of the United Nations, takes note:
>
> Of the agreements concluded at Geneva on July 20 and 21, 1954, between the (a) Franco-Laotian Command and the Command of the People's [Communist] Army of Vietnam; (b) the Royal Khmer [Cambodian] Army of Vietnam; (c) the Franco-Vietnamese Command and the Command of the People's Army of Vietnam and of Paragraphs 1 to 12 inclusive of the declaration presented to the Geneva conference on July 21, 1954;
>
> Declares with regard to the aforesaid agreements and paragraphs that (i) it will refrain from the threat or the use of force to disturb them, in accordance with Article 2 (4) of the Charter of the United Nations dealing with the obligation of members to refrain in their international relations from the threat or use of force, and (ii) it would view any renewal of aggression in violation of the aforesaid agreements with grave concern and as seriously threatening international peace and security.
>
> In connection with the statement in the declaration concerning free elections in Vietnam, my Government wishes to make clear its position which it has expressed in a declaration made in Washington on June 29, 1954, as follows: "In the case of nations now divided against their will, we shall continue to seek to achieve unity through free elections, supervised by the United Nations to insure that they are conducted fairly."
>
> With respect to the statement made by the representative of the state of Vietnam, the United States reiterates its traditional position that peoples are entitled to determine their own future and that it will not join in an arrangement which would hinder this. Nothing in its declaration just made is intended to or does indicate any departure from this traditional principle.
>
> We share the hope that the agreements will permit Cambodia, Laos and Vietnam to play their part in full independence and sovereignty, in the peaceful community of nations, and will enable the peoples of that area to determine their own future.

The disappointment and disapproval registered at Geneva was only confirmed and reinforced in Washington. On July 20

Defense Secretary Wilson described the cease-fire as hardly "something to enthuse about." The president admitted the next day that the agreement "was not satisfactory" to the United States "in certain of its features." That afternoon Mr. Dulles said that he too "regretted" many of its aspects. Though the displeasure was understated in the interest of maintaining a façade of allied solidarity, it was no less real; such faint praise, in these circumstances, was little better than damnation.

The Indochina armistice had by all accounts been a disaster, and on December 31, 1954, in a year-end review, Secretary Dulles cited it as a significant "setback" for American foreign policy. Yet thirteen months later, in a *Life Magazine* article in January 1956, he was described as regarding that settlement as a "major save for the free world." His deferred appreciation reflected the increasing probability that not all the unfortunate terms agreed upon would be carried out; specifically, that the scheduled July 1956, Vietnam-wide referendum would not be held.

Though the conference declaration had called for "Consultations" on the subject of elections to begin on "20th July 1955," that date passed without the establishing of any fruitful contacts between the two sides. The responsibility for that failure lay almost entirely with the leaders in Saigon, who simply refused to engage in any discussion with Hanoi. Their refusal, justified on the spurious ground that they had not signed the cease-fire, was sanctioned by Washington; United States officials had no apparent difficulty in adjusting to the possibility that the provisional demarcation line would lapse into permanence. On August 10, John Foster Dulles proposed a guarantee of the status quo at the truce line, should peaceful reunification prove unworkable, and on the thirteenth he expressed the doubt, earlier raised in South Vietnam, that genuinely free electoral conditions could be insured in the North.[31] By January a pattern that seemed likely to continue had been set: observance of the Geneva accords in Hanoi paralleled by flagrant defiance of them in Saigon.

In March 1956, the South Vietnamese National Assembly took the fully anticipated step of formally and unequivocally repudiating the 1954 agreements. In June[32] Assistant Secretary of State Walter Robertson lent American support to that move.

While the United States, he declared, "hopes and prays" the division of Vietnam "will speedily come to an end," it shares the opinion of Mr. Diem that provisions for reuniting the country were meaningless without the assurance that "intimidation or coercion of the electorate" could be precluded in the D.R.V. In July, forseeably, the planned national elections did not take place; though the North protested vigorously to the International Control Commission against what it regarded as a material breach by South Vietnam, it made no attempt at armed reprisal, and the armistice remained intact.

The Indochina truce became acceptable to Washington because it could not be enforced by the conference machinery, because it deprived the Vietminh of the political control which its military successes warranted, and because, contrary to all prophesies, it was the Communists, and, through 1956, only the Communists who observed its terms. It was ironic in light of that history that the government put such emphasis on alleged North Vietnamese noncompliance during the next decade; in the drama being played out in Southeast Asia, Hanoi was depicted as the international outlaw. Secretary Rusk talked in 1962[33] of the assistance being given "by North Vietnam—all in gross violation of the 1954 Geneva accords." In 1965[34] President Johnson spoke of "the refusal of the Communist forces to honor their agreement of 1954." In a speech at Howard University in 1967,[35] Arthur Goldberg pointed to Hanoi's "hostile activities against the South, which the Geneva accords explicitly prohibit." "Since the late 1950s," Ambassador Harriman insisted in 1968,[36]

> North Vietnam has violated the Geneva accords by sending armed men directly across the demilitarized zone, and in May-June 1966, massive numbers of North Vietnamese troops. . . .

Ironically also, in view of initial reactions, Washington regularly offered the 1954 pact as a model for any future solution. On July 10, 1964, the State Department contended that "a satisfactory political settlement for restoring peace to Vietnam was provided in the general agreements of 1954." Mr. Johnson maintained the following March,[37] "we seek no more than a return to the essentials of the agreements of 1954." In January

1966,[38] United Nations Representative Goldberg wrote that "the United States is prepared for discussions or negotiations" organized on "the basis of the Geneva accords of 1954." During the spring of 1967,[39] Dean Rusk recalled the government's proposal for "a reconvening of the Geneva conference of 1954 —a return to the agreement of 1954." At the Paris talks one year later,[40] Mr. Harriman stated, "We believe the Geneva accords of 1954 in their essential elements provide a basis for peace in Vietnam." On January 25, 1969, Henry Cabot Lodge, speaking for the new administration, recited that position again:

> The United States has, on more than one occasion, expressed its conviction that the essential elements of the Geneva accords of 1954 provide a basis for peace in Vietnam. We reaffirm this today.

The ultimate irony, however, lay in the subsequent treatment of Secretary Smith's unilateral declaration. Though it had been intended and delivered as a disavowal of responsibility for the conference results, it was presented as an instrument which effectively, if not legally, bound the United States to underwrite those terms. At a news briefing in early 1962,[41] Mr. Kennedy reminded reporters:

> in 1954 the Geneva Agreements were signed and, while we did not sign those agreements, nevertheless Under Secretary Mr. Smith—Bedell Smith—stated that he would view any renewal of aggression in violation of the aforesaid agreement with grave concern and as seriously threatening international peace and security.

Robert McNamara offered the same reminder in March, 1964:[42]

> Although the United States was not a party to those Geneva agreements the United States unilaterally declared that it would not violate them and that it would regard any violation by other parties as a serious threat to international peace and security.

On March 9, 1966, the State Department published a legal brief in defense of the war which cited the Smith statement as a commitment to the Republic of Vietnam, and on May 15, 1968, Averell Harriman defined that undertaking as the basis for

American aid. The government, he told delegates to the peace negotiations that spring, has "repeatedly made clear that we would have to take action in support of the people of the South if North Vietnam violated the [Geneva] accords." He went on:

> On the day that the accords were signed . . . [we] said that "any renewal of Communist aggression would be viewed by us as a matter of grave concern." Accordingly, we have responded to the request of the Government of the Republic of Vietnam for assistance as North Vietnam increased its aggression.

The Geneva Declaration was never anything other than supplementary to Washington's case for involvement in Vietnam, and is, therefore, not vitally important in itself. It becomes significant, however, when seen in conjunction with the other documents of that 1954–1955 period. Like the Eisenhower letter and the SEATO treaty, the Smith statement was made for clear and limited purposes. But, as with the other two, its very general language rendered it susceptible to extensive interpretation. These subsequent understandings ignored, if not wholly defeated, the original and essential intent in order to satisfy the more immediate and pressing demands of U.S. intervention.

INSTITUTIONS

The Presidency

At a news conference on February 14, 1962, President Kennedy was asked to respond to the accusation made by a Republican National Committee publication that he had been "less than candid with the American people as to how deeply we are involved in Vietnam." He began his reply with the observation that "the United States for more than a decade has been assisting the Government and people of Vietnam." He went on to recall, "Way back in December 23, 1950, we signed a military assistance agreement with France and with Indo-China. . . . We also signed in December 1951 an agreement directly with Vietnam." There were too General Smith's declaration of concern at Geneva and the SEATO pact in 1954, as well as the "logistical assistance, transportation assistance, [and] training" supplied to the Republic since 1960. "So that there is," he concluded, "a long history of our effort to prevent Vietnam from falling under the control of the Communists." In May 1963,[43] Mr. Kennedy noted that an American-Vietnamese relationship had existed for "a good many years."

The longstanding nature of U.S. interest in the Republic of Vietnam received regular attention during the first nine months of 1964. Lyndon Johnson stated on February 21 that "for ten years" Washington had been involved in Southeast Asia. That March[44] Secretary McNamara remarked, "the United States since 1954 has been providing assistance to the Vietnamese." Two months later[45] Secretary Rusk reviewed how "for the past ten years" his government had given the South Vietnamese government "every possible assistance."

The fact of a decade's participation was not presented merely as interesting and parenthetical data; it was adduced to support the contention that over a number of years the official American position had remained virtually the same. At a briefing on April 4, the president told the press that "we are trying to do what we have done for many years." Two and a half weeks after that, on April 21, he observed, though more equivocally, "I think that our policy there is somewhat like it was ten years ago in 1954." By August[46] all reservations had disappeared; "Our policy in Southeast Asia," President Johnson declared to the Congress, "has been consistent and unchanged since 1954." Three presidents were, according to these statements, implicated in the Vietnamese affair.

From June through September, the assertion of complicity was made continually. Mr. Johnson insisted in June,[47] "we are steadfast in a policy which has been followed for ten years in three Administrations." That July[48] he reported, "For ten years and in three different administrations, the United States has been committed to the freedom and independence of South Vietnam." "For ten years, three American Presidents—President Eisenhower, President Kennedy, and the present President," he repeated on August 5, "have been actively concerned with threats to the peace and security of the people of Southeast Asia." On August 12 he repeated it again: "For ten years, through the Eisenhower Administration, the Kennedy Administration and this Administration, we have had one consistent aim."

1964 was a presidential election year. It was a sound political tactic then to identify the problem of Vietnam as being of bipartisan character and thereby remove it from partisan debate. But the problem outlasted the campaign, as did the desire to deflect professional and popular criticism, and so the emphasis on bipartisanship was maintained. In his State of the Union Message, delivered on January 4, 1965, President Johnson referred to the promise given to South Vietnam "ten years ago . . . [which] three Presidents have supported." Passing from commitments to objectives, he commented on the eighteenth, "Our purpose under three American Presidents has been to assist the Vietnamese to live in peace." On March 13 he dealt with the question of continuity. "I would say," he insisted, "that our policy there is the policy that was established by President Eisenhower, and I've stated since I've been President forty-six times, the policy carried out by President Kennedy and the policy we're now carrying on." The next week[49] he again all but lectured newsmen on the point:

> One year ago this week on March 1, 1964 I made this statement, and I quote:
> "For ten years under three Presidents this nation has been determined to help a brave people to resist aggression and terror. It is and will remain the policy of the United States to furnish assistance to support South Vietnam for as long as it is required to bring Communist aggression and terror under control."
> Our policy in Vietnam is the same as it was one year ago. And to those of you who have inquiries on the subject, it is the same as it was ten years ago.

The "three presidents" line was stated once more in April, May, and June. Then, during a nineteen day period in July, it was recited no fewer than five times. On the ninth, Mr. Johnson said that the American commitment to Vietnam had "been reaffirmed by three Presidents." On the thirteenth he asked the public "to remember that three Presidents have made the pledge for this nation." In a *Newsweek* interview, reported in *The New York Times* on the twenty-sixth, he urged steadiness and resolve: "We cannot just get out. Eisenhower [promised help]. . . . President Kennedy put 33,000 American troops there and I put more." "Three Presidents—President Eishenhower, President Kennedy and your present President—over eleven years have committed themselves," he reiterated on the twenty-eighth, "and have promised to defend this small and valiant nation." Upon arriving in Saigon on July 16, Robert McNamara had cited the American obligation which "Three Presidents have backed."

Throughout July Washington was engaged in a comprehensive review of its program of assistance to Vietnam, which culminated in the disclosure at the end of the month of the assignment of 50,000 U.S. soldiers to duty in Southeast Asia. During that time, the constant reminders of Presidents Eisenhower and Kennedy's association with that program were intended to clarify four related points. First, that Lyndon Johnson had inherited,[50] not created, the issue of Vietnam. Second, that his predecessors had shared his concern about that issue and his conclusion that it was one whose implications were great for the future peace and security of Americans. Third, that each of the others had felt compelled to assume certain responsibilities and undertake certain action on behalf of the Vietnamese Republic. Fourth, and consequentially, that any decision arrived at by the Johnson Administration, whatever other responsibilites and actions it involved, should be regarded as an outgrowth of, not a departure from, that consistent U.S. position.

After 1965 the theme of the three presidents changed in several material ways. To begin with, there was a marked decrease in its frequency of occurrence as Mr. Johnson virtually abandoned the allusion: from 18 repetitions out of a total of 291 utterances in 1965, it dropped to 8 out of 366 in 1966, and 7 out of 299 in 1967. In the late winter and early spring of 1968 the pattern was temporarily broken. From March 12 through 31, with the Communists challenging America's military strategy and domestic critics attacking the policy in general, the government again turned to the historical record.[51] The secretary of state told a Senate Foreign Relations Committee Panel on the twelfth:

I think the [Southeast Asia] policy is a policy that was there before. It has been a longstanding policy of this country in the postwar period under different Administrations, Republicans and Democratic.

On the eighteenth, Vice President Humphrey wrote, "From President Eisenhower on, American Presidents have seen our involvement in Vietnam as a necessity in maintaining peace and stability in the whole of Southeast Asia." Mr. Johnson indicated on the thirty-first that the U.S. course had been steady "under three different Presidents, three separate Administrations."

But apart from March 1968, the broad trend was downward, and for reasons which were hardly obscure. Once the United States became a direct participant in battle, taking massive losses of material, suffering casualties on a large scale, it was less and less persuasive to state flatly that the American role had grown inevitably from Mr. Eisenhower's offer of aid and Mr. Kennedy's dispatch of advisers.

The theme of the "three presidents" changed after 1965 in content as well. On occasion, it was still repeated by Lyndon Johnson in its familiar, slogan-like form. He spoke on January 12, 1966, of the "pledge which has grown through the commitment of three American Presidents." Twenty-one months later, during the autumn of 1967,[52] he talked of "the commitment that three Presidents" had made. The following August[53] he remarked that the enormous stakes in Southeast Asia made clear "why three different Presidents have taken and have held the position they have taken." But from 1966 on there were many more vague references to "other Presidents"[54] and "successive Administrations,"[55] partly explained by the more significant and basic shift of dating the American connection with Vietnam to a time prior to 1954.

That tack had been taken before. Vice President Nixon had alleged on June 27, 1954, that "the Acheson policy was directly responsible for the loss of China. And if China had not been lost, there would have been . . . no war in Indo-China today." In the winter of 1962[56] John Kennedy had pointed to agreements made with the Republic of Vietnam as far back as 1950. Twice in June of 1964[57] Ambassador Lodge had noted that the "Vietnamese thing . . . involves the Eisenhower Administration and the Kennedy and Johnson Administrations, and the Truman Administration." These were, however, isolated instances. With 1966 they became, if not commonplace, at least no longer so exceptional.

On April 18, 1966, Dean Rusk called the original grant of aid to the French in 1954 and the SEATO treaty "expressions of a policy attitude initiated during the Truman Administration." Explaining in May[58] the "why" of America's commitment to an audience of foreign affairs experts, he argued that the

> determination that the peace and security of that [Southeast Asia] are extremely important to the security of the United States . . . [had been] made first, before the Korean war, by President Truman on the basis of protracted analysis in the highest councils of government . . . [and was] reexamined at least twice during his Administration.

That January,[59] asked to react to Secretary General U Thant's claim that no vital Western interests were threatened in Vietnam, he stressed, "Four Presidents have not taken that view and the United States does not agree with it."

The secretary of state was the principal but not the only exponent of this idea. On February 15, 1967, a department aide, Daniel Davidson, described the American mission in Southeast Asia as the extension of the Truman Doctrine. In March[60] the president stated, "We chose a course in keeping with the foreign policy of at least three Administrations." William Bundy maintained that fall[61] that to dispute the validity of the "so-called domino theory" was to call into question "the explicit view" of John Kennedy and "the broad judgment of three other Presidents and their advisers." On August 27, 1968, Vice President Humphrey discussed the "difficulties of Southeast Asia and Vietnam," contending, "It had been the problem of three Presidents by the time that Johnson became President."

Nor did the attempt to affix, or share, ultimate responsibility for the war end at Mr. Truman. On February 23, 1966, Lyndon Johnson declared:

> in Vietnam . . . we keep the faith of freedom.
> Four Presidents have pledged to keep that faith.

The first was Franklin D. Roosevelt in his State of the Union Message twenty-five years ago.

That May,[62] tracing his decisions to "every lesson that we've learned in this century," he turned to Mr. Roosevelt again:

> Standing in this great city of Chicago, one of our greatest leaders ever to be produced in America, on October 5, 1937, Franklin D. Roosevelt said, and I quote him:
> "When an epidemic of physical disease starts to spread the community approves and joins in a quarantine of the patient in order to protect the health of the community against the spread of the disease. . . ."
> That is what John F. Kennedy remembered when in the face of Communist aggression . . . in Vietnam he began to send American forces there as early as 1962.

The figure of the past presidents related in differing ways both to the commitment theory and to the allusions to Greece, Berlin, and Turkey. Its relationship with commitments, indicated by the regularity with which the two appeared together within the same sentence or paragraph of an official speech, grew out of the obvious role that America's leaders had had in creating America's obligations. Though the interplay between the men and the engagements was never uniformly or precisely defined, the process seemed to be described according to one of three models.

> The steps taken by Presidents Eisenhower, Kennedy, and Johnson over a period of years in promising and providing assistance and support to South Vietnam
> 1. constituted an evolving, dynamic commitment to which each administration had become a party: "Three Presidents . . . over eleven years have committed themselves";[63]
> 2. stood as the critical endorsement of a separate, preexisting congressional commitment: "Three American Presidents have backed the United States commitment";[64]
> 3. represented an initial presidential commitment confirmed, amplified, and strengthened by succeeding governments: "President Eisenhower made our first commitment there in '54. That was reaffirmed by President Kennedy many times in different ways. The present President has reiterated . . . that we expect to keep that committment."[65]

Much of this complexity and confusion was attributable to the changing interpretations of whether, or if, the president's 1954 letter or the Congress's 1954 treaty, or both, should be regarded as the basic commitment, as well as the chronic uncertainty about when commitment meant a legally binding pledge and when a purely moral undertaking.

The second relationship, between past presidents and Greece, Berlin, and Turkey, was grounded in the logical similarity of the arguments implicit in striking both these images: when Washington referred to either, it was making a positive appeal to precedent. It invoked the memory of Greece, Berlin, and Turkey, while stating that the Vietnam position was consistent with the broad tradition of post-1945 interventionism; it invoked the memory of Eisenhower, Kennedy, and Truman, while stating that the Vietnam position was consistent with a specific and established line of Southeast Asia involvement. To contend that the issues in Vietnam were the same as those in Europe after the Second World War, and that the policy of Lyndon Johnson was the same as that of his predecessors, was to say that ignoring or leaving the battlefield in Asia would be breaking fundamentally and irrevocably from the recent and successful past of the United States.

Congress

In the months from February to June 1954, as the Vietminh proved themselves more and more successful in their war against the French, Washington had to address itself repeatedly to the question of what it would do if the situation deteriorated any further; if the allies were on the verge of collapse, would the United States agree to dispatch combat troops? In its response, it was consistently and scrupulously deferential to legislative prerogative: not unless the issues were first considered and approved by the Senate and the House of Representatives.

Undersecretary Smith told members of the Foreign Relations Committee on February 16 that a Chinese invasion of Indochina would prompt the immediate submission of the entire matter to the Congress. The president refused on April 7 to speculate upon the actions he would recommend "as the last resort, because there was a Congress." "The thing," he said, had to be "settled and properly worked out with the people who also bore the responsibilities." At a June 11 briefing he assured newsmen that if Southeast Asia "came on the crest of some crisis," then "you would have to go and lay the problem before Congress and ask them."

That May Secretary Dulles had been even more direct. "In making commitments which might involve the use of armed force," he stated on the seventh, "Congress is a full partner." He continued, "Only Congress can declare war. President Eisenhower has repeatedly emphasized that he would not take military action in Indo-China without the support of Congress." On the twenty-fifth he insisted that it be "clear that one of the conditions [of intervention upon] which we have always stood is that there must be Congressional sanction of any such action."

John F. Kennedy was asked at a press conference in March 1963,[66] whether he would "go to Congress for approval before committing combat troops in Vietnam." He replied, "If there was a basic change in that situation in Vietnam which calls for a constitutional decision, I, of course, would go to the Congress."

On August 2, 1964, the Pentagon reported:

> While on routine patrol in international waters, at 4:08 A.M. EDT, the United States' destroyer Maddox underwent an unprovoked attack by three PT-type boats at lattitude 19–40 no., longitude 106–34 e., in Tonkin Gulf.

On August 4 there was another, similar announcement:

> A second deliberate attack was made during darkness by an undetermined number of North Vietnamese PT boats on the USS Maddox and the USS C. Turner Joy while the two destroyers were cruising on routine patrol in the Tonkin Gulf in international waters about 65 miles from the nearest land.

That evening, President Johnson disclosed to the nation, "Air action is now in execution against gunboat and certain supporting facilities in North Vietnam which have been used in these hostile operations."

The next day, addressing a joint session of Congress, he requested that a resolution be enacted "expressing the support of the Congress for all necessary action to protect our armed forces, and to assist nations covered by the SEATO treaty." Submitted formally on August 5, it was approved overwhelmingly on August 7 by a vote of 504 to 2. It declared:

> Section 1—The Congress approves and supports the determination of the President, as Commander in Chief, to take all necessary measures to repel any armed attack against the forces of the United States and to prevent further aggression.
>
> Section 2—The United States regards as vital to its national interest and to world peace the maintenance of the international peace and security in Southeast Asia. Consonant with the Constitution and the Charter of the United Nations and in accordance with its obligations under the Southeast Asia Collective Defense Treaty, the United States is, therefore, prepared as the President determines to take all necessary steps, including the use of armed force, to assist any member or protocol state of the Southeast Asia Collective Defense Treaty requesting assistance in defense of its freedom.
>
> Section 3—This resolution shall expire when the President shall determine that the peace and security of the area is reasonably assured by international conditions created by action of the United Nations or otherwise, except that it may be terminated earlier by concurrent resolutions of the Congress.

Though the Tonkin Resolution was passed under the impeller of emergency, the Johnson Administration was unwilling to take it as a dramatic but wholly symbolic gesture. In its terms of reference it was a useful, unambiguous affirmation of America's security interest in Southeast Asia, as well as an important reconfirmation of the obligations imposed by the SEATO treaty. In its substantive provision, whatever the circumstances of its origin, it was a far-reaching, unqualified endorsement-in-advance of any decision the president might choose to make, an explicit waiver of congressional bars to future action. On December 1, therefore, after disregarding it for four months, the White House concluded a statement on Vietnam by taking note that "the Congressional Joint Resolution of August 10, 1964" remained "in full force and effect." During the period which followed, as the United States escalated its role in the war, the resolution was cited repeatedly as the legislative authorization for that progressive involvement.

The State Department revealed on February 24, 1965, that

American crews were flying bombing raids against Vietcong concentrations in the South; the transition from providing advice and assistance to lending active support was described as "consistent with the Congressional resolution approving and supporting the determination of the President as Commander in Chief to prevent any further aggression." Charged on March 3 with committing United States forces to war without the required formal declaration, the department answered that Mr. Johnson was acting within the terms of the language of the August bill. When in June American combat responsibilities were expanded to include offensive patrolling to seek out the enemy, spokesman Robert J. McCloskey again[67] turned to Section 2 of that statute, which approved "all necessary steps including the use of armed force" to assist South Vietnam "in defense of its freedom."

On August 9, eleven days after ordering the massive buildup of United States troop strength, Lyndon Johnson recalled that Congress the year before had accepted legislation which "goes just as far as we know how to go" in allowing the president to conduct the war in Asia. "I have the authority," he added, "and I am exercising it." He wrote on January 28 to senators concerned about the dangers of his military course, "I continue to be guided in these matters by the resolution of the Congress, approved on August 10, 1964, Public Law 86–408, by a vote of 504 to 2." That afternoon, in an appearance before the Senate Foreign Relations Committee, Secretary Rusk recited the full text of the resolution to rebut the claim that its scope was intended to be specific and limited; concluding his testimony on February 18, he underscored "that [resolution] is the law of the land as far as the Secretary of State is concerned." In the summer of 1967,[68] as the same body investigated the government's authority to wage the war, Undersecretary Nicholas Katzenbach pointed out that the 1964 "resolution authorize[d] the President to use the armed forces of the United States in whatever way was necessary." He questioned, "What could a declaration of war have done that would have given the President more authority and a clearer voice of the Congress of the United States than that did?"

Though Washington maintained that the legal effect of the

Tonkin Resolution was obvious and broad, it never argued that its passage had been a constitutional necessity; had it never existed, the president would still have had the power to act just as he had. On June 17, 1965, Mr. Johnson stated, "the authority of the President is very clear and unquestioned without a resolution. The Commander-in-Chief has all the authority that I am exercising." In February 1966,[69] he reiterated:

> I think it's very clear to the members of Congress that the President has authority to take the actions he has taken, first as Commander-in-Chief. . . .If the resolution is repealed I think I could still carry out our commitments there,

Eighteen months later, in August 1967,[70] he was equally emphatic: "We stated then, and we repeat now, we did not think the resolution was necessary to do what we did and what we're doing."

On each of these three occasions he went on to explain why, nevertheless, he had sought congressional opinion. He spoke in 1965 of his "desire to have the support of Congress and to have them a part of any decision we make." In 1966, in more detail, he reviewed

> in light of what Senator Vandenberg had said about people being in on the takeoff as well as on the landing, in view of what Senator Taft had said about President Truman—"was justified in going to Korea but should have asked for a resolution"—in view of the advice I'd given President Eisenhower in connection with Formosa and Lebanon resolutions, I said to the Secretary of State and Secretary of Defense "before we go in there to a more advanced state or involve ourselves more substantially, I want the Congress to go in with me."

Paraphrasing Senator Vandenberg again, he said in 1967, "we thought if we were going to ask them to stay the whole route and if we expected them to be there on the landing we ought to ask them to be there on the takeoff."

President Johnson's wish to have the Congress informed about and involved in administration decisions was in part the product of a former colleague's understanding of legislative sensitivity and anxiety about the ultimate effect of executive encroachments upon the internal balance of power. It was, as

well, the expression of a consummate politician's efforts to create a national policy, a policy on which both levels of government would be united and for which, therefore, each would
share responsibility.

As the United States gradually intervened in Southeast Asia,
the August resolution stood as congressional sanction for that
intervention, effectively making the Congress a direct party to
it. At the extreme, its passage was represented as an independent promise by the Senate and House of Representatives, their
own obligation to defend Vietnam. "The how of the commitment [to Southeast Asia]," Mr. Rusk maintained in May 1966,[71]

> consists of various acts and utterances of successive Presidents
> and Congresses—. . .[Among them] the resolution of August,
> 1964, which the House of Representatives adopted unanimously
> and the Senate with only two negative votes.

On January 10, 1967, the President declared, "We are in Vietnam . . . because Congress has pledged by solemn vote to take all
necessary measures to prevent further aggression."

The Tonkin Resolution, like the names of Dwight Eisenhower and John F. Kennedy, was invoked to make clear that the
war in Vietnam could not be regarded as Mr. Johnson's war.
Conceived and implemented by two previous presidents,
codified and approved by the Congress, the course in Southeast
Asia had evolved from a collective judgment about American
interests. It was the product of over a decade of concern by
Democrats and Republicans in both branches of government,
the product of a deep, abiding concensus; it was not the liability
of a single man.

In the fall of 1967, the president continued to defer to the
1964 authorization. In September[72] he reminded a Texas audience:

> The Senate [sic] said, in a resolution that it passed in 1964 by a
> vote of 504 to 2, "the United States is, therefore, prepared as the
> President determines, to take all necessary steps, including the
> use of armed forces, to assist any member or protocol state of the
> Southeast Asia Collective Defense Treaty requesting assistance
> in defense of freedom."

He pledged on December 12 that he would not now

> nullify the word of the Congress . . . as expressed in the . . . Tonkin Gulf resolution where there were only two votes against it when they said they would support the President and whatever means it was necessary to take to deter aggression.

In an interview on the twentieth he talked of the program of assistance to the Republic of Vietnam that "we had agreed to . . . in the Gulf of Tonkin resolution." But by then, the credibility of that agreement had already been eroded.

The events of August 2–7, 1964, had had a quality of epic clarity: two senseless attacks on American vessels on the high seas, an impassioned presidential appeal for unity, a declaration by Congress of determination and complete support. In November 1967,[73] however, Mr. Johnson remarked for the second time,[74] "we began discussing at this table in May of that year [1964] the desirability of asking the Congress to join with us in deterring aggression." On December 21 the State Department made public testimony given by Assistant Secretary William P. Bundy in September 1966, which indicated that the administration "had contingent drafts [of a resolution] . . . for some time prior to [August 1964]."

Throughout February, as the Senate reexamined the August incidents themselves, other revelations were made. In the course of defending U.S. activities, Secretary McNamara admitted to the panel that the *Maddox* and *C. Turner Joy* had been on a mission of "visual and electronic surveillance of the area," that they had been "instructed to remain at least eleven miles from the coast," within, that is, the twelve mile territorial waters claimed by Hanoi, that their patrols were coincident with in time, even if unrelated in purpose, to "certain reconnaissance and bombardment activities of South Vietnamese patrol craft against North Vietnam."[75] He acknowledged, too, that the August 4 raid had "occurred on a very dark, moonless, overcast, night" and that Washington had been warned by the commander of the destroyer task force:

> Review of action makes many recorded contacts and torpedoes
> fired appear doubtful. . . . Freak weather effects and over-eager
> sonarmen may have accounted for many reports. No actual sight-
> ings by Maddox. Suggest complete evaluation before any further
> action.[76]

The Pentagon had conceded three weeks earlier[77] that that
second attack, confirmed largely by soundings taken aboard the
Maddox, had taken place only a few hours after that ship had
radioed that its sonar detection equipment had developed a
"material deficiency."

The disclosures posed several questions. How preliminary
and tentative were the drafts of the resolution framed in the
spring of 1964? Could Hanoi have perceived the patrol of
American warships as a threat to its security? Did the government satisfactorily confirm the August 4 engagement in advance of taking retaliatory measures? Had Lyndon Johnson,
that is, deliberately seized upon an ambiguous situation and
masqueraded it as a challenge of the nation's resolve in order
to obtain the permissive endorsement that he had considered
securing long before?

On March 12, 1968, asked about "the exact, precise plans
that you have with regard to the matter of this escalation,"
Dean Rusk observed that that decision was "basically for the
President to make." "Congress itself," he recalled,

> with two dissenting votes, resolved that the United States is
> therefore prepared, as the President determines, to take all
> necessary steps, including the use of armed force, to assist any
> member or protocol state of the Southeast Asia Collective De-
> fense Treaty requesting assistance in defense of its freedom.

On the thirty-first Mr. Johnson noted, "Resolutions of the Congress testify to the need to resist aggression in the world and in
Southeast Asia." Thereafter, the Tonkin Resolution was no
longer mentioned. The doubts about its validity, exacerbated
during the Senate hearings in February, and the dramatic reverse in the trend of ever-increasing escalation, heralded by the
partial suspension of bombing in March, had rendered it suddenly obsolete.

NOTES TO CHAPTER 5

1. Johnson, February 4, 1965.
2. Johnson, April 1, 1965.
3. Great Britain, April 13, 1954.
4. France, April 14, 1954.
5. Dulles, May 25, 1954.
6. Dulles, June 11, 1954.
7. Eisenhower, May 24, 1954.
8. Dulles, September 3, 1954.
9. Eisenhower, April 10, 1954.
10. Dulles, March 17, 1954.
11. Dulles, June 12, 1956.
12. Rusk, May 22, 1964.
13. Rusk, February 25, 1965.
14. Rusk, February 18, 1966.
15. On November 26, 1966, the Senate Foreign Relations Committee released a censored text of hearings which had taken place at the time of the Tonkin Gulf incident, two years before. Dean Rusk had then been asked by Sam Ervin whether United States assistance to South Vietnam had been granted "under an obligation assumed by us under the [Southeast Asia] Treaty." The secretary had replied that "the SEATO treaty is a substantiating basis for our presence there and our efforts there, although, however, we are not acting specifically under the SEATO treaty."

    The State Department, commenting on this testimony three days after its disclosure on November 29, 1966, insisted that Mr. Rusk had not intended to "minimize the importance of the SEATO Treaty" and pointed out that the senator was discussing the question of aid, not the "military and security aspects of the SEATO Treaty." It stopped short, however, of claiming that had the question been different his answer too would have changed, and entirely avoided the issue of whether that 1964 statement was consistent with the implications of his sweeping assertion before the same committee in 1966.
16. Humphrey, April 25, 1966.
17. Johnson, November 1, 1966.
18. Throughout all of 1966 and during the first three-quarters of 1967 SEATO was cited as a binding commitment in 4 percent of official speeches; during the final quarter of 1967, that figure rose to 9 percent.
19. Johnson, March 2, 1967.
20. Rusk, February 18, 1966.
21. State Department, March 9, 1966.
22. State Department, March 11, 1967.
23. Dulles, March 23, 1954.
24. State Department, June 30, 1954.
25. Eisenhower, May 5, 1954.
26. Dulles, July 12, 1954.
27. Smith, June 21, 1954.
28. Dulles, March 29, 1954.
29. Eisenhower, June 30, 1954.
30. Morton, July 11, 1954.
31. In October, in seeming disproof that such conditions could be insured in

the South either, Ngo Dinh Diem was elected president with a 98.2 percent majority. On the twenty-fourth, after reviewing the results, the State Department said it was "gratified" that "the referendum was conducted in such an orderly and efficient manner."

32. Robertson, June 1, 1956.
33. Rusk, March 1, 1962.
34. Johnson, January 18, 1965.
35. Goldberg, February 10, 1967.
36. Harriman, May 18, 1968.
37. Johnson, March 25, 1965.
38. Goldberg, January 5, 1966.
39. Rusk, May 1, 1967.
40. Harriman, May 13, 1968.
41. Kennedy, February 14, 1962.
42. McNamara, March 26, 1964.
43. Kennedy, May 8, 1963.
44. McNamara, March 26, 1964.
45. Rusk, May 22, 1964.
46. Johnson, August 5, 1964.
47. Johnson, June 2, 1964.
48. Johnson, July 24, 1964.
49. Johnson, March 20, 1965.
50. Johnson, April 1, 1965.
51. Four of the twenty statements issued during those two and a half weeks cited that history.
52. Johnson, September 29, 1967.
53. Johnson, August 19, 1968.
54. Johnson, June 30, 1966, and December 12, 1967.
55. Rusk, August 22, 1966.
56. Kennedy, February 14, 1962.
57. Lodge, June 23 and June 28, 1964.
58. Rusk, May 24, 1966.
59. Rusk, January 11, 1967.
60. Johnson, March 15, 1967.
61. Bundy, November 12, 1967.
62. Johnson, May 17, 1966.
63. Johnson, July 28, 1965.
64. McNamara, July 16, 1965.
65. Johnson, July 13, 1965.
66. Kennedy, March 14, 1963.
67. McNamara, June 8, 1965.
68. Katzenbach, August 17, 1967.
69. Johnson, February 26, 1966.
70. Johnson, August 18, 1967.
71. Rusk, May 24, 1966.
72. Johnson, September 29, 1967.
73. Johnson, November 1, 1967.
74. Johnson, August 18, 1967.
75. McNamara, February 20, 1968.
76. McNamara, February 24, 1968.
77. Defense Department, February 3, 1968.

CHAPTER SIX

IN THE FINAL ANALYSIS

WHAT WASHINGTON SAID

A thematic analysis of public language has two inherent limitations. First, by concentrating on how an individual theme evolves over time, the interrelationship among themes across time is necessarily obscured. The clarity about the way in which a particular chain of allusions is modulated and modified over two decades is achieved, but only at the expense of a real feeling for the overall verbal texture in any single year.

Second, the restricted focus upon content, upon what officials say, conveys an overwhelming and finally distorted impression of the complexity of official speech. It conceals the fact that in terms of the function of that speech there is an underlying and central unity. Lost is the sense that whatever the specific point being made, the basic reason for making it was always the same. North Vietnamese aggression, U.S. disinterest in territory, the commitment theory, President Eisenhower's 1954 letter—all were raised as integrated elements in an indivisible case. Each was advanced to further one argument: that America had to do exactly what it was doing in Southeast Asia.

In an effort therefore to restore this other perspective, the summary which follows is structured chronologically.

On February 7, 1950, Washington extended diplomatic recognition to the Republic of Vietnam, granting it military and economic aid in May and ordering the dispatch of an American advisory mission that June. On December 23, defense accords were signed between the United States and France, and the following September 1951, a direct agreement was entered into with the Associated States. These actions, which for the first time substantially involved America in the affairs of Southeast Asia, were accompanied by a minimum of publicity. Nevertheless, over thirty-six months, in thirty-four releases, the Truman Administration did make plain the assumptions upon which its Indochina initiative had been based:

1. Ho Chi Minh, the leader of the insurgency, was an agent of the Russians, and it was they who were responsible for orchestrating the conflict and who would be the prime beneficiaries of a Vietminh success.
2. The struggle was closely related to the war in Korea in that in each case there was Chinese assistance; there was a danger that in the south of Asia, as in the north, an armed attack by China might occur.
3. The objective of the United States was to maintain Vietnamese freedom and prevent the encroachment of international communism; it was not to foster French colonialism.
4. Vietnam was of enormous strategic importance to the free world, the key to the defense of the entire peninsula.
5. Victory for the Franco-Vietnamese forces was contingent upon the rapid assembly of an effective native army.

Though from 1953 to 1954 there were Republicans conducting foreign affairs, the scenario they offered was only a more elaborate rendering of that presented by the Democrats over the three years before. The Russians, in absolute control of Eastern Europe and Central Asia, sought to extend their hegemony to India and Japan. Since both nations depended heavily on Southeast Asia for their food, the capture of that region became a target of the Kremlin's revolutionary program.

In pursuit of this intermediate goal, Ho Chi Minh, a veteran operative with a long-standing Soviet affiliation, was dispatched to Indochina. His strategy had been set forth by Joseph Stalin in 1924: infiltrate dependent areas, foment rebellion, amalgamate the liberated peoples with the socialist community. His material and practical support—training, equipment, direction —came from Peking. The activities in Vietnam were part of a single aggressive pattern, extending from the Yalu River to the South China Sea.

Their appraisal carried three broad implications. First, it removed the Indochina conflict from the class of domestic uprising. The indisputable assistance of the U.S.S.R. and the C.P.R. totally destroyed any illusions that the Vietminh represented either nationalism or liberty. Second, it defused the charge of French colonialism. It was Moscow that was engaged in creating satellites and dependencies in Asia, not Paris which was withdrawing its influence and divesting itself of holdings there. Third, and most important, it established unequivocally that the Indochina war was a war against communism. Though it was also a war to maintain freedom and repel aggression, it was resistance to that international conspiracy which was the central issue.

Because freedom was "of one piece," the loss of Indochina would affect free people everywhere. Because the peninsula was weak and divided, and the Communists were ambitious and determined, the loss would, as well, set off a disastrous chain reaction throughout the area: Malaya, Thailand, and Burma would collapse; Indonesia would be seriously endangered; Australia, New Zealand, the Philippines, and Japan would come under enormous pressure; America's Pacific line of defense would be gravely imperiled. The result would be a substantial and direct threat to U.S. security. It was therefore in the national interest, both economic and judicious, to contribute to the effort to insure the survival of a pro-Western Vietnam.

The contribution to that effort was, in the end, almost entirely financial; between 1950 and 1954, America underwrote 80 percent of France's costs. The government did, however, explore the possibility of providing more direct military help in April 1954, to the accompaniment of the most intense publicity barrage of that war—a campaign based on the fact of Chinese intervention and the fear of falling dominoes. The exploration was revealing in that the points raised then were the same ones to be raised in other discussions of similar proposals in later years. Officials maintained during those weeks that

1. no commitment would be undertaken unless it was within a collective framework of action;
2. no commitment could be undertaken without the approval of the Congress;
3. no commitment should be undertaken in the absence of a suitable political and psychological background in Vietnam.

That summer a cease fire was reached, and in the days and months which followed, the United States expressed in several forms its interest in continuing to play a role in Vietnamese destiny. In July General Smith made his minimal declaration at Geneva. In September Mr. Dulles initialed the far-reaching SEATO treaty. In October President Eisenhower wrote offering American aid to President Diem. These expressions marked the beginning of the rapid transfer of responsibility for the fate of Southeast Asia from Paris to Washington, a transfer which by 1960 was a matter of history.

In its detail, the Kennedy war in southern Asia was very different from the war which Dwight Eisenhower had met in 1954. The battleground had narrowed from all of Indochina to a part of Vietnam. The Vietcong had succeeded the Vietminh as the local army of insurgency. The enemy's activity was closer to subversion—ambush, kidnap, murder—than to open aggression. Hanoi, not Peking, was the source of external support and direction; Chairman Krushchev, not Marshal Stalin, was the fount of revolutionary wisdom; "wars of liberation," not "amalgamation," was the doctrinal script.

In broad outline, however, the two wars were much alike. In both the United States was primarily interested in opposing communism and defending freedom. In both ostensibly national forces were waging a battle in fact manipulated from abroad. In both there was involvement by the U.S.S.R., C.P.R., and D.R.V.

Between 1961 and 1963 the American government took

various measures to assure the people of Vietnam of the importance it attached to their continuing struggle. The vice president was sent there in May 1961, on a mission which culminated in a June announcement that U.S. aid would be
significantly expanded. On December 15 it was disclosed that
the president had pledged to "increase our assistance" again.
That January the State Department revealed that a major new
socioeconomic program was being initiated. In February 1962,
a special military command was established for South Vietnam,
under the direction of a four-star general. Each of these not
insignificant engagements was presented without drama as a
limited and minor step, preserving the impression that the
situation in Southeast Asia while serious, was a thoroughly manageable one.

The rhetoric of the Kennedy Administration, when compared with that which followed, was in both its quantity and
content insubstantial. It was only on occasion that officials referred to the war at all; though there was a spate in May 1961,
February 1962, and September 1963, the total number of statements for those three years was exceeded by the number for
1964 alone. Of these occasional references, there was seldom an
effort to offer a coherent definition of American policy, rarely
an attempt to go beyond allusion to the domino principle and
accounts of Communist terror to a full-scale rationale. And, so
long as Washington believed, or the public could accept, that
the conflict in Southeast Asia was a low-risk, short-term operation, regular coverage and more detailed explanation were not
needed, and would not be forthcoming.

The period is nevertheless of interest, for on isolated instances remarks were made and interpretations advanced
which anticipated themes that would later become central in
the government's speech. In September 1961,[1] Mr. Kennedy
noted the threat posed by "wars of liberation," and asked
"whether measures can be devised to protect the small and
weak from such tactics." Commenting on the deaths of two
American advisers the next April,[2] he likened their sacrifice to
those of "World War II, World War I, [and] Korea." On March
14, 1963, he promised that he "would go to Congress" before
dispatching combat troops to Asia. That May[3] he stated, "We

have had a commitment for a good many years to the integrity of South Vietnam."

Secretary Rusk cited the "concern" of the members of the Southeast Asia Treaty Organization about the situation in Vietnam at a news conference on May 4, 1961. In March 1962,[4] he discounted a "desire for bases or other United States military advantages" in the area, insisting, "All we want is that the South Vietnamese be free to determine their own future." Evaluating the chances of eventual free world success in defeating the Communists, he observed that November[5] that "the reception, the support of the people themselves will be vital in this type of guerilla warfare. The attitude of the people becomes absolutely crucial."

In 1964 the war was discussed five times as often as in 1963, with the discussions taking on a much greater complexity. There was increased precision in the differentiation of responsibility among the four hostile parties: the Vietcong were the immediate agents of insurrection; North Vietnam was the primary source of control; China was the ultimate supplier of matériel; Russia provided moral and political support. Of the superpowers, China emerged as a more serious threat than Russia. Denounced far more regularly, its proclaimed militancy was contrasted with the moderation and reason being displayed by the Kremlin. The contrast was one form of recognition of the impact of the Sino-Soviet doctrinal rift; another was the relative decline in reference to communism.

The enemy's operations in Southeast Asia were in 1964, as between 1961 and 1963, characterized mainly in terms of guerilla warfare, in terms of sabotage and stealth, of assasination and terror. In March[6] Secretary McNamara introduced the idea that the adoption of this strategy by the adversary was a calculated test of American resolution, an experiment to determine whether modern and sophisticated technology could be confounded by such primitive maneuvers. Since both Mr. Khrushchev and Chairman Mao had endorsed these struggles for "liberation," it was unclear whether Moscow or Peking would benefit most if the United States failed in its trial. There was, however, a consensus that such a failure would inspire the outbreak of other, similar conflicts throughout the underdeveloped areas of the world.

Though the guerilla character of the war was given the major emphasis, there was a new and significant tendency to describe the whole affair as a case of "aggression." This description mediated the initial vague analogies, struck in March,[7] May,[8] and August,[9] between the situation in Asia in 1964 and that in Europe thirty years before; it heightened the relevance of the pregnant statements that the West had "learned" the dangers of acquiescence to armed force. The specter of general war raised by these allusions complemented the predictions of a Communist Far East, which officials insisted would follow a precipitate American withdrawal; the two together made plausible the parenthetical contention that national security was linked to the outcome in South Vietnam.

It was not only the negative experience of appeasement but also the positive implications of the confrontations of the Cold War which were cited for the first time in justification of U.S. policy. Vietnam, Adlai Stevenson said in May,[10] presented the same issues, and therefore required the same response, as were met "in Greece in 1947 and in Korea in 1950."

Nor was it only by historical inference that American assistance could be defended: aid had been given Saigon for a decade and had a history of its own. "Over ten years, in three different Administrations, Washington has acted to help protect the Republic of Vietnam," was the continual refrain. This longstanding bipartisan concern could be demonstrated in General Smith's declaration at Geneva, the SEATO treaty, and the letter from Mr. Eisenhower to Mr. Diem.

That letter represented more, however, than just an expression of a Republican leader's concern; on June 2 it was adduced as America's "commitment" to South Vietnam. It was upon the existence of solemn promises, an issue injected into the oratory in February,[11] that the United States principally rested its case in 1964. Twice in June[12] and once in August,[13] President Johnson explained the involvement in Southeast Asia as a function "first" of the fact that "America keeps her word."

Though it was unequivocal about its determination to aid the Vietnamese, the United States was careful that its resolve not be confused with imperial ambition. It denied any desire for conquest, or dominion, or political, military, or territorial advantage. It foreswore interest in the settlement of Saigon's internal disputes. It did not seek to choose the future of South Vietnam, but rather to insure that that future not be imposed from the North. America, it emphasized, was only exercising a supporting role, only helping the natives of the area to help themselves; the war could in the end only be won by the efforts and dedication of the people of Southeast Asia.

The August attacks on American warships by two enemy PT boats were the most spectacular events in Vietnam in 1964. They resulted in both the ordering of the first U.S. reprisal raids against the D.R.V. and the impressive passage by Congress of the Tonkin Gulf Resolution. What may finally be more significant, however, is that by then the Johnson Administration had unveiled all the themes which it would thereafter use to justify its inexorable intervention; Munich, Greece, Berlin, and Turkey, SEATO—all were elements in Washington's brief months before the actual program of escalation had begun. Whether these powerful arguments were cynically advanced in order to prepare the nation to accept extreme measures already approved, or whether the government presented an honest rationale for a limited program and became, tragically, the prisoner of its own perceptions—what, that is the dynamics of the interplay between military planning and public relations actually were—is a question which will remain a matter of controversy and speculation.

The assumption by Washington of a combat role in Southeast Asia in 1965 was attributed to increasing provocations by Hanoi. In February[14] the State Department officially depicted the war as an instance of illegal "aggression from the North," and thereafter stress was given to North Vietnam as an aggressor, seeking to impose itself on the South, rather than to North Vietnam as the source of direction and supply. This more serious estimate of the responsibility of the Democratic Republic was supported by reports of its growing infiltration and accounts of the presence of regular units below the Demilitarized Zone, and underscored by the generally more intense concentration of government attention on the D.R.V. It contrasted sharply with the decrease in attention given to the Vietcong, and heightened the impression that internal elements were of minor importance; the ratio of references of Vietcong to North

Vietnam had fallen from 34/41 in 1964 to 43/84 in 1965. The so-called indigenous rebels were dismissed as mere puppets of Hanoi.

The discussion of the U.S.S.R. and C.P.R. merely elaborated earlier trends. Though Moscow continued to aid the North Vietnamese, providing missiles and bombers, there was only the most sporadic and perfunctory criticism of its contributions; by July[15] W. Averell Harriman had concluded for the administration that Russia sought peace in Indochina and assisted the North merely to avoid the censure of Peking. China, in comparison, was attacked incessantly, despite its modest tangible help; it was China's doctrinal belligerence which, ultimately, had caused the war.

The most insistent period of Chinese denunciation came in October 1965, coincident with the discovery by the Pentagon of an article by Defense Minister Lin Piao. That article, like Joseph Stalin's lecture on amalgamation in 1924 and Nikita Khrushchev's party address of 1961, was evidence that the struggle in Vietnam was part of a larger program for Communist world domination. It confirmed the fact that Peking would be the real winner were the war to "liberate" Southeast Asia successful; victory would vindicate Mao Tse-tung's claim to be the true disciple of Karl Marx.

If the United States were unable to meet the test in Vietnam, however, not only would it have promoted China's bid for leadership of the Communist movement: it would have jeopardized as well the hope for stability of the weaker nations of the world. To the collapse of the peninsula and takeover of the Pacific islands, to the spread of peoples' wars over Africa and Latin America, was added the danger that one hundred small nations would be forced to accomodate with the enemy and realign with the East.

This addition was only one example of the parallel between the escalation of force and the escalation of oratory. On February 7, 1965, retaliatory strikes were launched against facilities in the North supporting infiltration, and on February 25 B-52 raids were conducted in the South and brought to a close the "advise and assist" phase of U.S. operations; during those weeks the government repeatedly disavowed any implication that those moves bespoke an aspiration for empire and emphasized its disinterest in material gains.

In March the continuous bombing campaign was begun and American reinforcements were sent to guard U.S. bases; that month the SEATO treaty became an operative commitment and it was suddenly a solemn international agreement, as well as a presidential promise, which bound the nation to intervene in Vietnam.

By April the air strikes had been expanded to include transportation equipment, radar, and all communications lines, and more troops had been dispatched to protect American installations. It was contended, then, that were the Southeast Asia pact dishonored the credibility of all the undertakings of the United States would be thrown into question; fulfilling its pledge in Asia became a matter which bore upon general security.

On July 28 Mr. Johnson announced that 50,000 American soldiers would be immediately deployed to the war zone; in the days which preceded the announcement officials underscored that any decisions taken would only be an extension of a long, bipartisan tradition, noting on five occasions that the same basic policy had existed in Vietnam for eleven years.

There were other, broader changes between February and July. The claim that the United States had to stand in Southeast Asia in order to keep its word was made incessantly. There was increased and increasingly specific invocation of the memories of Munich and more frequent reminders of the relationship between Vietnam and the national interest. The guarantee of the right of the South Vietnamese to shape their own destiny emerged, abruptly, as the central, positive aim of American intervention. There was also less insistence that the United States was just helping and supporting, playing a minor part in southern Asia.

In 1966 the overall number of statements dealing with U.S. involvement rose to 366. There were more references to the North Vietnamese and fewer to the Vietcong. Russia continued to be treated gently, and China was handled with equal harshness. The emphasis in rationale was shifted from honoring commitments to realizing affirmative goals, although commitments in general were still important and SEATO in particular was cited far more often. The Eisenhower letter disappeared as a referent after the general's clarification of its purposes the August before, and there was an overall decline in attempts to link President Johnson's position with those of his predecessors.

Disinterest in dominion was noted less frequently after March, and the Tonkin Resolution seldom after April. The vague talk of the fate of the hundred small nations and peripheral remarks about U.S. security remained at about the same level, while allusions to the lessons of the thirties, the dangers of wars of liberation, and the disintegration of Southeast Asia grew. More attention was given, also, to Greece, Berlin, and Turkey, the risk of a costlier conflict, and the romantic metaphysics of the indivisibility of freedom.

Most significant, however, was the electric quality of the rhetoric that year. Its tone was emotional, often strident. In characterizing Hanoi, clear stress was laid upon its "aggression," its intentions to "seize the South by force"; China was a "shadow"[16] looming over Asia, the Vietcong, a "Front,"[17] the Communists, "Reds."[18] There was, as well, a lack of subtlety— the appeals were more direct than ever before, and the language was of both greater and more immediate impact. In warning against appeasing the enemy, Washington warned about "Nazism, Poland, Hitler"; in urging that the South be allowed to choose its own future, it urged "self-determination"; in denying its desire for special positions, it denied a desire for "empire"; in maintaining that the struggle was not an internal uprising, it maintained it was not a "civil war."

The substance of many of the arguments was excessive and strained. There was the recurrent contention that if Washington disregarded its undertakings in southern Asia, it would undermine worldwide confidence in American reliability and rend the whole fabric of international peace. The eradication of hunger, poverty, illiteracy, and disease was dramatically designated the primary U.S. objective. By resisting aggression in Vietnam, it was declared, America had certainly contributed to and perhaps even inspired the social, economic, and political progress recorded throughout Asia. The war was compared with every engagement from Valley Forge[19] to Cuba,[20] the course related to that taken by every president since Franklin Roosevelt.[21]

As to their distribution, the themes were dispersed in an

irregular but not fortuitous pattern. There was a concentration upon SEATO, the right of choice, a better life, and peoples' wars in February 1966, when, at the United Nations Security Council, before the Senate Foreign Relations Committee, and in Honolulu with the leaders of Saigon, the government was called upon to define and defend its position. In May, attempting to put the large toll of American deaths in perspective with the approach of Memorial Day, officials underscored the connection between the crisis in Southeast Asia and the whole line of U.S. interventions since 1945. During the weeks after the start of bombing raids upon oil depots in Hanoi and Haiphong in late June, as if to obscure their novelty, Washington cited the "good" that America had achieved for that whole area by protecting Vietnam and, once again, the importance of not breaking its promises. President Johnson toured Asia that fall and conferred with his Pacific allies; impelled again to justify his decisions, he focused upon the significance of the experiences at Munich, the demands imposed by the national interest, and the limited goal of self-determination.

In texture, in content, and in intensity, 1966 marked an extreme. The government, in an enormous effort to clarify its case, to rationalize its policy, to enlist domestic and foreign support for a war which was beginning to impinge upon the lives of more and more people, offered a confused and desperate, almost baroque caricature of itself. Perhaps acknowledging this, realizing that emotional oratory was ruled by a law of saturation and understanding that its speeches were becoming divining rods for dissent, there was a deescalation and defusing of the rhetoric in the year which followed.

The signs of that process were various and abundant. The grossest index, total statements, reflected a 20 percent decline. Of particularly emotive language, references to aggression fell from ninety-seven to fifty-four; to self-determination, from sixteen to eight; to communism, from sixty-one to thirty-one. There was a halving of allusions to North Vietnam's ambitions for conquest, for takeover, for seizure. Concern for the fate of the hundred little countries entirely exhausted itself and the excitement about promoting a Vietnamese social revolution virtually did. There was less insistence that American fidelity was at issue and fewer specific denials that the battle was a civil war.

The Munich analogy was struck in twelve speeches, the test case rationale expressed in three, the comparisons with Greece, Berlin, and Turkey made in five—each having occurred seventeen, eleven, and sixteen times respectively the year before. Declarations of disinterest in bases was down two-thirds, and the aim of allowing Vietnam to select its own course was off by one half, though since it was cited on twenty-six occasions it continued, along with "commitments," to represent the core of the administration's position.

The moderation of the official message was one distinctive aspect of 1967; another was the launching of two offensives.

The first, which took place between February and April, was primarily a military phenomenon. On February 22 American artillery was fired across the demilitarized zone for the first time. Four days later the United States Navy began the unrestricted shelling of enemy supply routes and the Air Force, the mining of their rivers. On March 10 attacks were initiated against North Vietnam's iron and steel works; on April 21, against its power plants; on April 24, against its MIG bases. Some of these activities were reported by the Department of Defense, some by the command in Saigon. All were minimized and presented as natural extensions of established procedures.

The second offensive, which spanned the autumn months, was an entirely verbal affair. It began in San Antonio on September 29, somewhat after the commencement of strikes near the Chinese border and the disclosure that the president may have ignored a possible opening for negotiations, somewhat before the planned demonstration at the Pentagon, and in the midst of a rising tide of congressional and public criticism. It included all the familiar themes.

There was renewed concentration on the solemn obligations of SEATO and on the congressional approval symbolized in the Tonkin Resolution. There was much talk of the need that Washington fulfill its pledges and another spate of injunctions that the people of South Vietnam have the right of choice. Officials again stressed the strategic relationship between Indochina and Southeast Asia with the variation that the relationship was explained by quoting the warnings of Asian authorities. They also placed special emphasis on the likelihood that a defeat in Vietnam would foreshadow a larger and more expensive struggle—potentially World War III.

But the significance of the period was that it signaled a basic shift in the focus of U.S. justifications. The previously parenthetical line that American welfare was at stake in Southeast Asia became the central point in defense of U.S. actions. Self-determination was important, as were international agreements, but the principal factor, the reason for America's intervention, was that the national interest was directly and intimately involved.

"The key to all we have done," Mr. Johnson had declared in Texas at the end of September,[22] "is our own security." On October 12, asked to clarify that claim, Dean Rusk revived the menace of China, and China, which the cultural revolution had excised from the rhetoric the previous August, was briefly a major figure again. But even when, by November, China had submerged again, America's peril remained.

In terms of basic elements, the fundamental arguments advanced, there had been little substantive change in the government's rationale between 1964 and 1967. Nor was there much change in substance in 1968. Spokemen still cited dominoes, wars of liberation, Munich; still discussed national security, SEATO, the legacy of three presidents; still spoke of aggression and communism, larger battles and free choice. But in 1968, as in 1967, they dealt with these things at a generally diminished level of intensity. The process of defusing and de-escalating the oratory, which began in 1967, continued unabated the following year.

Allusions to Munich were less frequent and more moderate, and the predictions of a costlier war were down by a half. Comparisons of the Vietnam engagements with others met since 1945, professions of a lack of any desire for bases, both of which had dropped substantially in 1967, dropped again. References to Hanoi as a state bent on conquest decreased, far exceeded by neutral accounts of its infiltration and its regular troop strength in the South. Partly because of revelations made during the Senate hearings in February, which cast doubt upon the circumstances of its passage, the Tonkin Resolution ceased to be mentioned after March. The total number of attacks on the roles of Russia and China dwindled from twenty-one to five. The charge of "aggression" was leveled 55 percent as often.

Not every line, however, was marked by a decline. There was a relative increase in demands that the people of Vietnam be allowed to determine their own future; with the start of negotiations with the enemy, there was a fresh need to reiterate U.S. terms. There was an absolute rise in statements describing the growing South Vietnamese military responsibilities, a rise responsive to public insistence that the burden of the fighting be shifted to Saigon.

Nor was each line recited only on isolated occasions. An obscure version of the domino principle and a familiar one of the commitment theory were offered with regularity until December.

Nor were concerted efforts to enlist national support entirely abandoned. In March, after the disastrously impressive enemy offensive at Tet, the government engaged in a last major campaign to defend its position. In a barrage of commentary, it again underscored the bipartisan origins of its policy, the importance that America meet its obligations and comply with its treaties, and emphasized the primary influence of concern for the nation's welfare upon the decision to intervene.

None of these phenomena, however, marked a deviation from the general trend. Talk of self-determination and transfer of responsibility to Saigon was related not to pursuing the war, but to the process of disengagement from it; the themes that were still regularly recited had been recited even more regularly the year before; all of the issues stressed in March fell off sharply after April. There was no departure from the overall pattern of gradually deintensifying the justification of U.S. involvement in Asia.

This pattern was simply reconfirmed in the first five months of 1969, as the new administration sought to represent itself as occupied with effecting a withdrawal from Vietnam and, therefore, not interested in rearguing the case for entry. From January through May, Southeast Asia was given no more coverage than it had received in 1964, with policy statements being made less often than in 1953.

Nevertheless, the infrequent reviews of the warfare revealed a continuing tendency to focus on the role of North Vietnam, as opposed to the Vietcong, largely to ignore the help supplied by Moscow and Peking, and to avoid describing the struggle in terms of communism or aggression. There was as well the same insistence that the people of South Vietnam be permitted to decide their own course.

One major address on Southeast Asia was offered, delivered by the president in May.[23] Though it began with a plea for an end to the "old formulas and the tired rhetoric of the past," by the conclusion it had managed to recapitulate most of the lines of a familiar rationale: Asian opinion that America must remain in Vietnam if it would not weaken the security of the entire region; the necessity that the United States live up to its obligations and the danger that a failure to do so would destroy confidence in American credibility; the likelihood that a Western defeat would encourage and enhance the status of militants within the Communist world; the probability that it would also increase the eventual risk of a larger war; the renunciation of national advantages and the guarantee of free choice for the Vietnamese.

Perhaps the most striking thing about the defense of U.S. policy mounted in the years 1949–1969 was the enormous degree of underlying rhetorical continuity. There were recurrent broad themes: opposition to political change achieved through force which was central to the characterization of Russia, China, North Vietnam, and to the treatment of communism and aggression; disapproval of colonialism, embodied in the unqualified rejection of military or economic objectives, the foreswearing of a role in Vietnamese internal affairs, the stress on the right of self-determination. Some narrower themes recurred as well: the urging that Saigon be self-reliant, the emphasis on the importance of congressional support for presidential initiatives, the denial that the struggle was a civil war. And the principal justifications remained the same. Throughout officials defended American involvement by striking chords of fear, with prophesies of the strategic calamities which would ensue from a failure to stop the enemy in Indochina. And throughout they appealed to idealism and hope, implying that the United States had a responsibility as the greatest country in the world to look after those weaker and less fortunate, and insure them the chance to shape their own destinies and enjoy the minimal conditions of modern life.

In two very conspicuous ways, however, the rhetoric of the years after 1964 differed from that of the years before. First, there was the introduction of historical reference, with the implicit warning that the learning of the past must be applied consistently to the challenges of the present. What happened at Munich in 1939, in Korea in 1950, what Presidents Eisenhower and Kennedy decided about Southeast Asia, were experiences and facts with a bearing on current planning. Second, there was the advancing of another major justification, enlisting the values of honor and civilized morality. There was an insistence that the United States ought to act ethically in its dealings with other nations and ought to fulfill its obligations once undertaken because it was both right and honorable to do so. History and law became central elements in the official case once Vietnam became a pivotal problem in American foreign affairs.

Though there were no basic distinctions between Democratic and Republican oratory within each of the two decades, there were distinctions between the two decades in the manner in which respective governments divided the oratorical labors: in the 1950s the secretaries of state, Dean Acheson and John Foster Dulles, assumed the burden of discussing Southeast Asia; in the 1960s, in all three administrations, the presidents bore that onus. In only one year, 1964, did a secretary of defense have a greater public role to play than a secretary of state, and only in 1968 did a vice president have a larger one. The 1964 phenomenon may have reflected an internal decision that the Pentagon would be charged with overseeing the war, though this is unclear; the 1968 phenomenon was less obscure: in that year, Hubert Humphrey sought the presidency.

While on occasion every major administration official could be counted upon to provide a detailed rehearsal of his government's case, there were, over the long run, particular points with which each came to be associated.[24] Mr. Dulles, the thorough legal scholar, would often trace the impact of Stalinist and Leninist doctrine upon the revolutionary program of the Vietminh, and four-star General Dwight Eisenhower liked to discuss the relation between social and psychological factors and military victory. Ambassador Goldberg dealt especially with America's disinterest in Far Eastern gain and the principle of self-determination, key tenets of the U.S. position which he was called upon repeatedly to enunciate as United Nations representative, while Mr. Humphrey, consistent with his longstanding advocacy of improvements in social welfare, regularly heralded the goal of eliminating sickness, ignorance, and poverty from Asia. Robert McNamara, systems analyst and onetime automobile executive, introduced and was the main proponent of the argument that Washington had to meet wars of liberation, contending that this primitive, new line was designed to challenge America's resourcefulness and ingenuity. Former international lawyer Dean Rusk was preoccupied with the effect of U.S. abandonment of its treaty obligations in Vietnam upon the structure of world peace; he took great pains, as well, to review the gross similarities between the crisis facing the West in 1965 and that which it had faced, and he had misread, thirty years before. To Mr. Johnson, acutely aware that he was part of the ongoing tradition of the presidency, and concerned with the respect accorded that institution, it was the historical perspective—prewar isolationism and postwar interventionism—and the integrity of the American government—the need to observe the commitments and promises made by his predecessors—which emerged as the most significant themes.

THE TROUBLEMAKERS

The Dissenters' Line on the Government

Washington's case for Vietnam, outlined broadly in 1954 and elaborated and expanded a decade later, was stated in its most extreme form in 1966. In that year as well a series of books and articles began to appear which, more systematically than ever before, challenged the government's rationale. Of the spate of publications which emerged between 1966 and 1969, among the most interesting were Theodore Draper's *Abuse of Power*, Arthur Schlesinger's *The Bitter Heritage, The Arrogance*

IN THE FINAL ANALYSIS 195

of Power by J. William Fulbright, *American Power and the New Mandarins* by Noam Chomsky, and Carl Oglesby's *Vietnamese Crucible*.

Each of these writers offered an articulate and individualistic analysis of U.S. policies in Southeast Asia. Theodore Draper recapitulated in detail America's progressive involvement, interpreting it as a function of a misplaced reliance on military measures when confronted with what were essentially political problems. More briefly and discursively, Mr. Schlesinger discussed the war as the product of an unfortunate but not entirely incomprehensible moral commitment to Indochina made in the 1950s, a commitment which evolved and deepened largely through inadvertence. To Senator Fulbright, Vietnam was but another episode in the government's continuing mission to spread the gospel of democracy and oppose without qualification any movement associated at all with pagan communism. Professor Chomsky's was, in some sense, the only morally impassioned critique: he denounced the Southeast Asia adventure as a calculated and thorough attempt to reorganize the whole of Vietnamese culture according to the programs drawn by the self-proclaimed experts of the liberal, intellectual elite. By far the most fascinating and original treatment was that of Carl Oglesby, for whom intervention in Asia was only the paradigm case of a two-hundred-year quest for an American economic empire.

Each writer wrote from a unique and very personal perspective: Theodore Draper as an international historian; Arthur Schlesinger as a former adviser to President Kennedy; William Fulbright as chairman of the Senate Foreign Relations Committee; Noam Chomsky as a renowned academic; Carl Oglesby as a political activist of the New Left. Yet despite differences in their approaches and emphases, in their style and backgrounds, each, more often than not, struck the same basic themes.

All five, in various ways, disputed the existence of a universal Communist menace and, therefore, the implication that communism was the underlying reason for the Vietnam war. Mr. Draper and Professor Schlesinger dismissed the idea as an outmoded perception: a generation ago an international conspiracy did threaten the free world, but the process of decentralization, epitomized in the Sino-Soviet rift, signaled the end of an inflexible party line and invalidated the automatic assumption of hostility between Communist nations and the West. Mr. Draper[25] cited Washington's "continued reluctance to come to terms with the centrifugal forces in the Communist world," the "intersecting lines of tactics and doctrine."

Professor Schlesinger[26] was more specific and disparaging:

> The cliches about a centralized communist conspiracy aiming at monolithic world revolution are still cherished in the State Department in spite of what has struck lay observers as a rather evident fragmentation of the communist world. Thus, as late as May 9, 1965, after half a dozen years of vociferous Russo-Chinese quarreling, Thomas C. Mann, then No. 3 man in the Department, could babble about "instruments of Sino-Soviet power" and "orders from the Sino-Soviet military bloc." As late as January 28, 1966, the Secretary of State was still running on about "their world revolution" and again, on February 18, about "the Communists" and their "larger design."
>
> While the department may have finally accepted the reality of the Russo-Chinese schism, it still does not grasp the larger implications of the shattering of communist universality. For this schism has done a good deal more than simply to divide Russia and China: what it has done is to set all communist states free to pursue national policies. It has thereby transformed the character of the communist problem. . . . In the thirties or forties, if the communists took over a country, the result was to heighten the threat to the security of the democratic world. But in the age of polycentrism the extension of communism no longer means an extension of Russian, or of Chinese power . . . such a development, however deplorable, does not *per se* create a deadly strategic threat to the security of the democracies.

Senator Fulbright,[27] taking a more extreme position, denied that the "Communist menace" had ever been an appropriate description of reality; what was menacing was not Marxist theory but the revolutionary ardor with which it was practiced, and those excesses were more a function of revolutions in general than of the teachings of particular ideologies:

> The point that I wish to make is not that communism is not a harsh and, to us, repugnant system of organizing society, but that its doctrine has redeeming tenets of humanitarianism; that the worst thing about it is not its philosophy but its fanaticism; that history suggests the probability of an abatement of revolutionary

fervour; that in practice fanaticism *has* abated in a number of countries including the Soviet Union; that some countries probably are better off under communist rule than they were under preceding regimes; that some people may even want to live under communism.

The other two were totally skeptical, discounting the supposed peril as nothing more than a convenient ploy. Mr. Chomsky[28] dubbed the "international Communist conspiracy" a "perfect propaganda device." Mr. Oglesby[29] suggested it was only "a beauty mark" applied to mask "an unbecoming truth."

All were unanimous, as well, in rejecting the claim that the war was a simple case of aggression from the North. Their rejection rested on three grounds. First, that participation by Hanoi was minimal. "Until about 1960," Theodore Draper[30] wrote, "the Vietcong was strictly a Southern enterprise, and until 1965 the Northern contribution was mainly limited to training." Although thereafter, the North expanded its assistance, supplying Army regulars, Arthur Schlesinger[31] noted that the number of their soldiers "amount to only a small fraction of the total enemy force." Carl Oglesby[32] quoted the figure of "no more than 18 percent." Noam Chomsky[33] offered this comparison: "the role of North Vietnam in 'externally directed violence' has always been, and now [in 1967] remains, far slighter than our own."

Second, the mere presence of foreign armies, the bare fact of external influence, did not determine that the conflict was an armed attack. Mr. Draper[34] maintained that in deciding the issue of whether a battle was a civil war or aggression, it was "necessary to view the struggle as a whole, as a historical entity from beginning to end." Northern help, therefore, did not close the question. The war in Spain from 1936 to 1939, which he insisted "was integrally and profoundly a civil war," was also a war in which "foreign troops and matériel on a large scale were introduced on both sides." Mr. Oglesby[35] contended similarly that "the presence of outside troops or the making of alliances or the interference on either side of third party states proves nothing whatsoever about the internal political nature of the conflict." As evidence he adduced the American War for Independence:

Recall the extent to which our own revolution was directly and indirectly supported by France, Spain and Holland. Recall our national feeling for Lafayette. Recall the 3000 British freighters the French helped sink in support of our revolutionary cause. Recall that General Washington's troops were outnumbered at Yorktown by their French comrades under General Rochambeau. Recall that Washington chose to fight the battle of Yorktown largely because Admiral de Grasse promised to sail from the West Indies to land 3000 French troops with cannon on James Island, and that Washington won that battle largely because de Grasse searched out, engaged, and defeated the British fleet protecting Cornwallis' rear.

Third, the characterization of an invasion was inherently inapt since North and South Vietnam were parts of the same country. Mr. Draper,[36] Mr. Fulbright,[37] Mr. Chomsky,[38] and Mr. Oglesby[39] all reviewed the terms of the 1954 Geneva Agreement which explicitly stated, "the military demarcation line is provisional and should not in any way be interpreted as constituting a political or territorial boundary." Senator Fulbright[40] observed that what Hanoi was doing was no different "from what the American North did to the American South a hundred years ago."

Each of the five had equal difficulty in accepting the view that Peking was the actual threat in Vietnam. Chinese words, however belligerent, however much encouragement they gave the North, had not been translated into Chinese actions. Professor Schlesinger[41] called China's foreign policy "a compound of polemical ferocity and practical prudence." William Fulbright[42] urged that a "distinction must be made between what they say and what they do, between what they might like to do and what they are able or likely to be able to do"; he pointed out that even in 1966, when "the United States had some three hundred thousand troops, . . . the Chinese had only work teams supporting the North Vietnamese." Mr. Chomsky[43] spoke of Chairman Mao, "in his cunning way, committing aggression without troops" and Mr. Oglesby[44] talked of the China which "does nearly nothing for the Vietnamese but make speeches." Theodore Draper[45] summed up these impressions: "there is something hallucinatory about the theory that Communist China is the real enemy in Vietnam."

Professors Chomsky, Schlesinger, and Draper took specific

exception to the administration's analysis of Marshal Lin Piao's September 1965 article as proof that the Chinese specter in Vietnam was not illusory; disregarding the standard diatribe, it proved nothing other than China's unwillingness to involve itself directly in other peoples' wars. Mr. Chomsky[46] cited Peking's insistence "through the medium of Lin Piao, that indigenous wars of national liberation can expect little from China beyond applause." Mr. Schlesinger[47] reported that, after studying the document, the Rand Corporation had concluded that

> it was a message to the Viet Cong that they could win "only if they rely primarily on their own resources and their own revolutionary spirit," and that it revealed "the lack, rather than the extent, of Peking's past and present control over Hanoi's actions."

Mr. Draper[48] returned to the original text and the passage from which that conclusion had been drawn:

> "In order to make a revolution and to fight a people's war and be victorious, it is imperative to adhere to the policy of self reliance, rely on the strength of the masses in one's own country and prepare to carry on the fight independently even when all material aid from outside is cut off. If one does not operate by one's own efforts, does not independently ponder and solve the problems of the revolution in one's own country and does not rely on the strength of the masses, *but leans wholly on foreign aid—even though this be aid from socialist countries* which persist in revolution—no victory can be won, or be consolidated even if it is won." (my italics—T.D.)

There was no disagreement among them about the true relationship between Peking and Hanoi: government implications notwithstanding, twenty centuries of mutual suspicion and warfare made it unlikely that a victorious Ho Chi Minh would simply deliver his prize to Chairman Mao:

> Professor P.J. Horney, who has studied the subject more carefully perhaps than anyone else, reminds us that two thousand years of Vietnamese-Chinese relations have left the Vietnamese with feelings toward the Chinese "not unlike those of the Irish for the English of Oliver Cromwell's day." Though the Vietnamese have learned to respect and fear the Chinese, they dislike them even more.

THEODORE DRAPER, p. 129

North Vietnam [is] imbued with historic mistrust of China.

ARTHUR SCHLESINGER, p. 80

For our purposes, the significance of Ho Chi Minh's nationalism is that it is associated with what Bernard Fall called "the 2000-year old distrust in Vietnam of everything Chinese."

WILLIAM FULBRIGHT, p. 114

I will not dwell on the fact that all reputable authorities agree that the Vietnamese are strongly anti-Chinese.

NOAM CHOMSKY, p. 208

Maxwell Taylor has been . . . explicit about the alleged master-puppet relationship between China and North Vietnam. "To Hanoi," he told the New York Rotarians early in 1966, "China is the traditional, distrusted enemy." This must mean he is at least skeptical about the often insinuated, never proved surrogate theory, and when Taylor is skeptical others must be hardened nonbelievers.

CARL OGLESBY, p. 25

Challenging Washington for characterizing the battle for Vietnam as a struggle against international communism, a war of aggression from the North, a conflict to contain China, they challenged too the justifications imposed upon these characterizations. The affirmative goals that America set for itself were attacked for being essentially sham. Carl Oglesby[49] labeled "all the arguments about culture, freedom, and the rights of man . . . nothing but tactical positions which can always, if necessary, be exchanged." On the emptiness of the demand that South Vietnam be "free to determine its own future," Noam Chomsky[50] noted:

> that the regime we imposed excluded all those who took part in the struggle against French colonialism, "and properly so" (Secretary Rusk, 1963); that we have since been attempting to suppress a "civil insurrection" (General Stillwell) led by the only "truly mass-based political party in South Vietnam" (Douglas Pike); that we supervised the destruction of Buddhist opposition; that we offered the peasants a "free choice" between the Saigon government and the National Liberation Front by herding them into strategic hamlets from which NLF cadres and sympathizers were eliminated by police (Roger Hilsman); and so on.

Ridicule was also heaped on the proposition that the United States had come to Asia to eradicate hunger, illiteracy, poverty, and disease. Theodore Draper,[51] on the one hand, maintained, "No one, to be sure, was expected to take the 'Declaration of Honolulu' seriously," and dismissed it as "flights of social fancy." Arthur Schlesinger,[52] on the other, contended that "if meant seriously, the idea of a Great Society for Asia is surely a fantastic overcommitment of American thought and resources." Furthermore, Senator Fulbright[53] remarked,

> One wonders whether the "Asian Doctrine" will reap for the United States as rich a harvest of affection and democracy as has the Monroe Doctrine. One wonders whether China will accept American hegemony as gracefully as Cuba and the Dominican Republic have accepted it. And one wonders, whether anyone ever thought of asking the Asians if they really want to join the Great Society.

Though their objections were diverse, none of the five was any more persuaded by the domino principle, the Munich analogy, or the test case rationale.

Mr. Fulbright[54] criticized the domino principle for being wholly open-ended; accepting the premise that all Southeast Asia was unstable, he argued that the principle would justify either intervention or withdrawal:

> the domino theory . . . holds that if one country falls to the communists, so must another and then another. The inference we have drawn from this is that we must fight in one country in order to avoid having to fight in another, although we could with equal logic have inferred that it is useless to fight in one country when the same conditions of conflict are present in another, that the failure of subversion in one country might simply result in the transfer of subversion to another.

Theodore Draper,[55] by contrast, regarded the situation in Vietnam as unique, not duplicated anywhere else in the region, and precisely because it was atypical, he rejected the principle, not for being ambiguous, but for being too facile and simplistic.

> In order for a domino theory now to operate in Southeast Asia, it would be necessary to assume that conditions in at least several countries resemble those in Vietnam of the past twenty years. That is, it would be necessary to assume that a number of Com-

munist parties were capable of doing the equivalent of what the Vietnamese Communists had done—inaugurated an armed struggle against French colonial rule in 1946; inflicted a total of 172,000 casualties on the French armed forces in the next eight years; compelled a far larger French army to capitulate in 1954; resumed the struggle in South Vietnam five or six years later; drove the United States to intervene in force to stave off a South Vietnamese defeat in 1965; obligated most of the South Vietnamese forces to withdraw from the front lines in 1966. . . .

As far as I know, no other Southeast Asian Communist Party comes near to fulfilling these specifications.

"Victory" itself, he went on, was not finally decisive, despite the principle. A U.S. "victory" after all "the failures which have already marked American policy in Vietnam" could still "have adverse repercussions on American influence and interest elsewhere, especially in neighboring countries of Southeast Asia"; a North Vietnamese "victory" not consolidated with "economic as well as revolutionary success," which did not set an "irresistible example" for others to follow, might have no effects at all.

Theoretically unsound, the principle also defied reality. In the Western Hemisphere "the Latin American dominoes did not fall after Castro's victory." In the Far East, the loss of North Vietnam to the Communists in 1954 was "an undeniable reverse," but "it was not a dreadful or even a major catastrophe." Arthur Schlesinger[56] had taken a similar tack: in 1949 "the biggest domino of all, China, had fallen . . . without starting the chain reaction."

Like the others, Carl Oglesby[57] dismissed the domino theory, describing it as "primitive, paranoid, and mechanistic." As a formula for persuasion, he noted, it had had a long and celebrated past. In 1779, King George had defended his campaign against the colonies with the prediction that if America succeeded

> "the West Indies must follow them, not [toward] independence, but must for its own interest be dependent on North America; Ireland would soon follow the same plan and be a separate state, then this Island would be reduced to itself, and soon would be a poor island, indeed."

But what most disturbed Mr. Oglesby was not Washington's lack of subtlety or of inventiveness, but its lack of candor. In propounding the domino principle, a principle which, though overstated, had a core of validity, the government had deliberately mischaracterized the issues. The danger of revolutionary change arose not because communism threatened freedom but because "nationalism is a threat to imperialism." Hanoi, not Washington, was on the side of right, but for purposes of domestic consumption the truth had been obscured: the labels were altered and the poles of Good and Evil reversed.

Both Mr. Fulbright[58] and Mr. Schlesinger[59] began their treatment of the comparisons between Europe in the thirties and Asia three decades after with a warning about the hazards inherent in efforts to divine relevance from history. Each quoted Mark Twain's graphic injunction to

> "be careful to get out of an experience only the wisdom that is in it—and stop there; lest we be like the cat that sits down on a hot stove-lid. She will never sit down on a hot stove-lid again— and that is well; but also she will never sit down on a cold one anymore."

To equate "North Vietnam's involvement in South Vietnam" with "Hitler's invasion of Poland" or "a parley with the Vietcong" with "'another Munich'" was, Mr. Fulbright[60] continued, to treat "slight and superficial resemblances as if they were full-blooded analogies—as instances, as it were, of history 'repeating itself.'" As such, it was "a substitute for thinking."

"Historical generalizations," Mr. Schlesinger[61] observed more broadly, "make large-scale, long term prediction possible. But they do not justify small-scale, short term prediction." Proceeding from that maxim, he then denied there was a

> useful parallel between Hitler, the man on the bicycle who could not stop, a madman commanding vast military force and requiring immediate and visible success, and the ragged bands and limited goals of Ho Chi Minh.

Nor was there a parallel

> between Europe—a developed continent with well-defined national frontiers, interests and identities and a highly organized equilibrium of power—and Southeast Asia, an underdeveloped subcontinent filled with fictitious states in vague, chaotic, and unpredictable revolutionary ferment.

Carl Oglesby[62] also failed to appreciate the analogy, dismissing as "Munich-bemused" those officials who held "that the two halves of Vietnam relate to one another as Germany and Czechoslovakia of 1938." As for those who regarded China and not North Vietnam as the Asian Germany, they were in Theodore Draper's[63] mind not only hopelessly bemused, but utterly blind, totally missing the point of the lesson they so insistently claimed should be applied:

> And if there were anything to the analogy, the United States should have struck at the source of the trouble. Perhaps the last word on the misuse of the analogy with Germany and Czechoslovakia in 1938 was said by Hannah Arendt. . . . "It is as if France or England would have tried to stop Hitler, not by making war on him, but by making war on Slovakia as being somehow in collusion with the Nazi government against the Czech government. They would have started bombing Bratislava and intervening in what could only have been a civil war in Czechoslovakia."

Professor Chomsky's[64] demurrer was, by far, the most extreme:

> The unpleasant fact is that if one wishes to pursue the Munich analogy there is only one plausible contender for the role of Hitler. . . . Arnold Toynbee has put the matter quite succinctly: "The President manifestly feels that he is speaking with Churchill's voice—the Churchill of 1940—but to the ears of peoples who have suffered from Western domination in the past, his voice sounds like the Kaiser's and like Hitler's."

The test case rationale was attacked on three levels. First, a defeat for the United States would not necessarily or automatically encourage the outbreak of peoples' wars in other countries; that would depend mainly on the dynamics of the local situation:

> guerilla warfare is not a tactic to be mechanically applied by central headquarters to faraway countries. More than any other form of warfare, it is dependent on conditions and opportunities within the countries themselves. Defeating communist guerillas in Greece, the Philippines, Malaya and Venezuela . . . did not prevent guerilla warfare in Vietnam. Whether there are wars of national liberation in Uganda and Peru will depend, not on what happens in Vietnam but on what happens in Uganda and Peru.[65]

Second, wars of national liberation have been, by and large, a failure as a Communist tactic in underdeveloped areas; most upheavals for independence have not been directed by Marxists:

> The successes of the Viet Cong, Dr. Zagoria [a leading China expert] points out, should not "obscure the more fundamental fact that communists have been unable to seize control of a nationalist movement anywhere else in Asia, Africa or Latin America since the start of the Second World War."[66]

Third, an American victory would not preclude other, similar confrontations; an expensive triumph might well incite such struggles elsewhere:

> If the Communists of other impoverished, diminutive Southeast Asian countries could be sure of making us spend so much blood and treasure on frustrating them, . . . we might well be faced with an epidemic of such wars. In this sense, the Vietnamese war, however it may end, has been more an encouragement than a discouragement to other wars of "national liberation."[67]

Nor was the general contention that Washington had a vital national interest in the region any more credible or readily accepted. Mr. Draper[68] reported with approval Senator Richard Russell's appraisal that there was no " 'strategic, political, or economic advantage to be gained by our [Vietnam] involvement' "; on grounds of "strategic significance" and "cultural accessibility," Arthur Schlesinger[69] maintained, "Western Europe and Latin America are the parts of the world which matter most to the United States. We could survive the subjection of Asia . . . by a hostile power or ideology"; Mr. Chomsky[70] indicated that the welfare of the American people was hardly "served" by "100,000 casualties and 100 billion dollars expended in the attempt to subjugate a small country halfway around the world," and Mr. Fulbright[71] stated that "opposing communism" when, as in Vietnam, it was encountered along with "nationalism" was a "cruel and all but impossible task," distinctly not "in our interest." Carl Oglesby,[72] in contrast, demonstrated that Vietnam was indeed vital to America—if it were assumed that it was America's mission to establish a global economic empire.

While there was less discussion of purported U.S. commitments, what did occur was no less dissenting. President Eisenhower's October 1954 letter to Mr. Diem was discounted by Theodore Draper[73] as being quite clearly a "conditional" promise, a program of assistance to the Republic of Vietnam whose grant was expressly contingent upon " 'assurances as to the standards of performance it would be able to maintain in the event such aid were supplied,' " offered with the stipulation that " 'needed reforms' " be undertaken. Furthermore, Professor Schlesinger[74] reminded, "[It] contemplated only economic and political support for the Saigon government. It was not a warrant for military intervention."

Mr. Oglesby[75] found the Southeast Asia Treaty hardly any more "unambiguously binding," remarking that it had "even more escape clauses in it than has NATO's." Mr. Draper[76] concluded, similarly, that the pact was both "noncommittal" and "permissive." In support of that conclusion he adduced Secretary Dulles's November 1954 acknowledgment that the agreement " 'does not attempt to get into the difficult question as to precisely how we act,' " and Ambassador Lodge's unqualified concession eleven years later " 'that the action we are taking in Vietnam is not under the aegis of any international organization. It is not under the aegis of the United Nations or the Southeast Asia Treaty Organization—SEATO.' " The idea that America was required to intervene as a result of the treaty Arthur Schlesinger[77] dismissed as quite simply "audacious," a bald "excercise in historical and legal distortion." As for the eight-member organization itself, Senator Fulbright[78] judged that to be just "non-functioning."

The related argument, that the issue in Vietnam had become one of U.S. reliability as a guarantor of world security, that disengagement from Southeast Asia would undercut the confidence of America's allies in the value of all American pledges, was turned on its head. The assertion that "our global reputation is at stake," Mr. Oglesby[79] wrote,

> cuts both ways. No less than President Johnson, the dissenters consider themselves to be the partisans of America's prestige, which they define differently. The only question is, What kind of reputation do we want our country to have.

"It is contended by American policy-makers," William Fulbright[80] noted,

> that if the United States makes major concessions in Vietnam, the credibility of our other guarantees and commitments will be undermined and countries which depend on America's support, from Thailand to Germany, will lose faith in the United States.

He continued:

> There may be something in this but not much. In fact many of America's allies are more inclined to worry about an undue American preoccupation with Vietnam than to fear the consequences of an American withdrawal.

Mr. Schlesinger[81] made much the same charge—far from enhancing U.S. prestige, "the Vietnam obsession has stultified our policy and weakened our position in both [Western Europe and Latin America]"; there is "the spreading impression that the United States, in its preoccupation with Vietnam, has lost interest in its western allies."

All of them, in the end, denounced Washington's public defense. To Senator Fulbright,[82] it was "the official rhetoric"; to Professor Chomsky,[83] "the government's propaganda"; to Carl Oglesby,[84] "slogans of a hard-sell sales campaign"; to Mr. Schlesinger,[85] "flim-flam, showmanship and manipulation"; to Mr. Draper,[86] "a squirming mass of contradictions, evasions, half-truths, and worse."

They went, however, beyond sheer denunciation, beyond academic rebuttals, to launch an affirmative case of their own. The brief they argued was made up of five major points. First, the leadership of the Republic of Vietnam was authoritarian, unresponsive, and corrupt. Theodore Draper[87] described the ruling body as "a self-imposed military junta ... without a shred of legitimacy and social conscience"; Arthur Schlesinger[88] branded it a "shaky Saigon regime led by right-wing mandarins or air force generals." Mr. Fulbright[89] referred to the "weak, dictatorial government which does not command the loyalty of the South Vietnamese people," and Mr. Oglesby,[90] to those "elite Vietnamese sympathetic enough with our own politics to have been allowed their hour in the Saigon Presidential Palace." To Noam Chomsky[91] it was just an American "puppet government" which lacked "even the legitimacy of those set up [in the 1930s] by Germany and Japan."

Second, the Vietcong, while brutal and repressive, had continued to command the sympathy and respect of a large proportion of the native population. Mr. Draper,[92] Mr. Schlesinger,[93] and Mr. Chomsky[94] each included in his book a passage from a *New York Times* article by journalist Neil Sheehan, composed at the completion of his second Southeast Asia tour, attesting to the compelling power of the rebels:

> "idealism and dedication are largely the prerogative of the enemy....
>
> In Vietnam, only the Communists represent revolution and social change.... The Communist party is the only truly national organization that permeates both North and South Vietnam ... [and] despite their brutality and deceit, [the Communists] remain the only Vietnamese capable of rallying millions of their countrymen to sacrifice and hardship in the name of the nation and the only group not dependent on foreign bayonets for survival."

Third, the intervention by the United States, undertaken to foreclose or at least limit Chinese influence in southern Asia, had served only to expand it; American military action was mediating the historic antagonism between North Vietnam and China. The whole thrust of Washington's policy had not been "to pry Peking and Hanoi apart but to drive them together."[95] Its effect was the transformation of an "Asian Tito" into "a Chinese 'Ulbricht' "[96] and the destruction of "perhaps the only potential bulwark against Chinese domination of Vietnam."[97] "If we were really interested in containing Chinese expansionism," Professor Chomsky[98] advised, "we should presumably be supporting Ho Chi Minh, along with all popular, indigenous forces on the border of China."

Fourth, the United States was systematically destroying the land and people of the nation it had come to save. Senator Fulbright[99] reported that "American bombs [were] falling on Vietnamese jungles and villages in a volume equal to that of the bombing of Germany's great industrial cities at the height of the Second World War." Mr. Schlesinger[100] added another statistic:

Already our bombers roam over the hapless country dumping more tonnage of explosives each month than we were dropping per month on all Europe and Africa during the Second World War—more in a year than we dropped in the entire Pacific during the Second World War.

Theodore Draper[101] supplied a detailed description of a campaign mounted in January and February 1967, to clear out Vietcong concentrations in the South:

> When American forces moved in, they found few enemy troops, but they proceeded to complete the destruction of the homes and villages, to which the native inhabitants could never come back, as well as camps and tunnels. These operations were designed to make the areas unusable by the enemy or to destroy whatever usefulness they had had. In the process, however, increasingly large areas of South Vietnam were desolated, thousands of noncombatants were displaced from their ancestral dwellings, and where there had been for decades and even centuries a human culture, however simple or primitive, there was now a wasteland. . . . There was no way of denying land to one's enemy in South Vietnam without devastating the land of one's friends.

Mr. Chomsky[102] described the situation a year later:

> The savage battering of the Vietnamese continues without pause; in scale it is unique in the history of warfare. We learn that aerial bombardment alone exceeds 100 pounds of explosives per person, twelve tons of explosives per square mile, distributed almost equally between North and South Vietnam. Hundreds of thousands of acres have been subjected to defoliation, with what ultimate consequences no one knows. Refugees in South Vietnam are counted in the millions.

"A whole nation beholds itself in the act," Carl Oglesby[103] wrote, "the act being the incineration of a whole other nation."

Fifth, in the process, the United States was systematically destroying itself. Mr. Oglesby[104] cited

> a clear mechanical connection between the war and the problems of the American ghettos. . . . More important still is the spiritual connection. Black America, whose political actions have a complex impact on poor-white America, is at the moment being driven toward total alienation from white power and total

solidarity against a system whose hypocrisies have never before been so nakedly on view.

The war, Mr. Chomsky[105] stated, testified daily to America's "moral degeneration." "In the course of dehumanizing an enemy," William Fulbright[106] observed, "man dehumanizes himself." Professor Schlesinger[107] framed it as a question: "The war began as a struggle for the soul of Vietnam: will it end as a struggle for the soul of America?"

The onslaught of these writers was extraordinarily comprehensive. The heroes were villains. The villains were heroes. The United States in a crusade to defend freedom against communism in Vietnam had served to clear the path for communism in Asia and dim the prospects for the ultimate survival of freedom at home.

While there was agreement that by the middle of the 1960s Washington's course in Vietnam had devolved into a disastrous adventure, there was no consensus on how or where the mistakes had been made. To Mr. Schlesinger and Mr. Draper, the problems presented themselves as problems of execution. American involvement, while perhaps debatable from the start, had become unsatisfactory and impractical only after a time; the war had grown too expensive given the speculative benefits to be derived. To Mr. Oglesby, Mr. Chomsky, and Mr. Fulbright, the program had been flawed in its conception. It had been immoral from the beginning.

All were unanimous, however, in regarding American insolence, American arrogance, and American pride as factors significant to understanding the course of the adventure. Whether they advanced these factors as fundamental causes, or accompanying symptoms of later difficulties, each critic related those difficulties to the tendency of the United States to seek to impose itself upon others, to convert them to its system. Theodore Draper[108] ended his critique with the warning: "All great powers which have overestimated, over-indulged, overextended their power have come to grief." Senator Fulbright[109] opened his with the same caution: "Other great nations . . . have aspired to too much, and by over-extension of effort have declined and then fallen." "Power," he went on to explain, tends to confuse itself with virtue and a great nation is peculiarly susceptible to the idea that its power is a sign of God's favor, conferring upon it a special responsibility for other nations—to make them richer and happier and wiser, to remake them, that is, in its own shining image. Power confuses itself with virtue and tends also to take itself for omnipotence. Once imbued with the idea of a mission, a great nation easily assumes that it has the means as well as the duty to do God's work.

It was imperative, Mr. Schlesinger[110] maintained, for America to confront that issue of

whether this country is a chosen people, uniquely righteous and wise, with a moral mission to all mankind; or whether it is one of many nations in a multifarious world, endowed with traditions and purposes, legitimate but not infallible, as other nations have legitimate and fallible traditions and purposes of their own, and committed not to an American century but to what President Kennedy used to call a world of diversity. . . . The ultimate choice is between messianism and maturity.

Mr. Chomsky[111] bemoaned and decried the "colonialist mentality":

the tolerance by even enlightened American opinion of the notion that we have a perfect right to intervene in the internal affairs of Vietnam, to determine the legitimate elements in South Vietnamese society, and to direct the development of social and political institutions of our choice in that unfortunate country.

"The war is being fought," contended Carl Oglesby,[112] "to determine how and by whom the Vietnamese political economy is to be developed." He concluded:

America's Vietnam policy does not merely illustrate American imperialism, it is a paradigm instance of it; . . . in its fusion of imperialist motive and anti-communist ideology, the war is not only exemplary, it is also climactic.

The Government's Line on Dissent

Highly literate rebuttals, these and others, were one expression of popular disapproval of the Johnson Administration's course in Vietnam. There were also community discussions, teach-ins, partisan addresses, as well as the more dramatic mass demonstrations and rallies. The government was outspoken in its defense of the right of its opponents to make their views known in such ways. Freedom of speech, it said, was the necessary prerogative of men living in a truly democratic society; in America, dissent was a central value, a privilege guaranteed by law and supported by two centuries of tradition.

The initial affirmation of this position came in the late winter of 1965, in the wake of the first sustained wave of public criticism directed at the decision to bomb North Vietnam continually. "Debate's healthy," President Johnson declared unequivocally in March,[113] "It's good for us." In April[114] he rejected the implication that "participants in the national discussion of Vietnam could be appropriately likened to the appeasers of twenty-five or thirty years ago." He maintained on the morning of June 1, "discussion is one of the great strengths of American democracy"; that afternoon he told newsmen, "I am hopeful that every person will always exercise the free speech that the Constitution guarantees him."

In the autumn, in the weeks before and after Armistice Day, there was another spate of opposition activity, inspiring another series of assurances. Commenting on student denuciations of the war, Ambassador Goldberg stressed on October 26 that it was "the role of youth to ask pointed questions." In early November[115] the secretary of state reasserted that the "Government should not interfere with the normal process of democratic discussions in our system." "In a vigorous and thriving democracy such as ours," he went on, "we must have debate and an opportunity for dissent. It would be wrong to try to restrict these opportunities in any way." At the end of the month[116] Presidential Press Secretary Bill Moyers underscored this assertion: "The right of the minority to disagree with . . . [administration] policy is unquestioned." He added that it was Mr. Johnson's view that the exercise of that right was "a healthy sign for the nation."

There were more of these pronouncements the next year. Responding on January 10, 1966, to the possibility of a full-scale congressional investigation of the war, the White House noted that the president had "always welcomed in the past careful

and thorough discussions." Shortly after the Foreign Relations
Committee had concluded their hearings, on February 23, Mr.
Johnson himself reaffirmed that support:

> in these last days there have been questions about what we're
> doing in Vietnam and these questions have been answered
> loudly and clearly for every citizen to see and hear. The strength
> of America can never be sapped by discussion, and we have no
> better nor stronger tradition than open debate.

On March 11 the vice president strongly defended again the
right of U.S. senators to criticize the government.

The graduation period directed the country's attention to
the young, the source of much of the sustained and most vocal
protest; capitalizing on that seasonal interest, officials issued a
barrage of statements attesting to the inviolability of the First
Amendment during the late spring. Speaking at a commencement program at Chatham College on May 22, Robert
McNamara said emphatically, "let us be perfectly clear about
our principles and priorities. This is a nation in which the freedom of dissent is absolutely fundamental." A week later[117]
Secretary Rusk contended that "full and free discussion is essential to the conduct of an effective foreign policy in this age." At
a reception for high school scholars on June 7, President Johnson declared, "No American young or old, must ever be denied
the right to dissent. No minority must ever be muzzled. Opinion and protest are the life breath of democracy." On the eighth
in an address at New York University, Arthur Goldberg insisted
that the United States was "passionately devoted to free expression"; four days after that, at Brandeis ceremonies, he praised
"the freedom of expression that is being manifested by students
in the colleges and universities." Hubert Humphrey described
dissent on June 14 as an integral part of the American way of
life.

The testimonials went on into the summer and the fall. In
August[118] the president pledged, "we defend, and we intend to
defend, the right of everyone to disagree with what we urge or
do." That September[119] Mr. Humphrey repeated the pledge
through a quotation from Henry David Thoreau: " 'If a man
does not keep pace with his companions, perhaps it is because

he hears a different drummer. Let him step to the music which he hears, however measured or far away.' " On November 6 Mr. Goldberg observed, "Free debate and discussion obviously must be the keystones of . . . [American foreign] policy, and the right to participate in them must not be limited only to voices that agree." "The price of our freedom," he continued, "includes that of criticizing our elected officials and of disagreeing with their policies." On the tenth Secretary McNamara called dissent "both the prerogative and the preservative of freemen everywhere."

In 1967 there was a sharp decline in the number of these stirring declarations, indicating Washington's growing impatience with the critics and their ever more frequent criticism. There were other indications too, less abstract and ambiguous. For despite the unqualified support of "freedom of inquiry, [and] freedom of expression,"[120] despite the encouragement of "suggestions from committees, commissions, from Congress, from private individuals, from clubs,"[121] despite the injuctions to "behave towards the minority with a tolerance and with courtesy and with a gentlemanliness and with ordinary respect,"[122] the administration, in fact, regarded dissent as an irritant and from the start, from the spring of 1965, sought to limit the credibility and impact of those who disagreed with the official course.[123] The attacks, interspersed among and delivered along with the assurances of constitutional guarantees, were most frequent at times of unusually vocal and voluble protest. They were as carping in tone as the assurances were balanced, and their scope was enormous.

To begin with, the government questioned the capacity of the university community, locus of much of the early opposition, to make meaningful judgments about complicated matters of international affairs. In April 1965,[124] Dean Rusk dismissed most of the academic analysis on the "nature of the struggle" in Southeast Asia as "nonsense." "I sometimes wonder," he mused, "at the gullibility of educated men and the stubborn disregard of plain fact by men who are supposed to be helping our young to learn—especially to learn how to think." Thomas Conlon, a State Department adviser, reported on May 7 that many of the professors he had encountered on college campuses who were critical of U.S. actions were men "out of their field," generally teachers of "psychology, the exact sciences and literature, rather than political science." He explained, "They have often not read far enough to realize the implications of what they are advocating." Mr. Rusk was no less condescending in the autumn of 1967:[125]

> as friends used to say of Einstein . . . he was a genius in mathematical physics, an amateur in music, and a baby in politics.
> Now I think that an idea stands or falls on its own merits and the fact that a man knows everything there is to know about enzymes doesn't mean that he knows very much about Vietnam or how to organize a peace or the life and death of nations.

Vice President Humphrey was hardly any more complimentary about the undergraduate contribution to the discussion of the war: their enthusiasm was misplaced, their energy misdirected, their efforts finally an avoidance of the really pressing problems facing American society. "Many of those who demonstrate," he commented patronizingly on October 21, 1965, "are just sincere, idealistic youth whose idealism could well be channeled" into humanitarian work. On the twenty-eighth he asserted:

> The voices that are raised outside [in protest] could do more for the good of their country if they would do something for those who suffer rather than try to proclaim themselves as experts on matters of national security and foreign policy.

Three years later, in August, 1968,[126] he had concluded that "a lot of the talk we've had on Vietnam [from students] is escapism engaged in by those who don't want to go out" and confront the harsh realities of the world.

The government also struck at what it regarded as the dissenters' lack of objectivity: their criticism was distorted and grossly misrepresented the facts; the inadvertent errors of the allies were underscored, the calculated atrocities of the other side, totally overlooked. On April 1, 1965, the president appealed to those in the United States who were

> concerned by the roar of a plane that may destroy a building but kill no people, to be equally concerned when bombs are thrown

in our embassies, and American citizens are carried out on stretchers and American lives are taken.

In July 1966,[127] he scored dissidents for being so eloquent in their denunciation of American strikes against Hanoi and Haiphong, but so "strangely silent" about terrorist attacks on a U.S. naval hospital at Danang: "I just wish they would ask themselves if their standard of judgment is really fair." The next March,[128] in an address to the Tennessee legislature, he reported how "tens of thousands of innocent Vietnamese civilians have been killed and tortured and kidnapped by the Vietcong. . . . Yet, the deeds of the Vietcong go largely unnoted in the public debate." He concluded, "It is this moral double bookkeeping which makes us get sometimes very weary of our critics."

In terms of its value, the offerings of the opposition were discounted as being "irrelevant,"[129] a "concoction of wishful thinking and false hopes"[130] that was ultimately a "waste of time."[131] Moreover, and more importantly, they were said to be having a detrimental effect on the prosecution of the war. The protest, uninformed and biased, was denounced for being irresponsible as well.

The demonstrations were, first, demoralizing the American forces in combat. Critics "are very disheartening to the troops over there facing death" wrote a United States sergeant in a letter cited by Mr. Johnson on August 24, 1965; "I don't think they have really helped our marines a whole lot up there on the DMZ," he remarked in November 1967.[132]

Second, they were encouraging the enemy, inducing him to persist in his aggression, postponing, rather than advancing the progress toward peace. On October 15, 1965, General Maxwell Taylor, then special consultant to the president, warned that rallies being held across the nation against U.S. involvement might persuade the leaders in Hanoi that "there is a real division in this country and that may tempt them to prolong the war." Lyndon Johnson disclosed on June 18, 1966:

> our intelligence indicates that the aggressor presently bases his hopes, we think, more on political differences in Saigon and Washington than on his military capacity in South Vietnam.

Returning to the United States in the spring of 1967,[133] after completing his second tour as ambassador, Henry Cabot Lodge declared, "disunity in America prolongs the war. . . . [It makes] Hanoi think all they have to do is hang on and we'll fall apart." On October 15 Mr. Humphrey repeated, "The hope of victory for the enemy is not in his power but in our division." Nine days after that, Secretary Rusk asked a Los Angeles audience, "How do we prevent . . . [North Vietnam] misunderstanding the news that forty or fifty thousand people are demonstrating in front of the Pentagon?"

The fundamental danger of dissent was that it revealed division within the nation—division which inspired "their" side and discouraged "ours." Yet, to object, as Washington did, to this effect was to object to the very essence of the First Amendment. It was inevitable that once restrictions on expression had been removed differences would become apparent. Indeed, it had been to provide unrepresented minorities with a voice, and thereby allow factions to emerge, that the Constitution's framers had at the outset undertaken to protect speech.

Though the government insisted that it had no doubts about the sincerity or the motives of its opponents, to maintain that their impact was to dishearten U.S. soldiers and encourage those of the North Vietnamese could not help but awaken such doubts in others. And despite the disclaimers, the impression that the opposition was enagaged in un-American activities was fostered and reinforced, heightened by official commentary verging on vilification that transcended any reasonable standard of "fair exchange."

Eugene Rostow dismissed the protest as "the counsel of despair"[134] and Secretary Rusk contended that it was motivated by "the thoughts of another generation," "the old discredited ideas of yesterday."[135] In a more obvious allusion to 1930s Appeasement, the vice president described the dissenters' program as "the new isolationism" produced by youngsters for whom the "old isolationism, depression, Nazism, Fascism and Hitler are just words."[136]

The rebels were variously labeled "cussers" and "doubters,"[137] "anarchists,"[138] "calamity hawkers,"[139] "Communists,"[140] "Nervous Nellies,"[141] "damned fools."[142] Mr. Johnson

remarked that the group as a whole was one which had "always
been blind to experience and deaf to hope."[143] He contrasted
their "hostile placards and debating points" with the real "bul-
lets and mortal shells of aggressive armies"[144] faced by men at
the front. He said he was neither "angry" nor "sorrowful" about
their behavior. "But," he admitted, "I sometimes think, God
forgive them for they know not what they do."[145]

The tradition of dissent in America was a tradition of compounded error, a history of a small band of willful men who had
always been wrong. At a news conference in the autumn of
1967,[146] the President provided a detailed account of that past.

> I think there was [difference of opinion] in the Revolutionary
> War when only a third of the people thought that was a wise
> move, and a third of them were opposing it and a third on the
> sidelines. I think that was true when all New England came
> down to secede in Madison's Administration in the War of 1812
> and they stopped over in Baltimore, and they didn't quite make
> it because Andrew Jackson and the result of New Orleans came
> in, and they were having a party over there that night and the
> next morning they came over and told the President that they
> wanted to congratulate him, they thought he'd been right all
> along, although they'd come from Boston to Baltimore in the
> secessionist move.
> I think that was true in the Mexican war when Congress
> overwhelmingly voted to go in and later passed a resolution that
> had grave doubts about it and some of the most bitter speeches
> were made—they couldn't be published they were so bitter.
> They had to hold up publication of them for a hundred years.
> I don't need to remind you of what happened in the Civil
> War. People were here in the White House begging Lincoln to
> concede to work out a deal with the Confederacy when the word
> came to him of his victories. They told him that Pennsylvania was
> gone, that Illinois had no chance, those pressures come to a
> President.
> I think you know what President Roosevelt went through,
> President Wilson in World War I. He had some Senators from
> certain areas that gave him very serious problems until victory
> was assured, and I think now when you look back upon it, there
> are very few people that would think that Wilson or Roosevelt
> or Truman were in error.

The intended inference was plain: though there were critics
during every war, in each case the outcome had exposed their

position and vindicated the official line. The pattern would, doubtless, be repeated again. In the national experience dissent was nothing more than a tolerated aberration. Oliver Wendell Holmes's notion that the First Amendment would create an opportunity for divergent views to be objectively considered in an unemotional forum had been replaced by what appeared to Lyndon Baines Johnson's, that speech should be protected largely because of the cathartic effect it would have upon the speaker. The romantic nineteenth-century vision of the "market place" had given way to the pragmatic, twentieth-century concept of the "safety valve." "The right to be heard," it was explained, "does not automatically include the right to be taken seriously."[147] More to the point, opposing ideas were likely to have little impact on the conduct of U.S. foreign policy.

By the late 1960s Washington had served notice that dissent was a hindrance, a source of frustration, and attempted by aspersion more than by argument to minimize its force. Critics were charged with being something less than loyal and little more than fools. Criticism was dismissed as misinformed and misguided, as well as potentially dangerous. The First Amendment, which insured what was in theory the central and absolute American freedom, was, as applied to opponents of the Vietnam war, becoming an increasingly empty and peripheral abstraction.

To Capture the People

Manipulation

Between 1965 and 1968 the government reaffirmed the right of dissent and reviled the dissenters, and with that apparent contradiction announced that while it would not violate basic principle, neither would it deviate from official policy. In its treatment of the protestors, Washington sought to convince the American public, its allies, the enemy, and, perhaps, itself that protest would not weaken U.S. resolve. There were, however, other far more direct and dramatic expressions of that determination.

They began suddenly to appear in 1964, a year before the organized opposition to the war had surfaced. In April[148] Mr. Johnson declared to an Associated Press convention: "The situation in Vietnam is difficult. But there is an old American saying that 'when the going gets tough, the tough get going.' " "If anyone has the illusion," Ambassador Stevenson told delegates to the United Nations that May,[149]

> that my Government will abandon the people of Vietnam, or that we shall weary of the burden of support that we are rendering these people, it will be only due to ignorance of the strength and conviction of the American people.

Secretary Rusk underscored that point the next month:[150] "we certainly do not intend to abandon the people of . . . Vietnam."

During the spring of 1965 there was a not surprising spate of such assurances, verbal reinforcement of the military implications of that winter's escalation. On April 1, President Johnson stressed to newsmen that if "diplomatic and political leadership" did not succeed in ending the conflict, "we do not plan to come running home and abandon this little nation." Less than a week later[151] he reiterated to university students, "We will not be defeated. We will not grow tired. We will not withdraw." In similar fashion he insisted on May 4, "we cannot, and will not, withdraw or be defeated. . . . We will not surrender."

In 1966 the number of these proclamations more than doubled, an increase consistent with Washington's general tendency that year to overstate and oversell its case. "We shall not be forced out of Vietnam," Arthur Goldberg promised on January 1; on April 27 he emphasized again America's "determination and our strength not to be forced out," and in mid-September[152] repeated the same pledge, in the same language, for the third time: "The United States will not be forced out of Vietnam."

Hubert Humphrey on February 3 notified "those who live by force" that Americans can and would demonstrate that "we are too strong to be afraid, too determined to be defeated"; on the thirteenth he reaffirmed to the leaders of Thailand that the nation had no thought of pulling out of Southeast Asia. Four weeks later[153] he was utterly unequivocal: "Let me, as Vice President of the United States, make it once more clear. We will not tire nor withdraw. . . . We will remain in Vietnam."

The line which most clearly exemplified the spirit of those twelve months and best conveyed the government's mood, was the familiar slogan, America will "see it through." "We will not tire, we will not flag, we intend to work with you," the president began on February 7. He went on to say that there was no question about "our resolution and our determination to see this thing through." In a Memorial Day statement, released on May 26, he reminded the public, "This nation has never left the field of battle in abject surrender of a cause for which it has fought." "We shall not now do so," he continued. "We shall see this through." He was equally emphatic in Omaha, Nebraska, on June 30: "[to] those who would try to pressure us or influence us or mislead us or deceive us, I say this afternoon there can only be one decision in Vietnam and that is this: We shall see this through." On July 11, Dean Rusk remarked to reporters that the "key point" of administration policy in Vietnam was the "determination to see it through." On July 17 he said, "We are determined to see that South Vietnam is not seized by the North militarily. We have a commitment to see that through and we're going to see it through." Speaking in Saigon that December[154] he recited the formula again: "we are going to see this thing through."

These declarations of dedication, aimed manifestly at impressing friendly and unfriendly foreign listeners, were also designed to rally the people back home. There was an element of exhortation in proclaiming "we shall stand in Southeast Asia" —a definite strain of "we should" or "we must" stand there. Though the impact of these calls for resolution and patience depended in part upon reaction to the underlying substantive rationale, it did not do so entirely. For resolution and patience were recognized virtues, in the sense that their opposites, irresolution and impatience, were recognizable vices. The demand never to yield, to remain firm was therefore to an extent compelling in and of itself, independent of the merits of the given situation for which it was demanded. There was something right about "seeing it through"; not doing so, whatever the particular circumstances, was a sign of weakness and timidity.

In the fifteen months between January 1967 and April 1968, officials were increasingly apt to phrase the still recurrent talk of persistence in the form of directed appeals to the nation; it was less and less "we will persist" and more and more "we should persist."[155] In his January 10, 1967, State of the Union Message Mr. Johnson counseled "patience. I mean a great deal of patience." That spring[156] Ambassador Lodge predicted an American success "if we have the patience." In September[157] Defense Secretary McNamara warned of the danger posed by the growing "lack of patience" in the land. "Let's have some patience," the vice president urged on November 1.

Patience was not, however, the only quality which Washington sought to inspire. On March 2, 1967, President Johnson contended that ultimate victory "requires courage, perseverance and dedication." He declared in November[158] in remarks at Fort Benning, Georgia, that

> peace will come more quickly when the enemy of freedom finds no crack in our courage—and no split in our resolve—and no encouragement to prolong the war in the shortness of our patience or the sharpness of our tongues.

"I think," he observed the following March,[159]

> if we are steady, if we are patient, if we do not become the willing victims of our own despair, if we do not abandon what we know is right when it comes under mounting challenge—we shall never fail.

The point was sometimes made with less eloquence, but more force. "If we stick with it," Ambassador Bunker asserted in early July 1967,[160] "we will have some reasonable success." Mr. Humphrey adopted the same phraseology six weeks later:[161] "If we stick with what we're doing . . . this struggle is going to come to a halt." "Sad but steady," Mr. Johnson began his 1968 Lincoln's Birthday[162] address, "—always convinced of his cause—he stuck it out." "And we," he insisted, "must stick it out—just as Lincoln did."

These statements, declaratory as well as hortatory, were

meant to stir, to move, to galvanize the nation, to forge a concensus behind which the United States could best wage battle. It was the desire for unity which competed with and finally outweighed the right of dissent; dissent may have been "a cornerstone of democracy,"[163] but unity was its "bedrock."[164] Its importance was attested to in all the homilies which had become part of the American folklore and which officials dutifully paraded forth:

> Where there is unity in the land there is strength.
>
> NOVEMBER 2, 1966

> He deserves the gratitude of the American people for maintaining our great tradition that politics stops at the water's edge.
>
> APRIL 7, 1967

> I think every American will want to say, "I stood up to be counted."
>
> FEBRUARY 27, 1968

> And in these times, as in times before, it is true that a house divided against itself by the spirit of faction, of party, of region, of religion, of race, is a house that cannot stand.
>
> MARCH 31, 1968

To achieve this unity, Washington not only appealed to that collection of what have passed for the "manly virtues"—steadfastness, courage, restraint—but also tried to arouse more volatile, patriotic feelings, feelings of devotion to and love for the homeland. The mode at times was to touch upon the mystique of American success—America's heritage and destiny as a chosen people. There was a profound and widely shared belief that the United States could solve any problem, deal with any situation it encountered, "that when the United States puts its hand to something . . . something gives."[165] As the president expressed it in the fall of 1967,[166] "We have a tremendous confidence in this country, in ourselves, in our capacity to surmount any obstacle, to remove any injustice, to settle any issue."

Against this background, the crisis in Southeast Asia was

another attempt, by yet another adversary, to undermine that confidence and challenge America's preeminent position in the world. To defend the freedom of South Vietnam was, therefore, to defend the prestige and standing of the United States as well. "I ask every American," Lyndon Johnson said in a speech in Chicago in May 1966,[167] "to put our country first if we want to keep it first." During the late winter of 1968, in the aftermath of the enemy's massive offensive and in the face of rival candidacies mounted from within his party, in the midst, that is, of enormous military and political pressures, he resorted to this line twice in thirty-six hours. On March 19, he concluded an address to the National Farmer's Union, noting that the government was "trying to preserve the American system, which is first in the world today." "I want it to stay first," he submitted, "but it cannot be first if we pull out and tuck our tail." The next day he exhorted, "Today we're the number one nation and we're going to stay the number one nation."

Another tack was for the president to close his reports on Vietnam with direct, personal pleas for support, the beleaguered wartime leader seeking the help of his nation, to ease the lonely and agonizing decisions which lay ahead:

> In all of this [that we try to do] I ask for the understanding, the support and the prayers of our countrymen.
>
> OCTOBER 27, 1966

> So with both your confidence and your support, we are going to persist and we are going to succeed.
>
> JANUARY 10, 1967

> So I ask you not only for your prayers, but for the courageous and understanding support that Americans always give their President and their leader in an hour of trial.
>
> OCTOBER 31, 1968

The most frequent and poignant appeals, however, were those which played on the services being performed by America's soldiers;[168] in a variety of ways, both obvious and subtle, Washington called attention to the hardships endured by the U.S. forces operating in Vietnam. In his annual Thanksgiving message to the troops of autumn 1965,[169] President Johnson wrote to those who would be spending the holidays "away from your families," stationed "in a lonely and dangerous land." At a Medal of Honor ceremony that April[170] he talked of the valor of a dead hero:

> In all this there is irony, as when any young man dies. Who can say what words Private Olive might have chosen to explain what he did? Jimmy Stanford and John Foster, two of the men whose lives he saved that day on that lonely trail in that hostile jungle 10,000 miles from here are standing on the White House steps today because this man chose to die.

That July [171] he spoke to the press about the men "out in the rice paddies." "Let's realize," he urged on November 17, 1967, "that we're in the midst of a war, let's realize that there are 500,000 of our boys out there giving their life to win that war."

Given such sacrifice, the least those left behind could do was refrain from divisive criticism; if some were called upon to die in the jungles of Asia, the others could at least be patient in the safety of their refuge. On July 23, 1966, after praising the courage of Americans fighting in Vietnam, Mr. Johnson declared:

> We at home must ask ourselves this question: Have we the same strength of spirit, the same commitment to resisting oppression, the same willingness to endure the long and uncertain days that may pass before peace returns?

"I think," he told reporters on November 1, 1967, "[the road ahead] is going to be exacting, difficult, and going to require the best that is in all of us. . . . But," he reminded, "not nearly as much from us as it is from the men fighting out there." On the tenth, the contrast was elaborated:

> For these Americans [at the battlefront], Vietnam is no academic question. It is not a topic of cocktail parties, office arguments, a debate from the comfort of some distant sidelines.
>
> These Americans . . . do not live on the sidelines. Their lives are tied by flesh and blood to Vietnam. Talk does not come cheap to them. The cost of duty is too cruel. The price of patriotism comes too high.

And it was only by supporting government action that such sacrifice could be redeemed; to deny the government that support was to pronounce the suffering meaningless. On May 30, 1966, the president pledged:

> to those who have died there and to those who have been wounded there and to those who are now fighting there and to those who may yet fight there . . . we shall help the people of South Vietnam to see this through.

He promised his army in December 1967,[172] in Camranh Bay, as Abraham Lincoln had promised at Gettysburg, 102 years before, "We shall not fail you. What you have done will not have been done in vain." "We are there," he maintained to the American Legion at the end of the summer of 1968,[173] "to bring an honorable—to bring a stable—peace to Southeast Asia, and no less will justify the sacrifices that our men have died for."

In these passages the question of unity was framed not in terms of the acceptance of an abstract foreign policy, but in terms of a concern for the fate of very real men risking their lives out in the field. It was given its most clear and dramatic expression in a speech by Mr. Johnson to the Veterans of Foreign Wars on August 19, 1968:

> One day, and I pray—I pray every night that it will be soon—the men who bear the brunt of battle are going to come back home and when they do they are going to ask an accounting of us for the support we gave them or that we denied them in the hour of greatest need, when we sent them away to protect us and defend us, and I hope and I pray that we are not going to be found wanting in that judgment.

These statements represent the most purely emotional rhetoric in which the administration engaged. Certainly the Munich analogy and allusions to self-determination had strong emotive aspects. Each, to be sure, was associated with an event or experience—the tragedy of appeasement on the one hand, the enlightened idealism of Woodrow Wilson on the other— which elicited unequivocal and vivid responses. But the emotions excited merely heightened the impact of a substantive rationale. The recollection of the horrors of the Second World War made it harder to dismiss the warning against a precipitate withdrawal from Southeast Asia; popular awareness of the object of the Fourteen Points in general and the specific vision embodied within them of eliminating colonial exploitation made it easier to accept representative democracy and native rule as a major aim in South Vietnam. References to communism and aggression were also heavily loaded. "Aggression" suggested the activities of the Nazi Wehrmacht; "communism," the excesses of Joseph Stalin. Both, that is, had highly charged associations. Yet the memories stirred again only reinforced an underlying message: if the North Vietnamese were guilty of open aggression, did seek to communize southern Asia, then the United States had better move with determination and in force.

In contrast, the invoking of American supremacy, the talk of the boys in the jungles, the appeals by the president for forbearance, offered no reason for approving official actions other than some vague, moral obligation to be "loyal" citizens. The fact that the United States was involved overseas, and apparently that fact alone, imposed a responsibility to heed "the call to the colors." Even if the particular arguments were not particularly persuasive, that the commander-in-chief had asked for assistance, that some Americans were dying in answer, that the national reputation had, therefore, been put on the line, demanded that the general public at least close ranks in the rear. On occasion, such peroratory was disturbingly reminiscent of an earlier century's romantic and absurd devotion to the ideal, "my country, right or wrong."

These unrestrained attempts to generate a consensus were not entirely unsuccessful, and until late 1966 officials took pride in regularly noting that their policies were fully approved by most in the nation. "The large majority of Americans support our efforts everywhere to stop aggression," the president contended on June 1, 1965, as some reacted against his decision to raid the North continuously. On August 10, a week and a half after the announcement that 50,000 U.S. troops were being immediately deployed to South Vietnam, the White House revealed, "There is a feeling of general support" for Mr. Johnson's actions. Three months thereafter,[174] on the eve of antiwar demonstrations to be held in the capital city, Mr. Moyers repeated that the "overwhelming opinion" of Americans was that Washington's course was correct. "I think the country overwhelmingly supports the position that we have taken," President Johnson remarked to newsmen on February 10, 1966; he reiterated on May 21, "a substantial majority [of our people] . . . do approve of the course of action that we have taken, and they do support their Government." Again, on October 22, he reported "the vast majority of the American . . . people are together."

Beginning in 1967, these self-serving accounts were discarded and a new line substituted: support while desirable was not a necessity. The president, in reaching his decisions, would be influenced by the merits of alternative proposals, not by any anticipated public response. White House Press Secretary George Christian stressed on November 13, 1967, that Mr. Johnson would "proceed on what is right—not popularity." As Lyndon Johnson himself explained on December 12, he would not alter his position, "regardless of my polls." "We don't," he had said that July,[175] "base our action on the Gallup poll."

This change in emphasis coincided with the findings of the American Institute of Political Research, that from the end of December 1966 on, the percentage of those disapproving of President Johnson's conduct of the war exceeded with fair consistency the percentage approving.[176] By 1967 the support which the president said he no longer needed, he no longer had. There were sharp rises in the polls at times, often when Mr. Johnson took decisive military or diplomatic steps, and correspondingly sharp declines, as the war continued to drag inexorably on. But despite these successive ups and downs, an overall trend did emerge: the American government gradually and progressively lost the approval of the American people. The "infinitesimal fraction,"[177] the "extremists"[178] who had opposed the war in 1965, had by 1968 wrought "very deep and very emotional divisions in this land."[179]

The Peril of Propaganda

The Johnson Administration reacted publicly to the spectacle of growing disillusionment with its policies with more dismay than alarm. Though it sought tirelessly to rekindle the waning popular enthusiasm, it repesented that disenchantment as unfortunate but inevitable; "We will expect dissent in any period like this. We have always had it."[180] It arose for two reasons:

> The longer we are there, the more sacrifices we make. The more we spend, the more discontent there will be, the more dissatis-faction there will be.

LYNDON JOHNSON, MAY 21, 1966

> Our American people, when we get in a contest of any kind, whether it's in a war or an election or in a football game, or what it is they want it decided and decided quickly and get in or get out and they like for that curve to rise like this, and they like for the opposition to go down like this.

LYNDON JOHNSON, NOVEMBER 17, 1967

The greater the degree of sacrifice, the larger the amount of money expended or lives lost, the more inconclusive the strug-gle, the longer assistance was advanced without apparent effect, the higher the level of opposition. That American boys were being killed in a conflict without an imminent end was all that had been needed to turn large masses of people against the government, or so Washington suggested.

There clearly was a connection between increasing U.S. battle fatalities, the continuingly remote prospects for peace, and the steadily declining support for the administration. To describe that connection was not, however, to explain it. The casualties doubtless brought grief and sorrow; the seeming in-terminability of it all bred frustration. But neither alone was responsible for the resulting protest. Grief and frustration may well have contributed to criticism by lowering the threshold of tolerance; they were not, however, its equivalent. Whatever the official representations may have been, there was neither a necessary nor a direct relationship between the growth of dis-sent and the waging of war.

In a less automatic and more involved fashion, however, the sacrifices and the complexity of the conflict in Southeast Asia did bear on the rise of opposition. On the one hand they precipi-tated an examination of the premises upon which U.S. involvement was based. The deaths suddenly made the crisis in Vietnam more immediate and serious for Americans; the lack of dramatic military progress made apparent the difficulties with which that crisis was fraught. Each stimulated a more thorough analysis of Washington's rationale. Together they raised the question, "Would the principles justify the costs?" Not all who undertook the inquiry pursued it with the same vigor or to the same depth. Nor did each finally conclude that the official case was wanting. But some did; the most articulate expression of their conclusions was presented among the collection of dissenting publications which began to emerge after 1966, publications which in turn focused the thoughts and influenced the opinions of others uneasy about the justifications for the war. In addition the manner in which the nation was made aware of the escalations and of the elusiveness of success had the effect of eroding public confidence in the government's management of policy.

Presidential administrations have traditionally started by enjoying a substantial amount of popular trust, which has accrued primarily because of two assumptions made about the personnel responsible for ruling the country. The first is that they are experts, men privy to highly specialized information, professionals for whom the affairs of state are a daily preoccupation; the second is that they are candid and forthright individuals, conscious of the obligation to disclose fully all that may be safely disclosed, sensitive to the people's "right to know" in a genuinely democratic society. The way in which Mr. Johnson, Mr. Rusk, Mr. McNamara, and their subordinates conducted the expansion of America's involvement in Asia undermined the assumptions of expertise and candor, and finally destroyed the atmosphere of trust.

To begin with, officials were exceedingly prone to define U.S. commitment in terms which seemed expressly to preclude the measures eventually taken. On January 29, 1964, in testimony to the House Armed Services Committee, Secretary McNamara reaffirmed his October prediction that most American troops would be removed from Southeast Asia by the start of 1966. Citing that earlier statement, he told the congressmen:

We continue to be hopeful that we will be able to complete the training responsibilities of many of the other United States personnel now in Vietnam and gradually withdraw them over the period between now and the end of 1965.

In mid-summer[181] the State Department confirmed that 5,000 additional men would be sent to reinforce the U.S. mission.

On June 5, 1964, Ambassador Lodge dismissed calls for enlargening the war or "going north" as "Mother Hubbard phrases that cover everything and touch nothing." In a report delivered that August[182] to the Security Council on the Tonkin incident, Adlai Stevenson insisted " 'we still seek no wider war.' " The next month, on September 9, Maxwell Taylor, asked by newsmen whether he foresaw any shifts in America's position, said, "we are on a given beam and we are going to stay on that." Mr. Johnson declared three weeks later,[183] "We're not going north and drop bombs at this stage of the game, and we're not going south," and he emphasized these objections to a "big offensive"[184] in the days that followed. Robert McNamara commented on November 10, "we have no plans at present to send combat units to South Vietnam." In an interview in early January[185] Secretary Rusk again ruled out a major extension of the war. In February the United States initiated a bombing campaign against North Vietnam. In March the first American combat battalions were introduced in the South.

On June 26, 1966, Undersecretary of State George Ball appeared on "Meet the Press" to announce unequivocally, "There is no decision on the part of the United States Government to bomb Haiphong or to bomb the [fuel] installations in Haiphong-Hanoi." On June 29, the initial raids upon these depots were launched.

On August 25, 1967, at hearings held by the Senate Armed Services Committee, Mr. McNamara argued strongly against the destruction of the harbors at Haiphong, Hongai, and Campha. Destroying these facilities, he contended, would not "eliminate seaborne imports" nor would it "prevent movement in and through N.V.N. [North Vietnam] of the essentials to continue their present level of military activity in S.V.N. [South Vietnam]." On September 11, strikes were directed against two of the three ports.

The uncanny failure of the United States to forecast its requirements was disturbing no matter how it was explained. If it was all a charade, a deliberate attempt to prepare the public for a known future by discussing and apparently rejecting all unpopular options in advance, then the government was simply perpetrating a fraud. If some spokesmen were themselves being misled, so that in describing what ostensibly was official policy they no longer reflected official thinking, then there was a telling division within the administration, the cause of which may not have been merely the merits of a particular military venture, but the wisdom of the overall course. And if Washington just could not predict or limit the scale of its assistance from one month to the next, then there was nothing to insure that it would remain in control of the unforseeable events, nothing to prevent the skirmish from blooming into World War III of its own irresistible momentum.

Such doubts were only compounded by the government's extraordinary attempts to minimize the significance of the previously precluded steps—and others not anticipated—once taken. On March 7, 1964, President Johnson offered a reinterpretation of the statement issued that autumn[186] on plans for withdrawal, a statement noting the "judgment" of Secretary McNamara and General Taylor "that the major part of the United States military task can be completed by the end of 1965." "I don't think," the president began, "that the American public has fully understood the reason for our withdrawing any advisers from South Vietnam, and I think that they should." He went on:

> We have called back approximately one thousand people. A good many of those people—several hundred—were there training guards and policemen. Once these people were trained, why we thought that they could act as well as policemen as our people could act, so we withdrew these people.
> From time to time, as our training mission is completed, other people will be withdrawn. From time to time as additional advisers are needed or as people to train additional Vietnamese are needed, we'll send them out there.

The object of the exercise was to preserve the illusion of consistency with the past. "The policy should continue," it was recommended on the seventeenth, "of withdrawing United States personnel where their roles can be assumed by South Vietnamese, and of sending additional men if they are needed." A program of disengagement was thereby suspended and transformed into a license for intervention.

Eleven months later, as that process began with the inauguration of U.S. raids against communication and transportation facilities in the North and the assignment of American crews to fly missions against rebel concentrations in the South, Washington sought then, too, to deny the fact of change. America's policy was still the same, Dean Rusk maintained on February 25, 1965, though how that policy was translated into action "depends upon the circumstances from time to time." Mr. Johnson repeated that emphasis on March 13:

> Although the incidents have changed. In some instances the tactics and perhaps the strategy in a decision or two has changed. Our policy is still the same and that is to any armed attack our forces will reply. To any in Southeast Asia who ask our help in defending their freedom, we're going to give it.

The tenuous claim rested on a definition of its policy in Southeast Asia as the utterly open-ended and unqualified objective of safeguarding the Republic of Vietnam.

The government was no less obscure on the issue of the increasingly direct involvement of U.S. fighting men. When on March 6 the Pentagon announced that two batallions of marines were being dispatched to South Vietnam to defend American bases, it made no effort to relate that very new and broader responsibility to the still presumably operative "advise and assist" restriction on the U.S. role. When on June 9 the White House confirmed that these marines were permitted to engage in offensive operations, in "active patrolling and securing action," despite Secretary Rusk's earlier[187] assurances that they were solely to relieve the South Vietnamese for combat and would themselves only fire if fired upon, it stated that the disclosure signified "no change in the mission of U.S. ground combatants." When on July 28 President Johnson revealed that 50,000 soldiers were being immediately deployed to South Vietnam, cautioning that "additional forces will be needed later" and

and pledging that "they will be sent as requested," he refused to acknowledge that these measures, as a newsman phrased it, implied

> any change in the existing policy of relying mainly on the South Vietnamese to carry out offensive operations and using American forces to guard American installations and to act as an emergency backup.

"It does not," he remarked simply, "imply any change in policy whatever. It does not imply any change of objective." Nor was that acknowledgement ever made; the drastic rise in American casualties, however, made such an admission superfluous.

In November 1965,[188] Dean Rusk noted that, except perhaps in "nuance," the U.S. position had remained steady within the preceding year, and in February 1966[189] the president declared in assent, "our American purpose and policy are unchanged." Over the months that followed, with deftness and skill, officials attempted to maintain that fiction.

The scope of the air war widened with no notice at all given by Washington, announcement of the operations being made at regular briefings of the Military Command in Saigon. None of the moves, spokesmen contended when pressed, suggested any dramatic shifts, either in philosophy or tactic. The strikes against oil dumps in Hanoi and Haiphong, begun in late June 1966, were described by presidential assistant Walt W. Rostow on July 3 as "wholly consistent" with all past efforts to prevent a Communist success. The Department of Defense denied on February 26, 1967, that the mining of North Vietnamese rivers for the first time represented any expansion of the war. The next day President Johnson refused to embrace a reporter's characterization of new Navy shelling and long-range artillery fire as a "step-up," going no further than to concede that such measures were somewhat more "far-reaching" than those taken before.

On March 10 State Department press officer Robert McCloskey was asked if the attacks upon a previously avoided steel fabricating plant constituted an escalation of or an alteration in the bombing program. "No it does not," he replied. On August 14, at the White House, George Christian was questioned as to whether the raids conducted on targets ten miles from the Chinese border fitted into "the context of no wider war." "Yes," he answered.

The repeated decisions to send more and more American soldiers to Southeast Asia were also treated in a routine manner. The assumption was: "There will be additional men needed and they will be supplied."[190] Future deployment was to be regarded as the implementation of a continuing and unlimited authorization; the troop ceiling was always provisional.

It was the defense secretary, no longer the president, who bore the responsibility for breaking the news to the public. On February 23, 1966, Mr. McNamara told the Senate Armed Services and Defense Appropriations subcommittees, "In view of the continued build up of Vietcong and North Vietnamese forces, we now believe we should be prepared to deploy additional forces to that area if required." He added, "President Johnson has stated categorically that we will give our commanders in Vietnam all the resources they need." He commented at a session with members of the National Chamber of Commerce in May[191] that the United States "probably will have to send additional troops." "We will meet whatever requirements the military commanders submit to us," he reaffirmed during the summer,[192] "and I do anticipate that it will be necessary to increase the size of our ground and air force there before the end of the year." On July 12, 1967, at an informal meeting with newsmen he reported that "some more" units would be dispatched.

By the fall there were 470,000 Americans stationed in South Vietnam. At a press conference on November 1, this exchange was transcribed:

> Q. Mr. President, sir, one of the main points in the domestic arguments about the policy of the war has been the fact that in 1964, when you were campaigning, you spoke of not wishing to send American boys to fight a war that Asian boys should fight. Then a year later the Government did that. I wonder if you could give us your thinking on the change in policy.
> A. There has not been a change in policy. You have quoted one sentence in a speech that contained many sentences and many paragraphs. We always said—and we repeat now—that we

> do not want American boys to do the fighting that South Viet-
> namese boys ought to do or that Asian boys ought to do.
>
> We are asking them to do all they can. But that did not imply
> then and does not imply now that we would not do what we
> needed to do to deter aggression.

In political terms there was good reason for the Johnson
Administration to seek to divert attention from its burgeoning
military commitment in Asia; concentration upon such a program could only breed dissent and controversy. To attempt to
disguise its actions in a cloak of words, however, was not to
distract the public; as a strategy it created rather than solved
problems. The presence of one-half million U.S. combat troops
in South Vietnam where there had previously been 16,000 advisers, the daily aerial bombardment of virtually all of North
Vietnam, which before was a restricted sanctuary, however
justifiable, represented an escalation, a change in policy, a wid-
ening of the war. To dispute that conclusion was to declare that
conventional rules of language had been suspended.

The use of common words in an uncommon way has the
effect of arousing suspicion and does not either cushion realities
or allay fears. If Washington would engage in verbal subterfuge
and "doublespeak," masking the truth about its activities when
that truth was known, would it not be equally capable of with-
olding the truth when discovery was unlikely? Could Washington be trusted any more?

The uncertainty was only deepened by the contrast between the bleak, inconclusive battlefield situation and the constantly hopeful appraisals being released at home. The tendency towards optimism was not in any way new. During the
1950s it was evident in the assessments made by members of
the Truman and Eisenhower Administrations about the prospects in the struggle with the Vietminh. On June 18, 1952,
Secretary of State Acheson cited the "distinguished" performance in combat of the Vietnamese army and the "vital
security functions" they were carrying out "in many parts of the
country." He went on to observe that what America was doing
in Indochina proved "once again the policy of meeting aggression with force is paying off." Two years after that, on February
9, 1954, Defense Secretary Charles Wilson informed newsmen
that a French victory was "both possible and probable" and that

the war was going "fully as well as we expected it to at this stage." Fourteen days later Undersecretary Smith described the military situation as being favorable. "There is no reason," John Foster Dulles contended that April,[193] five weeks before the debacle at Dienbienphu, "to question the inherent sound-ness of the Navarre Plan."

The Kennedy era was marked by the same proneness to-ward overconfidence. Robert McNamara was undoubtedly the most indomitable enthusiast. On February 19, 1962, he in-dicated that conditions in Southeast Asia appeared "to be stabil-ized," adding on the twentieth that government forces "are hitting the insurgent Communists harder" and "pursuing them harder." In May[194] he detected "nothing but progress and hope for the future"; in July[195] he was encouraged by the shift in the "ratio of killed and captured" to more greatly favor the South Vietnamese. He was still convinced that January[196] that opera-tions were going well, and on July 19, 1963, adjudged the cir-cumstances there to be "very satisfactory."

His was not, however, a voice in the wilderness. Elvis J. Stahr, secretary of the army, stated in the spring of 1962,[197] that he believed the enemy would be defeated "in a few years." On January 13, 1963, President Kennedy declared, "The spear point of aggression has been blunted in Vietnam." Dean Rusk told the press on March 8 that the conflict in Southeast Asia was "turning an important corner" and noted that loyalist forces "clearly have the initiative in most areas of the country." "The corner has definitely been turned," Assistant Secretary of De-fense Arthur Sylvester remarked that May.[198] On August 11, Ambassador Lodge reported that the campaign against the Communists was "going well" and predicted some "very im-pressive victories" in 1964.

Given this background it was not surprising that hopes re-mained so high in the succeeding years, although perhaps by then the perils of forecasting an Asian guerilla war should have been more apparent. Throughout the period from December 1963 to April 1968, from Lyndon Johnson's elevation to the presidency to the announcement of his impending retirement, there was an almost uninterrupted stream of buoyant commen-tary:

1964

"I'm encouraged by the progress of the last two weeks."

ROBERT MCNAMARA, JANUARY 28

"I have no doubt myself about the longer-range outcome of [the]
. . . situation."

DEAN RUSK, FEBRUARY 7

"So I think we're beginning to move ahead on a front that involves the military."

HENRY CABOT LODGE, JUNE 29

There are indications that allied forces have driven the "Vietcong into covert as opposed to overt operations. This is a tremendous accomplishment . . . today, compared to a month or two ago,
we can look ahead with greater confidence."

ROBERT MCNAMARA, NOVEMBER 10

1965

The U.S. military effort in Vietnam is "impressive."

MCGEORGE BUNDY, FEBRUARY 8

American raids against the North have produced a "very clear
lift in morale" in South Vietnam; in general, "things are turning
for the better."

MAXWELL TAYLOR, MARCH 28

There has been "real progress" in the last ten months. "It is
simply inconceivable that we should be defeated."

HENRY CABOT LODGE, APRIL 29

It is "very clear in my own mind" that the rapid deployment of
U.S. troops has "blunted an expected Communist offensive to cut
the country in two." I am "cautiously optimistic" about the overall situation.

ROBERT MCNAMARA, SEPTEMBER 16

American plans are "progressing well."

DEAN RUSK, NOVEMBER 5

"We have stopped losing the war."

ROBERT McNAMARA, NOVEMBER 29

1966

"The enemy is no longer closer to victory. Time is no longer on his side."

LYNDON JOHNSON, JANUARY 12

"The tide of battle has turned . . . the rate of casualties of the Vietcong is high." I return from Southeast Asia "with a spirit of restrained optimism and confidence, with encouragement."

HUBERT HUMPHREY, FEBRUARY 24

"Well, we've had military—very considerable military success beginning last—last summer, and we showed that we knew how to overcome the main-force units of the Vietcong. We showed that we know how to overcome the battalions of the Army of North Vietnam."

HENRY CABOT LODGE, APRIL 22

There is "great basis for real encouragement" in all military phases of the war.

GEORGE BALL, JUNE 30

"North Vietnam and the Vietcong will be defeated." There are "flickering bits of evidence" that some of Hanoi's leaders are "wondering if there is a way out. . . . On the military front, the good news is that we are gaining each day."

HUBERT HUMPHREY, JULY 6

"South Vietnamese forces, vigorously supported by American and other allied units, are steadily gaining ground."

CHESTER BOWLES, AUGUST 17

Military plans have "progressed very satisfactorily" in the last year, "the rate of progress exceeded our expectations." Enemy casualties, "destruction" of his combat units, declining Communist morale were all "greater than we anticipated."

ROBERT McNAMARA, OCTOBER 13

Indications are mounting that the other side is suffering "serious manpower, supply and moral problems."

HAROLD BROWN, DECEMBER 11

"In Vietnam, the tide of battle has turned . . . aggression has been blunted."

LYNDON JOHNSON, DECEMBER 15

1967

This year, efforts against main force enemy units "will achieve very sensational results."

HENRY CABOT LODGE, JANUARY 8

"There are many signs that we are at a favorable turning point." The allies "now hold the initiative and are striking heavy blows against the [Communist] strongholds and refuges."

LYNDON JOHNSON, MARCH 20

I have seen "a tremendous change" for the better in American ground and air operations since October; the large scale campaigns have been "going very well."

ROBERT MCNAMARA, JULY 10

The enemy is "hurting very badly"; the Vietcong and North Vietnamese have "suffered very substantial loses" to the extent that they were unable to stage "a major offensive in June and July as all indications indicated they planned to."

DEAN RUSK, JULY 19

"There is progress in the war. . . . The campaigns of the last year drove the enemy from many of their interior bases. The military victory almost within Hanoi's grasp has now been denied them. The grip of the Vietcong on the people is being broken."

LYNDON JOHNSON, SEPTEMBER 29

"I think that we are winning the struggle." Since last February there has been "general progress in every area."

HUBERT HUMPHREY, NOVEMBER 1

1968

"The enemy has been defeated in battle after battle."

LYNDON JOHNSON, JANUARY 17

The South Vietnamese Army "has turned in an excellent performance," during the recent barrage of attacks.

ELLSWORTH BUNKER, FEBRUARY 18

The Communists "failed to achieve their objectives" in the Tet offensive. The Vietcong and the North Vietnamese did not "seize and hold the cities . . . [or] set up a revolutionary administration . . . [or] destroy the Government in Saigon." In fact, the Saigon government "if anything has been strengthened by the attacks," and the people of the capital have suddenly a "feeling of this war" and a "greater solidarity."

HUBERT HUMPHREY, FEBRUARY 19

These reports were not all entirely fanciful; there was undeniably some evidence to support most of the claims being made. Nor was the optimism unqualified; Washington acknowledged that the war was "confusing"[199] and "difficult"[200] and warned repeatedly that it would be "long and hard,"[201] that it was a "serious," "agonizing"[202] affair. Nevertheless, it was all very misleading. Given human nature, given the fact that people would rather hope than despair, the public was forever awaiting an elusive, chimerical success. Over and over expectations were raised only to be shattered by another reversal and a new escalation. Promise was followed by disappointment; disappointment by discontent; discontent by cynicism. How could the government appraise a situation whose contours it had not yet recognized? How could the government devise a solution to a problem it did not—and perhaps could not—understand?

The establishment of limits on operational strategy and their summary abandonment; the insistence that a changing policy remained essentially fixed; the expression of confidence in the face of a defiant reality; each of these contradictions was intimately related to American escalation, and as that process gradually unfolded, each was exposed in turn:

> Option A has been rejected as too extreme and of speculative benefit.
> Option A has been implemented as part of our continuing mission to defend the nations of Southeast Asia.
> Option A has substantially enhanced the prospects for an eventual peace.
> Option B has been rejected as too extreme and of speculative benefit. . . .

The conclusion which emerged from the recurring sequence was that the Johnson Administration did not know what it was doing and was not telling all it knew; that in its approach to the war it was demonstrably lacking in both ability and candor. That impression was confirmed in other ways: in the failure of the supposedly "successful" pacification program; by the nonofficial disclosures of South Vietnamese repression and corruption. Yet its source and fundamental association was with the course of military expansion, in which context it was revealed again and again.

There was no single nor simple path to dissent and it is impossible, therefore, to apportion or ascertain the precise impact of oratory upon the growth of opposition. Certainly for some it had little or no impact, for those who remained insulated from the media and those who presumed at the outset that rhetoric was all lies. For others, who were unalterably opposed to America intervening in world affairs and those who rejected on principle the resort to force as a means of settling international disputes, the impact was negligible.

But there was a group that was affected, a group which as a result of what it heard came to disapprove of the war, either because it decided on moral, intellectual, or political grounds that involvement was unjustifiable, or because it had, in the end, lost faith in the men who controlled the government. The extensive sacrifice of lives and money and the lack of progress on the battleground were, as officials suggested, significant factors in their disaffection. They were significant, however, only because they occurred against the background of what Washington said.

NOTES TO CHAPTER 6

1. Kennedy, September 25, 1961.
2. Kennedy, April 11, 1962.
3. Kennedy, May 18, 1963.
4. Rusk, March 1, 1962.
5. Rusk, November 8, 1962.
6. McNamara, March 26, 1964.
7. McNamara, March 26, 1964.
8. Rusk, May 22, 1964.
9. Johnson, August 5, 1964.
10. Stevenson, May 21, 1964.
11. Johnson, February 21, 1964.
12. Johnson, June 2 and June 23, 1964.
13. Johnson, August 5, 1964.
14. State Department, February 27, 1965.
15. Harriman, July 24, 1965.
16. Johnson, June 30, 1966.
17. Humphrey, April 26, 1966.
18. Harriman, November 11, 1966.
19. Johnson, October 26, 1966.
20. Johnson, May 30, 1966.
21. Johnson, May 17, 1966.
22. Johnson, September 29, 1967.
23. Nixon, May 14, 1969.
24. The extent to which selected themes were struck by each of the Johnson Administration's five major spokesmen. (Figures in the first five columns represent percentages.)

	pres	vp	sec st	sec def	amb UN	all spkrs
post-war interventions	76	7	3		7	29
not colonialism/ no bases	38	6	19	11	17	63
choice of destiny	46	9	13	3	13	126
better life	52	22	6	4		67
domino principle	44	13	13	8		64
munich analogy	54	8	29	2	2	52
greater cost /larger war	67	7	10	3	3	30
test case rationale	23	4	15	23	4	26
national security	58	11	15	5		62
honor commitments	58	5	22	5		83
breach causes catastrophe	41	7	41			29
ten years past presidents	59	2	17	5	3	59

25. Theodore Draper, *Abuse of Power: U.S. Foreign Policy from Cuba to Vietnam* (Great Britain: Pelican Books, 1969), p. 133.
26. Arthur Schlesinger, *The Bitter Heritage: Vietnam and American Democracy 1941-1966* (New York: Fawcett World Library, 1967), pp. 78-79.
27. J. William Fulbright, *The Arrogance of Power* (Great Britain: Pelican Books, 1967), p. 84.
28. Noam Chomsky, *American Power and the New Mandarins* (Great Britain: Pelican Books, 1969), p. 207.
29. Carl Oglesby and Richard Shaull, *Containment and Change* (New York: MacMillan Co., 1967), p. 45.
30. Draper, p. 97.
31. Schlesinger, p. 50.
32. Oglesby, p. 11.
33. Chomsky, p. 199.
34. Draper, pp. 97-98.
35. Oglesby, p. 12.
36. Draper, p. 98.
37. Fulbright, p. 116.
38. Chomsky, p. 194.
39. Oglesby, p. 12.
40. Fulbright, p. 108.
41. Schlesinger, p. 51.
42. Fulbright, p. 149.
43. Chomsky, p. 299.
44. Oglesby, p. 18.
45. Draper, p. 143.
46. Chomsky, p. 299.
47. Schlesinger, p. 82.
48. Draper, p. 142.
49. Oglesby, p. 57.
50. Chomsky, p. 299.
51. Draper, p. 114.
52. Schlesinger, p. 87.
53. Fulbright, p. 111.
54. Fulbright, p. 181.
55. Draper, pp. 115-121.
56. Schlesinger, p. 25.
57. Oglesby, p. 13.
58. Fulbright, p. 41.
59. Schlesinger, p. 99.
60. Fulbright, p. 41.
61. Schlesinger, pp. 82, 99.
62. Oglesby, p. 12.
63. Draper, p. 127.
64. Chomsky, p. 210.
65. Schlesinger, p. 82.
66. Fulbright, pp. 176-177.
67. Draper, p. 115.
68. Draper, p. 152.

69. Schlesinger, p. 86.
70. Chomsky, p. 299.
71. Fulbright, p. 119.
72. Oglesby, pp. 128–129.
73. Draper, p. 46.
74. Schlesinger, p. 30.
75. Oglesby, p. 7.
76. Draper, pp. 155–157.
77. Schlesinger, pp. 29–30.
78. Fulbright, p. 109.
79. Oglesby, p. 8.
80. Fulbright, p. 127.
81. Schlesinger, p. 68.
82. Fulbright, p. 108.
83. Chomsky, p. 298.
84. Oglesby, p. 14.
85. Schlesinger, p. 75.
86. Draper, p. 113.
87. Draper, p. 213.
88. Schlesinger, p. 85.
89. Fulbright, p. 25.
90. Oglesby, p. 8.
91. Chomsky, p. 209.
92. Draper, p. 103.
93. Schlesinger, p. 58.
94. Chomsky, p. 197.
95. Schlesinger, p. 85.
96. Draper, p. 212.
97. Fulbright, p. 114.
98. Chomsky, p. 208.
99. Fulbright, p. 128.
100. Schlesinger, p. 59.
101. Draper, pp. 174–175.
102. Chomsky, p. 186.
103. Oglesby, p. 4.
104. Oglesby, p. 162.
105. Chomsky, p. 17
106. Fulbright, p. 136.
107. Schlesinger, p. 62.
108. Draper, p. 215.
109. Fulbright, p. 15.
110. Schlesinger, pp. 87–88.
111. Chomsky, pp. 201, 196.
112. Oglesby, pp. 112–113.
113. Johnson, March 20, 1965.
114. Johnson, April 27, 1965.
115. Rusk, November 5, 1965.
116. Moyers, November 26, 1965.
117. Rusk, May 28, 1966.
118. Johnson, August 26, 1966.
119. Humphrey, September 22, 1966.

120. Johnson, May 1, 1967.
121. Johnson, March 18, 1968.
122. Johnson, October 23, 1966.
123. Though on thirteen occasions in 1965 and nineteen in 1966 government officials expressed their devotion to First Amendment freedoms, during the same period—on twenty-one and seventeen times respectively—they also made statements which in various ways discredited those who had taken advantage of these privileges. They continued to assume these contrasting positions the next year, offering, however, far more discouragment than encouragement to potential protestors; there were twenty-seven denunciations to nine appreciations of the ongoing dissent. By 1968 the disparity in emphasis reached an extreme, as spokesmen attacked the critics in thirteen speeches, affirming their right to criticize in only one.
124. Rusk, April 23, 1965.
125. Rusk, October 12, 1967.
126. Humphrey, August 13, 1968.
127. Johnson, July 23, 1966.
128. Johnson, March 15, 1967.
129. Johnson, October 21, 1966.
130. Johnson, December 12, 1967.
131. Humphrey, April 25, 1966.
132. Johnson, November 1, 1967.
133. Lodge, April 26, 1967.
134. Rostow, October 17, 1967.
135. Rusk, April 29, 1967.
136. Humphrey, August 25, 1966.
137. Johnson, June 27, 1967.
138. Humphrey, September 2, 1968.
139. Johnson, November 9, 1967.
140. White House, October 18, 1965.
141. Johnson, May 17, 1966.
142. Humphrey, September 22, 1968.
143. Johnson, February 6, 1966.
144. Johnson, May 2, 1967.
145. Johnson, June 30, 1966.
146. Johnson, November 17, 1967.
147. Humphrey, August 23, 1965.
148. Johnson, April 20, 1964.
149. Stevenson, May 21, 1964.
150. Rusk, June 14, 1964.
151. Johnson, April 7, 1965.
152. Goldberg, September 19, 1966.
153. Humphrey, March 11, 1966.
154. Rusk, December 10, 1966.
155. Of the expressions of determination to remain in Southeast Asia, the proportion that were aimed at animating home audiences grew steadily during the middle years of the decade: from 14 percent of fourteen in 1964, it moved to 16 percent of nineteen in 1965, 20 percent of forty-six in 1966, and a dramatic 51 percent of fifty-one between 1967 and the end of the first quarter of 1968.

156. Lodge, April 25, 1967.
157. McNamara, September 7, 1967.
158. Johnson, November 10, 1967.
159. Johnson, March 12, 1968.
160. Bunker, July 7, 1967.
161. Humphrey, August 22, 1967.
162. Johnson, February 12, 1968.
163. Rusk, May 28, 1966.
164. Johnson, February 7, 1966.
165. Rusk, September 8, 1967.
166. Johnson, September 22, 1967.
167. Johnson, May 17, 1966.
168. In the period from 1965 through 1968, while there were but three statements about keeping America first and six presidential plaints for compassion, there were a substantial forty-six references to the plight of the men of the United States military, nineteen of them coming in the peak year of 1966 alone.
169. Johnson, November 24, 1965.
170. Johnson, April 21, 1966.
171. Johnson, July 5, 1966.
172. Johnson, December 22, 1967.
173. Johnson, September 10, 1968.
174. Moyers, November 26, 1965.
175. Johnson, July 31, 1967.
176. Representative Gallup surveys for the months from summer 1965 through spring 1968, in response to the question, "Do you approve or disapprove of the way President Johnson is handling the situation in Vietnam?" (Figures represent percentages.)

year	65	66					67				68		
month	jul	jan	mar[a]	jun[b]	aug	oct[a]	dec[a]	mar	may[b]	jun[a]	nov	feb	apr
approve	48	56	56	41	43	44	41	37	43	43	35	35	41
disapprove	28	26	26	37	39	42	47	49	42	43	52	54	48
no opinion	24	18	18	22	18	14	12	14	15	14	13	11	11

[a]polling done late in the month
[b]polling done early in the month

177. State Department, October 15, 1965.
178. State Department, May 7, 1965.
179. Johnson, April 1, 1968.
180. Johnson, May 3, 1967.
181. State Department, July 28, 1964.
182. Stevenson, August 5, 1964.
183. Johnson, September 28, 1964.
184. Johnson, October 9, 1964.
185. Rusk, January 5, 1965.
186. White House, October 2, 1963.
187. Rusk, March 7, 1965.

248 WHAT WASHINGTON SAID

190. Johnson, February 11, 1966.
191. McNamara, May 2, 1966.
192. McNamara, July 11, 1966.
193. Dulles, April 5, 1954.
194. McNamara, May 12, 1962.
195. McNamara, July 6, 1962.
196. McNamara, January 30, 1963.
197. Stahr, April 16, 1962.
198. Sylvester, May 7, 1963.
199. Johnson, May 30, 1966.
200. Johnson, April 7, 1965.
201. McNamara, May 19, 1964.
     Vance, August 8, 1964.
     Bundy, April 14, 1965.
202. Johnson, March 21, 1967.

APPENDIX

The following tables offer quantitative evidence to support most of the qualitative assertions made throughout the book. The first chart indicates the number of official statements in which selected dominant words or themes appear in a given year; the second chart, the comparable percentages. The sequence of headings corresponds to the order in which these issues are presented in the text.

DOMINANT WORDS AND THEMES

NUMERICAL OCCURRENCES

RHETORIC	1950	1951	1952	1953	1954	1960	1961	1962	1963	1964	1965	1966	1967	1968	1969*
Chapter 1															
communism	5	1	3	12	52	4	12	9	13	46	63	61	31	24	5
enemy, foe				2	9	1	6	3	3	15	29	50	46	51	13
aggression			1	6	17		3	6	4	30	79	97	54	30	2
subversion	1		2		5	1	15	13	6	48	39	32	27	18	4
freedom, liberty	5	1		4	27	1	9	6	11	34	39	36	25	17	
Chapter 2															
Russia	5		1	7	17		1	3		8	8	12	6	2	1
China	2	1	3	6	18	1		2	2	23	38	45	15	3	2
North Vietnam							7	5	3	41	84	96	102	108	21
Vietminh/Vietcong	4		1		8		2	2	4	34	43	30	27	31	3
Chapter 3															
inside powers	4		1		8	1	2	2	4	34	43	30	27	31	3
outside powers	7	1	4	13	35		8	10	5	72	130	153	123	113	34
not a civil war					4					2	3	10	3	3	
post-war interventions								1		2	5	16	5	2	
help, aid, assist	6		2	7	12	1	12	9	9	28	29	28	13	13	1
not colonialism/no bases	7	1	1	10	14		1	1	1	9	22	20	7	6	1

Chapter 4															
choice of destiny					6		1	1	2	3	23	48	26	26	8
self-determination				7	2			1	2		3	16	8	9	1
better life				3	4		4	5	3	5	10	44	3	6	
domino principle	2			1	14		1	2	1	11	6	18	16	12	1
Munich analogy		5	5	2			1	1	1	5	13	17	12	5	
greater cost/larger war				4	3		1	1		1	5	8	11	5	
test case rationale			1				3				7	11	3	2	1
hundred little countries					7							6			
economic losses					8					4	5	5	3	4	
human costs												1	1		
national security							1			5	14	16	15	12	
freedom is one piece					6					3	2	8	2	4	
honor commitments			1	4			2				23	19	18	14	
breach causes catastrophe					2					10	7	12	6	4	
Chapter 5															
Eisenhower letter							1			1	4	15	15	6	
SEATO obligation										1	6	33	27	37	
allies						1				2	2	2		1	4
Geneva declaration							1	1							
ten years/past presidents							1			15	18	8	7	10	
Tonkin resolution										1	11	11	9	3	
total statements	15	6	13	31	118	10	32	39	33	168	291	366	299	269	68

*Sample covers period from 1/1 to 5/15 only.

DOMINANT WORDS AND THEMES

PERCENTAGE OF TOTAL STATEMENTS

RHETORIC	1950	1951	1952	1953	1954	1960	1961	1962	1963	1964	1965	1966	1967	1968	1969
Chapter 1															
communism	33	17	23	39	44	40	38	23	39	27	22	17	10	09	07
enemy, foe				06	08	10	19	08	09	09	10	14	15	19	19
aggression			08	19	14		09	15	12	18	27	26	18	11	03
subversion	07		16		04	10	47	33	18	29	13	09	09	07	06
freedom, liberty	33	17		13	23	10	28	15	33	20	13	10	08	06	
Chapter 2															
Russia	33	17	08	23	14			08		05	03	03	02	01	01
China	13	17	23	20	15	10	03	05	06	14	14	12	05	01	03
North Vietnam							22	13	09	24	30	26	34	40	31
Vietminh/Vietcong	27		08		07		06	05	12	22	15	08	09	12	04
Chapter 3															
inside powers*	36	100	20	100	19		20	17	45	32	25	16	18	22	11
outside powers*	64		80		81	100	80	83	55	68	75	84	82	78	89
not a civil war					04					01	01	03	01	01	
post-war interventions								03		01	02	04	02	01	
help, aid, assist	40		16	23	10	10	38	23	27	17	10	08	04	05	01
not colonialism/no bases	47	17	08	32	12		03	03	03	05	08	05	02	02	01

Chapter 4															
choice of destiny							03	03	06	02	08	13	09	10	12
self-determination					05			03		03	01	04	03	03	01
better life					02		03			07	04	12	01	02	
domino principle	33		40	23	03		03	13	06	03	02	05	05	04	01
Munich analogy				10	12			05	09	01	05	05	04	02	
greater cost/larger war					03					02	02	02	04	02	01
test case rationale											02	03	01	01	
hundred little countries											02	02			
economic losses			08	03	06							01	01	01	
human costs			08	06	07										
national security				13	05		03		03	03	05	04	05	04	
freedom is one piece					02		09			02	01	02	01	01	
honor commitments									03	06	08	05	06	05	
breach causes catastrophe							03				02	03	02	01	
Chapter 5															
Eisenhower letter											01				
SEATO obligation										01	02	04	05	02	
allies						10				01	01	09	09	14	06
Geneva declaration							06	03	03		06	01	02	04	
ten years/past presidents								03		06	06	02	02	04	
Tonkin resolution											04	03	03	01	
total statements	15	6	13	31	118	10	32	39	33	168	291	366	299	269	68

*The denominator for these percentages is not the yearly number of total statements but the yearly number of references to inside and outside powers.

73 74 75 76 77 10 9 8 7 6 5 4 3 2 1